Not the Camilla We Knew

———

Not the Camilla We Knew

One Woman's Path from Small-Town America
to the Symbionese Liberation Army

RACHAEL HANEL

 University of Minnesota Press
Minneapolis • London

The University of Minnesota Press gratefully acknowledges the generous assistance provided for the publication of this book by the Margaret S. Harding Memorial Endowment, honoring the first director of the University of Minnesota Press.

Published by the University of Minnesota Press
111 Third Avenue South, Suite 290
Minneapolis, MN 55401-2520
http://www.upress.umn.edu

ISBN 978-1-5179-1345-8 (pb)

A Cataloging-in-Publication record for this book is available from the Library of Congress.

Printed in the United States of America on acid-free paper

The University of Minnesota is an equal-opportunity educator and employer.

28 27 26 25 24 23 22   10 9 8 7 6 5 4 3 2 1

to CAMILLA

I hope this is the story you wanted told

to GEORGE and LORENA

CONTENTS

PROLOGUE   Camilla Is Killed: May 17, 1974   1

INTRODUCTION   The Woman in the Picture   7

Part I. Camilla Established

1 "We Begin When We First Met"   19

2 "Their First Concern"   27

3 "It Was a Troubled Spring, Heavy with Grief"   34

4 Camilla Goes to College   39

5 Camilla Gets a Job   46

6 A Turning Point   52

Part II. Camilla Transformed

7 Camilla Moves to California   59

8 Camilla and Mizmoon   65

9 The SLA Forms   72

10 Camilla Moves to Francisco Street   81

11 Camilla Joins the SLA   88

12 The SLA Kidnaps Patty: February 4, 1974   94

13 Camilla Slips Away   103

14 Camilla inside the SLA   107

Part III. Camilla Revealed

15 Crumbs on the Trail   123

16 The Missing Letters   127

17 "A Perfect, Loving Daughter"   132

18 The Last Christmas   139

19 The Sole Survivor   145

20 "She Was a Pacifist"   154

21 "I'm Not Surprised"   161

22 Camilla Reveals Herself   165

23 A Parallel Story   177

24 A Visit to Chowchilla   185

25 Nan   197

26 Good Girls Gone Bad   206

EPILOGUE   "It Has Been a Wonderful Life"   213

Acknowledgments   219

Notes   223

Camilla Is Killed

May 17, 1974

CAMILLA HALL darted out of the burning house in South Central Los Angeles in the early evening of May 17, 1974. Her eyes burned from the tear gas lobbed inside the home by some of the more than four hundred Los Angeles police officers who, along with dozens of Federal Bureau of Investigation (FBI) agents, surrounded the place. She took a big breath of fresh outdoor air.

Around her, glass shattered as bullets rained through windows and punctured stucco walls. Police helicopters swirled above the house. Journalists reported from behind police barricades down the street. A producer from KNXT-TV sent a crew to the scene with brand-new technology: the minicam. It was the perfect opportunity to test the device. After all, this was the Symbionese Liberation Army (SLA) trapped in the house. The small band of fighters had eluded police for six months, ever since their murder of Oakland, California, school superintendent Marcus Foster in November. And now, it could very well be that the SLA's famous hostage, Patty Hearst, was in the house. For the first time in history, breaking news was broadcast live across the nation. Hundreds of onlookers gathered as word spread quickly.

According to the Los Angeles Police Department (LAPD) report issued two months after the shooting, when Camilla came out of the house she fired her .380 Mauser directly at members of LAPD SWAT Team no. 2. The shots didn't hit anyone. A torrent of gunfire greeted her; one bullet hit her squarely in the forehead. The twenty-nine-year-old died instantly. Someone reached from inside the house, grabbed Camilla's ankles, and dragged her body back inside, down into a crawl space. The blaze engulfed the structure and spread to the homes on either side. It was nearly 7 p.m.; the battle had raged for more than an hour, the television crew on the scene the whole time. Gunfire from inside the house ceased; Camilla and five other SLA members were now dead.

In the days following the shooting, the families of those killed and members of the public raised questions about the overwhelming show of force. On behalf of the families, noted attorney Leonard Weinglass (defender of the Chicago Seven, Daniel Ellsberg, and Angela Davis) commissioned an independent investigation. Investigators said they discovered the presence of a working telephone in the house, which was not used to attempt negotiations. Investigators also heard that police had a letter of surrender from Camilla, but if it existed, it was never released by the police.

Though mainstream media went with the official story supplied by the LAPD, alternative media explored other theories behind the shoot-out. A headline in the *Berkeley Barb* from the June 21–27 edition proclaimed, "Report Says SLA Was Deliberately Massacred," referencing the Weinglass report. And a *New York Post* editorial of May 24, 1974, read:

> Looking at the site, it also became clear to a visitor that a force of about 75 cops could have easily sealed off the house, cleared the surrounding area and waited out the SLA. The street in front could have easily been lighted through the night, providing a clear field of fire for strategically located marksmen across the street who could have shot any fleeing SLA members in the leg. Behind the house, there is a small courtyard. . . . Six well-placed cops could have held this area against a real army; six amateurs should have been easy. There were almost 500 Los Angeles cops and FBI men

in the area last week, and it's astounding that they felt required to destroy the place in order to save it.

The day she died, Camilla chatted amicably with the people who lived at and visited 1466 East Fifty-Fourth Street, the home at which the SLA had found refuge early that morning. The SLA had hopped from a series of houses in the San Francisco Bay Area until they felt squeezed and decided to hide in Los Angeles. But they didn't do a very good job—the majority-white SLA chose to hide in predominantly black South Central Los Angeles, a place where police regularly patrolled the streets. Oddly enough, the mood inside the house was relaxed, and residents and guests walked in and out. With all the activity, someone was sure to talk, and it would be only a matter of hours before the police discovered the SLA.

Camilla must have known this was the end.

Over the previous months, Camilla had had many chances to end her involvement in the SLA. She could have simply walked out of one of the safe houses and turned herself in. She could have called her parents to let them know what was going on. She could have driven far away, set up a new life, taken a new name. This had worked for a few former SLA associates, who by then were living quietly in places like Texas and Florida.

Instead, Camilla sat in the house in Los Angeles, weapons at the ready, biding time until the inevitable police raid. Witness accounts from that day described Camilla as others had described her throughout her life: friendly, charming, warm, gregarious. She didn't appear anxious or depressed. The witnesses said Camilla had acted like a den mother, making sandwiches for her SLA comrades as well as for the home's residents and visitors. Camilla had always had a tender heart, a softness, a penchant for helping others, which did not abate even on her dying day.

Police released one letter they said was found in Camilla's backpack at the charred site. Although partially burned, the piece of thin paper somehow escaped total destruction in the inferno. While a surrender letter, if it had

existed, would have elicited sympathy for Camilla, the letter that was released shows Camilla in a radical state of mind.

Camilla's parents, the Reverend George and Lorena Hall, hadn't heard
from Camilla for several months, not since she went underground in
February after the Hearst kidnapping. The letter demonstrates a marked
change from the tone of Camilla's earlier letters to her parents over the years,
in which she never revealed radical viewpoints. In this letter, she displays revolutionary thought. She explains the actions of the preceding few months:

> I want you to remember that I'm with really good people and that we've
> trained ourselves in a great many ways because we realize the importance
> of the people's forces surviving and gaining victory after victory (you know
> I never do anything half-assed!). Our attitude is very positive and our
> courage comes from our love for the people and hatred for the enemy.
> You know well that I have worked for change all my conscious life. I went
> through many stages of development, attacking the enemy on many dif-
> ferent fronts only to see change co-opted into reformism.

Camilla encourages her parents to read stories about the SLA beyond
what the mainstream media was reporting. She worries that they would
not get an accurate portrait of the group through the usual media channels:

> I don't know what press coverage we've gotten in your area or what kind
> of distortions they've been [illegible] people with, but I strongly recom-
> mend that you check into underground news sources to get a better idea
> of what's really happening. The [Berkeley] Barb has published all our
> communiqués as well as people's responses to our actions and it would
> be very helpful to you in understanding all this to subscribe to it.

Camilla ends the letter by saying that she would not be contacting her parents for a while:

> Please try to understand that I won't be able to communicate with you
> again for quite a while for security reasons. Security not only involves me

but my comrades. We all face the same problems of wanting to communicate with our loved ones but not being able to do so for security reasons. So don't feel you're alone—there are lots of other parents and friends and lovers going through the same thing. I trust your courage and [illegible] to understand these things and keep them [illegible] in your heart.

It's difficult to discern the veracity of this letter. The house was burned to the ground, making it hard to believe a backpack, let alone a piece of paper, survived the inferno. Could the letter have been a police decoy, just one more piece of "evidence" that allowed them to justify using more than four hundred officers to destroy six people? Plus, Camilla hadn't been in contact with her parents for months. That she just happened to be ready to send a letter to them—the words describing, for the first time, her life inside the SLA—on one of her last days seems like too much of a coincidence. And its tone doesn't reflect the tone in Camilla's previous letters to her parents. Camilla wrote to them regularly. Most of her letters are perfunctory and mundane, reporting on the minutiae of her everyday life. She touches on the political, but not in any discernably radical way. The government frustrated her—the involvement in Vietnam, the seeming disregard for the poor and disadvantaged—but this didn't set her apart from millions of other protesters in the 1960s and 1970s.

This letter is just one mystery of many regarding her life. Perhaps she did write it. If she knew that police were closing in and that she was likely to die, maybe she did take a few moments to scribble her final thoughts. In some ways, the words in this letter do sound like Camilla (she was often funny and blunt—"half-assed" is a term she would have used). But in other ways, the letter sounds as if someone else wrote it. And to a degree, that could be true. The Camilla who died on May 17, 1974, was a different Camilla from years, or even months, past. She underwent a seismic shift in thought and behavior in just a few months that almost no one—not her parents, not her friends—saw coming.

The Woman in the Picture

WHEN I SAW CAMILLA'S PHOTOGRAPH for the first time in 1999, in a *Minneapolis Star Tribune* article, I stared at it for a good long while. Here was a woman in her midtwenties, the same age as I was. When I was little I pored over my older sister's high school yearbooks, captivated by the even teeth and feathered hair of her classmates. I was trying to divine what made them beautiful, as if the secrets to popularity and success would leap from the page if I looked long enough. I stared at Camilla's photo not to divine beauty but to try to understand her. Here, in the black and white of the newspaper, was a mystery waiting to unfold: how a soft Minnesota girl, the daughter of a Lutheran pastor, became a revolutionary.

I was conceived around the time of Hearst's kidnapping and born five months after the shoot-out that killed Camilla, in southern Minnesota just forty miles from where Camilla grew up. But the SLA had a way of sticking around, so that I grew up knowing its defining story line: that of Patty Hearst.

My family and I watched the television news every night. Dad was a gravedigger and cemetery groundskeeper, and his work depended on the weather. He used the forecast to plan his next day's schedule. Before the meteorologist spoke, though, we had to sit through fifteen minutes of news. On January 29, 1979, the top news story was President Jimmy Carter's commutation of Patty's sentence for bank robbery, which freed her from prison. I was probably watching those news reports; although I was young, the name "Patty Hearst" entered my subconscious.

Patty became an instant celebrity by virtue of both her family's wealth and status and her famous kidnapping. Her words on SLA communiqués ("Mom, Dad, I'm OK"), images of her (especially the one of her holding a machine gun, posed in front of the SLA emblem), and her multifaceted narrative (the friction between her parents, her kidnapping, her months on the run and subsequent trial) played well on TV and in newspapers and magazines. Patty was everywhere. She popped up again on news programs and talk shows in 1982 for the release of her book *Every Secret Thing*, in which she recounted her time in the SLA. The director John Waters became so enamored of her that he cast her in several films. And throughout the 1980s and 1990s, the SLA story would appear on tabloid shows like *A Current Affair* and *Inside Edition*. But Patty was always the blinding sun, and all the other SLA members orbited in the shadows. How easy it was to forget there were others, or to never even know of them in the first place.

───

The SLA story resurfaced again in 1999, and this time, the attention would stick, especially in Minnesota. When I first saw Camilla's photo, she was again overshadowed by a big name, but not Patty's this time. Camilla was just briefly mentioned in the June 17, 1999, edition of the *Minneapolis Star Tribune*; the main story's headline was "'70s Revolutionary Arrested in St. Paul."

That article was about Sara Jane Olson, who had joined the SLA after the shoot-out that killed Camilla. She was arrested on charges stemming from a bank robbery that killed a woman and for allegedly planting pipe bombs (none of which went off) on police cars. At the time of her arrest, Olson was a doctor's wife, a community volunteer, an amateur actress, and a mother of three. While in the SLA, she was known by her birth name,

Kathleen Soliah. The FBI arrested her on a leafy street in her affluent neighborhood in Minnesota's capital city. In terms of media attention, Olson would become a modern-day Patty Hearst, dominating headlines for the next three years through her trial and sentencing.

I started my search into Camilla's story the same day I saw her picture. That afternoon at the *Mankato Free Press*, the newspaper where I worked as a reporter, I went into the back room that passed as our archives—a small space cluttered with old newspapers, boxes of negatives, and a microfilm machine. A filing cabinet stuffed with index cards sufficed as a rudimentary cataloging system; its organization was always tasked to part-time news clerks who rarely agreed on what heading a story should be filed under or who forgot to do the indexing half the time. But with some luck, I found information on Camilla filed under "Hall, Camilla," and "Symbionese Liberation Army." A couple of stories had run after her death and burial in St. Peter, Minnesota. Another story had run a few years later on the anniversary of the shoot-out. I found the issues on microfilm and printed them out.

I made a case to my editor for writing a story on Camilla, since it could function as a local angle to the larger story of Olson's arrest. "Sure, go for it," she said. I made a couple of calls and discovered that George Hall, a professor at Gustavus Adolphus College in St. Peter for nearly two decades, had left materials related to Camilla's life in the college archives. I arranged to visit a few days later.

Gustavus Adolphus College is a private school founded by Swedish Lutheran immigrants in 1862. It's a small college in a small town, elite and expensive. Today it's far more liberal than it was when George Hall taught there from 1938 to 1956, but the school's mission has always focused heavily on social justice and fostering compassion within its students. Since 1981, its annual MAYDAY! Peace Conference has continued to promote the college's social justice mission.

The campus is compact; the walk to the library from the parking lot is a short one. It's a school where buildings are named not only after former Gustavus presidents and professors but also after Swedes of note. The library is named after Count Folke Bernadotte, a nephew of King Gustav V of Sweden, who was assassinated by Zionists in 1948 after trying to broker peace between Israel and Palestine. I went through the library's front doors and climbed the steps to the second floor, passing a portrait of Bernadotte, and went to the archives office in the back corner.

I had spoken to Mike Haeuser, the archivist, on the telephone, and he was as kindly in person as he was on the phone. He looked like a slimmer, shorter version of Santa Claus. He retrieved the box of documents, then chatted with me for almost an hour. It was a crash course in Hall family history.

I learned that George Hall had been a pastor before he accepted the faculty position teaching theology and religion at Gustavus. His wife, Lorena, a talented painter, taught art part-time at the college and raised their children while in St. Peter. George left Gustavus in 1956, when he took his family to Tanganyika (now Tanzania) to do mission work. They returned to Minnesota a couple of years later, eventually settling in Minneapolis. After Camilla graduated from high school, she attended Gustavus her freshman year but then transferred to the University of Minnesota, graduating in 1967. After working for two years as a county welfare case officer in Duluth and Minneapolis, Camilla moved to California in 1970. In 1971, in Berkeley, she met the woman who would become her lover and who would be Camilla's entry into the SLA: Patricia "Mizmoon" Soltysik.

The more Mike and I talked about Camilla, the more mysterious her actions seemed. We kept coming back to the oddity that a small-town Minnesota girl, a pastor's daughter at that, would become involved in such a violent movement. On the surface, it didn't make any sense. Then again, we were talking about the 1970s, with all that decade's political upheaval and societal restlessness, frequent hijackings, and bizarre events like the Jonestown massacre.

My article appeared in the July 3, 1999, *Mankato Free Press* under the headline "She Said She Wanted a Revolution," which was, I suppose, the headline writer's attempt to be clever by co-opting a Beatles song. We ran the same small picture of Camilla that had appeared in the *Star Tribune* a few weeks earlier, along with a photo of Camilla's gravestone at Resurrection

Cemetery. Next to my article was a smaller story, written by a coworker, about a former police chief in a town near St. Peter who had kept the original FBI Wanted posters featuring mug shots of SLA members. When he headed the department in 1974, he had wondered if the SLA might try to hide in Minnesota, drawn there through Camilla. "I surely kept an eye open for California plates," he said in the article. The police chief had winnowed his belongings over the years, but twenty-five years later he still had the Wanted posters. Some pieces of history are impossible to let go of.

———

All the media accounts that mentioned Camilla after her death, and even those from more recent years, focus on her time in the SLA rather than her life before the SLA. They look at the end result and fail to consider the nuanced decisions that led to her death. It's like looking at a dilapidated, abandoned house and not seeing the gleam and promise it once had or the sad stories that led to its decline.

How willing we are to look only at the surface, to quickly ascribe the most simplistic explanation, call ourselves satisfied, and move on. In newspapers published in the immediate aftermath of the shooting, Camilla was variably described as overweight (as she had been earlier in life, but she had slimmed down while living in California) and homely (who describes someone so cruelly?) and was categorized simultaneously both as a militant lesbian who wholeheartedly embraced revolution and as someone inept with a gun who joined only because she wanted to be near her former lover. Reporters struggled to find an easy narrative to explain her life, and when they couldn't find one, they made one up.

Even today, when someone writes about the SLA, they don't devote much time to anyone other than Patty. The other members are lumped together, stereotyped in one fell swoop. In *The Symbionese Liberation Army and Patricia Hearst, Queen of the Revolution* (2019), Gregory Cumming and Stephen Sayles write that the SLA was "a small clique of young, self-absorbed, guilt-ridden, emotionally scarred white men and women who found their salvation in the ideas held by a black escaped convict." In *American Heiress: The Wild Saga of the Kidnapping, Crimes and Trial of Patty Hearst* (2016), author

Jeffrey Toobin reduces Camilla to adjectives: gentle, zaftig, arty, erstwhile, ungainly, otherworldly, weary. These keywords allow readers to quickly assess her character. The simple adjectives make her transformation to radical terrorist mysterious—why did she do it? But when one looks at the entirety of her life and acknowledges its complexities—the loss of her siblings, her isolation from her parents, her disappointment in love, her growing frustration with the government, the loss of her job because she was a woman—her transformation becomes less mysterious. Her depth forces us to admit there's a side to Camilla that we may identify with. It forces us to confront a part of ourselves that doesn't always make the right choices. It's so much easier to pass judgment, to say that we'd never be like her. But had we lived in that time and place, had we experienced the grief and abandonment Camilla did, had we been looking for love and affection, had we been forced to the margins of society because of our gender and sexual orientation, it becomes possible to understand Camilla or others like her who make choices that, to them, don't seem wrong at all.

———

We all have, within ourselves, the ability to do good in the world. Some people choose to honor that, while others push it away. Those who choose to help do so in many ways. They may volunteer at a food bank or serve as mentors to youth. They may give money to causes that help the poor. They may get a job as a teacher, nurse, or social worker. They may enter politics to try to effect change from within the system. They may start a nonprofit.

My good works don't go beyond volunteering or making charitable contributions. I can give bits of my time or money without causing major sacrifices to my comfort or way of life. I like to think I'm generous, but how much am I truly willing to give up?

Camilla tried to work within the system for a few years. She was one of those good people who was always helping, always giving. She worked for county welfare offices, primarily assisting young unwed mothers. She wrote for an underground political newspaper. She attended political rallies for Eugene McCarthy. In September 1973, Camilla was leading the fight to bring female workers into the union in the Oakland/Berkeley East Bay Regional

Park District. Her picture was in the newspapers at the time; she beamed, surrounded by the workers at a protest. She could have stopped there and been a success. I wish I could travel back in time, to that scene, and say to her, "Let this be all you do, and you will have done good." But four months later, she bought a gun and had the grip customized for her small hand. She was the last SLA member to go underground, a few days after she and the others kidnapped Patty. What had changed in those few short months?

Her conversion to violent, radical domestic terrorist didn't make sense when I first visited with Mike Haeuser at Gustavus. But after more than twenty years, I've come to an understanding about this woman. There's no one explanation for why Camilla did what she did. It's a complicated story formed by grief, loss, adventure, independence, love, and a wish to leave the world a better place than she found it—in short, what almost all of us experience and desire.

———

It's hard to explain the hold Camilla Hall has on me. After more than two decades, she's still a big part of my life. When I first came across her story in 1999, I felt instant sympathy for her. Perhaps because of the way she was killed in 1974, in an overwhelming show of force. Perhaps because she was only twenty-nine when she died. Or perhaps because we shared a rural, southern Minnesota identity.

At the same time, I felt guilty about my sympathy. I knew the facts about the SLA: they were a small band of revolutionaries bent on violent overthrow of the government. They armed themselves with an array of weapons. They plotted and carried out a kidnapping, robbed banks, injured bystanders, planted pipe bombs on police cars, and killed two people. They were domestic terrorists.

This book is the culmination of the journey I took to find out more about Camilla, to discover why a mild-mannered Lutheran girl from Minnesota would get wrapped up in a world of revolutionary zeal. She was dead before I was born. Her family—the people who knew her best—are also gone. Her three siblings died before her. Her mother died in 1995. I had one brief correspondence with Camilla's father when I first started this research, before he died in 2000. I relied on archival material, old newspapers, books about the SLA, and a distant Hall relative. I traveled to the Bay Area in California to see the places where Camilla had lived. I visited a women's prison in Chowchilla, California, to interview a former SLA associate. I flew to Taos, New Mexico, to meet a friend of Camilla and drove to Lincolnwood, Illinois, to see the house where Camilla visited her parents for the last time. Camilla's father, the Reverend George Hall, wrote an account, never published, of his family's life that contained a wealth of information. I started this project with seven letters from Camilla to her parents; by the time I finished, I had more than fifty. A dissertation that probed Camilla's psychology proved immensely valuable. Since all the players in this story are dead, I also turned to more unconventional sources to infer Camilla's state of mind, such as her poetry and her artwork. And I looked at the lives of two women whose trajectories were similar to Camilla's: Diana Oughton of the Weather Underground and Sara Jane Olson (Kathleen Soliah) of the SLA.

This is a work of nonfiction, though elements of it are speculative. I ground the reader in verified facts, but at times I attempt to see events unfold through Camilla's eyes, though of course I do not know for certain what she was thinking. This speculation is one of my favorite aspects of creative nonfiction, and I realize others may feel differently.

I am a presence in this book; you will learn about Camilla as I learned about her, starting from her childhood and young adult years in Minnesota and shifting to her fateful move to California and her entry into the SLA, searching for reasons that might explain the choices she made. In some ways Camilla and I are alike, and I offer slices from my own life where I think they illuminate something about Camilla.

When I first started the research on Camilla, we were at the cusp of the twenty-first century, looking forward with hope and anticipation to what the new era might bring. The SLA was twenty-five years in the past, the stories safely ensconced in old newspapers and black-and-white television footage. Surely antiwar and equal rights protests were behind us. As a country, we thought we had moved on from the strife.

But in recent years, the agitation present in the 1960s and 1970s has resurfaced. Back then it was the Left fighting with revolutionary zeal; now, similar fervor comes more from the Right. I see Camilla in every news report I read about women who become radicalized and are willing to give their lives for what they see as worthy causes. I can draw a direct line between Camilla and the young women in the United States who sought to join the Islamic State of Iraq and Syria (ISIS), or the women involved in the January 6, 2021, Capitol insurrection. These women are not unlike you or me. At times we've all lost our way and made unwise choices. Some of us find our way back to the path; others do not. The question I sought to answer when I first came across Camilla's story—*How does a woman like her become a domestic terrorist?*—has now changed to *Who's next? And when?*

PART I

Camilla Established

It's incredible how impossible it is to project the future these days. I used to at least have a concept of the next few years, but now I don't have any way of even thinking of the next few months, weeks and even days. So much is happening in the world and in America and on so many levels and all seeming to point to either fascism or chaos.

—Letter from Camilla Hall to her parents,
December 8, year unknown but probably 1972

CHAPTER 1

"We Begin When We First Met"

Oh, that my words were written!
Oh, that they were inscribed in a book!
That they were engraved on a rock
With an iron pen and lead, forever!

Job 19:23–24 (New King James Version)

TO COMPARE SOMEONE WHO IS SUFFERING to the biblical Job is a tired cliché. Job lost everything—his family, his house, his possessions, his land, his health—yet he remained devoted to God. It's almost as if he were put in the Bible to stop us from complaining: *Look at how much pain and loss Job bore. Certainly your problems are no worse.*

Job's losses take place right away in the first chapter of the Book of Job. But stop there, and you miss Job's meaningful meditation on life. The additional forty-one chapters lyrically ponder the nature of human suffering. Job laments his lot, talks to his friends, and complains to God; God answers, and Job then triumphantly proclaims his love for the Lord. Job's losses aren't the center of the story; they are the catalyst for Job to see God's goodness and grace no matter what comes.

Camilla's father, George Hall, was more than the loss of his children. Unlike Job, he went through life with his wife at his side, he basked in a wide circle of friends, he always held a job, and he lived in modest comfort. But like Job, George was a contemplative and thoughtful writer, and his losses, too, were a catalyst for him to see God's love. In Job 19:23–24, Job abruptly stops his complaints to proclaim the importance of the written word. In effect, he says his words must be written for future generations, so they can understand him and his faith. And written not in sand or on parchment but in stone, engraved and lasting through the ages. Job worried that no one would remember his story if he only spoke the words; he wanted his words recorded.

The verse that immediately follows Job 19:23–24 has been immortalized in hymns, trotted out most frequently at Easter: "For I know that my Redeemer lives." A deep desire to write, to express his thoughts, leads to a simple, but powerful, proclamation of faith in God.

George and Lorena Hall had been married fifty-eight years when Lorena died in June 1995. By September of that year, George had typed out a one hundred–page ode titled "I Remember Lorena—A Love Story." Some people process events through talking, and some don't take time to process events at all. Then there are people who can only make sense of the world through writing. George was one of those people.

George was born to be a writer and thinker. His first book was published while he was still in college; he wrote about his European travels while a member of the Augustana College band (*The Augustana Band and Its Tour of 1928: The Story of Augustana's Greatest Brotherhood*). Throughout his life, he was a prolific author, writing sermons, papers, books, and curricula. George was a scholar, a lover of history. He knew the importance of transferring memories to paper, of getting them out of one's head, of creating a historical record.

Perhaps he thought that words written down would make his life seem more real. In his quiet moments, did he by chance think it had all been a dream? What did he have that proved his existence? The children he and

Lorena had created were gone, dead before they could carry on the family name. The only proof that the marriage existed would be photographs and a marriage license. But those ephemera were scattered, even lost. One thing George could control: he could write his memories. Today, at Gustavus, in the deep recesses of the library, lives a manuscript that testifies to the depths of love and faith even while grief and loss attack from every shadow.

———

Almost immediately after Lorena's death, George sat at his typewriter and tapped out the first words in "I Remember Lorena": "We begin when we first met."

George had been ordained as a pastor in the Augustana Lutheran Synod in 1934. While he worked on his doctorate in theology, he served a congregation in Gary, Indiana. When the president of Bethany College in Lindsborg, Kansas, encouraged George to take a position teaching Christianity and Greek, George didn't hesitate. He desired a teaching career. He was one of the few people in the small synod who could take the call, anyway. The salary was not large enough to support a married man and his family, so the college was specifically seeking a bachelor for the post.

George spotted Lorena Daeschner, a senior art student, in September 1936 at one of the first campus mixers soon after he arrived. Students and faculty had gathered at a local farm for a hot dog roast and fellowship. In the crowd of co-eds, Lorena stood out. She was surrounded by young women of Scandinavian descent, midwestern beauties with blond hair, blue eyes, and fair skin. By contrast, Lorena looked almost exotic. She was of German heritage and had the olive skin, dark hair, and warm brown eyes common in the southern regions of Germany. Lorena was older than her classmates, too—she had delayed college for a couple of years in order to work and save money. George and Lorena found themselves standing next to each other; they exchanged pleasantries but went their separate ways.

George saw Lorena frequently on the small campus. In the cafeteria, she sat with her friends, while he dined with fellow male faculty members. Protocol dictated that even if George was interested in Lorena, he could not make any overt gestures toward her. A professor dating a student is verboten even today; at a small Christian campus in the 1930s, George could hardly entertain the thought.

But George would not be deterred. In February 1937 he and Lorena stood beside each other in line in the cafeteria to pay, and he suggested they take a drive because the day was so beautiful. They drove to a hillside, where George read a book while Lorena sketched. He asked her for a date the next week, and they dated regularly after that. Their dates in Lindsborg were chaste: going to the bakery after they were finished with classes and George walking Lorena back to her apartment. George could not be her date at campus events. The scandalous nature of their relationship demanded quiet outings. As much as possible, they tried to get away from judgmental eyes; they took drives into the country or to neighboring towns. When Lorena's sorority held a formal dinner in May, she had to invite a friend as her escort. But the next day, George proposed to Lorena. One week later, after Lorena's graduation, they were married by the college president. The young couple soon left Bethany for George's new job at Gustavus.

———

St. Peter is a town of ten thousand people nestled on the banks of the Minnesota River in south-central Minnesota. From St. Peter, the river flows northeast until it meets the Mississippi in St. Paul, about sixty miles away. Downtown St. Peter is on the flood plain, while other parts of town, including the campus of Gustavus, sit atop the limestone bluffs overlooking the valley. The town is serene, and each distinct season offers picturesque views: the budding trees of spring, the lush greenery of summer, the blazing colors of fall, and the crisp monochromes of winter.

St. Peter, both in George's time and now, is sophisticated and refined. He fit in well. It's a place where ideas flourish. Five Minnesota governors have hailed from St. Peter. People there are hopeful and creative. For them, changing the world is not just an abstraction; it's a real possibility. The prestigious Nobel Foundation has supported an annual conference at Gustavus since 1965, where world-renowned thinkers gather to discuss scientific issues and their moral and social implications.

St. Peter is so emblematic of "Americana" that it could serve as the backdrop to a Norman Rockwell painting. This is where America's iconic folk singer John Denver met his wife, Annie, a St. Peter girl made famous in the chart-topping "Annie's Song" the year Camilla died. The town hosts a massive Fourth of July parade each year, and dozens of American flags stand as sentinels in the town park. Even today, late-nineteenth-century brick buildings dominate Main Street. A series of small, locally owned shops line the street—a rarity for a town just ten miles away from Mankato, a major retail hub with a mall, big-box retailers, and franchise restaurants. The people of St. Peter take pride in their town's individuality. St. Peter is home to the only food co-op in southern Minnesota, and the coffee shop serves locally grown and organic fare almost exclusively. People there do things their own way.

That included George. Even though he was a professor and an erudite man, he served as the general contractor when his home was built on Seventh Street, directly across from the college. He helped the crews with carpentry and painting and the cement work for the walks, patio, and terraces. The house, a rambler with a walk-out basement, was set into a slope. George had no difficulties supporting his family, but he was not inclined toward extravagance. The Halls built a cabin on Lake Superior north of Duluth, a rich man's luxury by today's standards but not in the 1940s. Cabins then were small and rustic, not the second homes they are today. People didn't vacation en masse to the outdoors, and property even on the glorious Lake Superior was inexpensive owing to its remoteness. George bought 125 feet of shoreline from a friend for one dollar a foot. The cabin, one-quarter mile north of the landmark Split Rock Lighthouse, was where George and Lorena could retreat in complete privacy and isolation.

George's autobiography is deeply understated. He tends to downplay the negative and seems hesitant to criticize anyone. In his first chapter, he paints a rosy picture of those early days with Lorena as they courted and got married. But then he describes returning on occasion to the Bethany campus. "[We] were always welcomed with warm Christian affection by the very persons we thought so critical of us." This revelation is a surprise, because we get only the subtlest hints that some might have viewed George and Lorena's teacher–student relationship as inappropriate.

The writing sets the tone for the entire manuscript. It's not a memoir; it's a report. It's a recollection of who, what, where, and when but not so much the why. The hallmarks of memoir are missing—the reflection, the narrative voice commenting on the past, the transformative moment. Stoic midwesterners of Swedish descent are not known for their effusiveness. Yet a strong current of love runs throughout, a muted love story more evocative than one obviously passionate.

I've raked through George's manuscript seeking clues that would unlock Camilla's story. When I first read it, I hoped that amid George's recitation of acquaintances and minutiae about jobs there would be a stunning, yet subtle, flash of insight that would explain Camilla's decisions. But not only does the manuscript as a whole yield few insights into Camilla's life, it also offers little revelation into the depths of grief George and Lorena must have felt when their children died. George titles chapter 4 "Terry and Peter's Deaths" as if he's an observer watching a film about a tragic family. On Terry's death from a virus, he writes about buying the cemetery plots. Three years later, after Peter's death from familial nephritis, a kidney condition, George recounts the facts—the church service, who sang there, the clearing of snowy cemetery roads, and the food and coffee served after the service. A small glimpse of emotion emerges when George explains how he taught his regularly scheduled class at Gustavus the morning after Peter's funeral: "As I went on in the lecture I grew stronger and even managed a feeble joke I had used many years. When the class was over there were feelings of relief and warm embraces of sympathy and support."

———

Camilla was three years old when Terry died and six when Peter died. By 1951, it was just George, Lorena, and their two girls, Camilla and Nan. While Camilla was healthy, Nan was not. Physical problems plagued her from birth. She was born with a joint disorder and underwent several surgeries. She spent much of her childhood in full leg casts.

What must it have been like for Camilla to grow up in a household so familiar with death? Children are astute. As George and Lorena went on with their everyday lives, Camilla surely would have absorbed her parents' grief. How does one view the world of the living when it's overlaid with the world of the dead? Camilla's siblings in their absence still were a presence. George ends chapter 4 with this sentence: "Less publicly, at home, Lorena went about the normal duties of a mother, trying to answer the profound questions of life and death raised by her little girls." That's the only commentary he provides. No sense of what those questions were, no description of how Camilla and Nan reacted to the deaths of their brothers. But he recognizes the burden that was placed on Lorena's shoulders.

A childhood suffused with death colors one's actions and thoughts. My dad's job as a gravedigger showed me, at a young age, that people die—not only old people, like grandparents, but also young people. Graves of youngsters who died of disease—like Terry and Peter—peppered the cemeteries near us. Teenagers also claimed spaces in our cemeteries, often the victims of accidents—Brad, Wanda, Brent, Linda, Chris. In rural areas, before laws required seat belts, rough gravel roads marked with sharp curves posed fatal dangers to young, inexperienced drivers.

You live your life differently when you grow up with a clear sense of mortality. I felt like something dark lurked around every corner. When would the Grim Reaper reach out to pluck my dad, my mom, my sister, or my brother? Nothing made us special. We didn't live in a bubble that would protect us. Look at Job: wealthy, successful, healthy, and he lost it all.

I was fifteen years old when death touched my family. My dad died unexpectedly from a fast-growing cancer. His death was a shock, but it also felt like the bad thing I had been waiting for. After that, I felt somewhat protected. I would be safe now. Surely God wouldn't take more from me when I had lost someone I had loved so much.

It's not a stretch to think that as a young woman, Camilla, who was her family's lone survivor of childhood, would have a preoccupation with death. The SLA expected death to arrive at any moment. They were convinced that law enforcement would beat down their door and kill them all, and they were right. But could Camilla have felt protected by her siblings' deaths—a feeling that allowed her to take risks, to feel invincible? Maybe she thought, *My parents have already endured so much grief. Surely I will not be taken from them, too.*

Or did she feel cursed, from a cursed family, far exceeding her allotted time on earth? Maybe she was willing to hasten what she figured would be an early death; maybe she felt that she, like her siblings, was fated to die young. And if that was the case, why not go out with guns blazing? Why not die for the revolution?

CHAPTER 2

"Their First Concern"

IN 1951, church leaders asked George Hall, who chaired the Board of Missions for the Augustana Church, to serve the mission in Tanganyika. Church leaders had asked George the same question years before, but he hadn't thought the work would suit his young and growing family. But now, after Terry's and Peter's deaths, it was just him and Lorena, Camilla and Nan. They still faced the challenges of Nan's health issues, which he and his wife took into consideration when they received the call.

"We thought about it for a few days. Staying home from Africa had not served to protect us from the losses of our two boys or to save Nan from her disability," George wrote. "These things had happened in an 'ideal world.' If this is God's will we will not have different fortunes of life wherever we are." George decided to accept the call to serve as education secretary for the northern provinces in Tanganyika. The Halls left St. Peter and set out for Africa in early 1952. Camilla was about to turn seven years old.

When Swedish immigrants founded the Augustana Lutheran Synod in 1860, mission work was at its core. In 1984, George wrote a book titled *The Missionary Spirit in the Augustana Church*, in which he said the intent of the first Augustana preachers was not to serve only Swedish immigrants; rather, "their first concern," as early as 1868, was to minister to former slaves. But this population was almost nonexistent in the upper Midwest, where the Augustana Synod was based, and the idea was abandoned.

As the country became more urban in the early twentieth century, Augustana adopted a cohesive "home mission" plan to serve nonwhites. Augustana churches in the heart of cities were encouraged to remain in their locations rather than follow white families to the suburbs. The churches embraced the shifting demographics. Augustana churches in Houston, New York, and Chicago were at the forefront of racial integration not only within the congregations but in surrounding neighborhoods as well. Mission work was about lending a helping hand, especially in poverty-stricken areas. Missions focused on self-help, not charity; on teaching, not just giving.

After World War II, Augustana was one of many Lutheran synods that joined forces to resurrect "orphaned" missions overseas. In places like Tanganyika, organized mission work flourished throughout the late nineteenth and early twentieth centuries, but church officials had largely abandoned African countries in the political chaos that plagued the continent immediately after the war.

———

Each time Camilla stepped outside their house in Marangu, in the very northeast corner of Tanganyika, she soaked in the stunning view of snow-capped Mount Kilimanjaro. The landscape offered beauty the likes of which the Halls had never seen. They also were not accustomed to such a rustic way of life. In Marangu, they drank glacier water that was pumped into the house, and kerosene powered the refrigerator in the absence of electricity. Shortages of paper had marked the World War II era, and it was still in short supply. Items like butter were wrapped in banana leaves or old newspapers. As was the custom, villagers were employed to do household chores for missionary families. Lorena at first bristled at the help—she was used to doing the cooking and cleaning herself—but she had no choice but to accept it. The Halls had three workers, all men: a cook, an outdoor handyman, and a housekeeper. Their work was physical and demanding—splitting and stacking wood for the stove, scrubbing clothes in a washbasin, ironing with a heavy charcoal-heated iron. After a time, Lorena was no doubt glad for the assistance.

The Halls lived a simple life, but they could not escape their privilege as whites in Africa. Camilla and Nan had their own textbooks, while in the schools George oversaw, students had access to only a few very old textbooks. The most widely available book was the Bible, but often an entire church shared one copy. To teach geography, teachers drew maps in the dirt of the schoolyards and children answered questions by jumping to the correct country.

Camilla and Nan played as little girls do around the world. The Halls acquired an old bicycle for Camilla and a tricycle for Nan. The girls quickly found playmates in the village. It was an early lesson in cooperation and cross-cultural sharing, the girls forced to communicate in ways that didn't involve language. They devised simple games out of sticks and strings, rocks, and bits of old wrapping paper. Camilla and Nan learned to play the shepherd's flute. They taught the village's children American songs, and the children taught the Hall girls their own songs. George and Lorena took the girls on safaris to Kinampanda and Bumbuli, and in the cities of Mombasa and Tanga they enjoyed the beaches and markets.

———

Something else was happening to the Halls in Tanganyika beyond the mission work, beyond learning about a new culture and making new friends. The family of four was becoming exceedingly close. No distractions in their small home, no outside entertainment options, no television or radio. In the evenings, George and Lorena would read by candlelight and the girls would do their homework. After the work was done, the family would play records on an old phonograph left by a previous missionary. Camilla and Nan twirled and sang along to the songs. "It was a wonderful family time as we read stories to the children and put them to bed with prayers. It was a good life for us as a family," George recalled.

But George was often gone. His territory covered schools in a 120-mile radius, and he was away for days at a time. Lorena's sole focus was on Camilla and Nan. The three spent almost every moment together for the eighteen months they were in Tanganyika. No dropping the girls off at friends' houses to play; no grandparents, aunts, or uncles to watch them; no job for Lorena; no solo shopping trips. Lorena was their teacher, their nurse, their friend. After the deaths of her two boys, she couldn't help but bond with her remaining children in those close quarters.

But even halfway around the world, the family couldn't escape sorrow. George and Lorena carried the heaviness of Terry's and Peter's deaths no matter where they went. The mission work may have given them a new focus, a diversion that, for brief moments, perhaps let them think their family had always been the way it was then: father, mother, and two girls. And for those brief moments, perhaps they hoped it would always be that way. In Tanganyika, they had never been closer as a family. They never would be again. George wrote that Africa would change the family more than they knew.

Nan continued to battle health problems. After a year and a half, it became clear that Nan needed medical attention from specialists back in the States. They took their time going home, traveling by ship from Dar es Salaam up through the Red Sea and the Mediterranean Sea. The cruise offered sunshine, good food, and time by the pool. They stopped in Europe to visit England, Germany, and relatives in Stora Aby, Rok, Sweden.

When the family arrived back in St. Peter after an almost two-year absence, they found much had changed. Camilla and Nan encountered these changes most directly. Their classmates had already formed bonds. It would have been hard for Camilla and Nan to break into a clique no matter where they had been, but their travels in Africa marked them as radically different. In St. Peter, they became the "other." And if there's anything children seize upon, it's someone who's different. George wrote, "The girls were ridiculed for their African experience by other children so they withdrew and were ashamed of it and wouldn't talk to anyone about it. Also, their own small cliques were established and our girls were left out. So they spent more time at home with Lorena." Camilla and Nan grew silent. They would not speak about Tanganyika to anyone, not even to adults who asked out of innocent curiosity. They retreated into their home, into the comforting arms of Lorena, with whom they had spent so much time over the past several months. The Hall home in St. Peter became a cocoon, a place of safety and nurture. The girls' bond with Lorena grew stronger, but it would be tested in the face of more tragedy.

———

The Halls did not stay in St. Peter for long after their return from Tanganyika. St. Peter was no longer the place George had first envisioned when he moved there, a safe and welcoming small town where the family would spend the rest of their lives. Now he had lost two children, one daughter faced serious medical issues, and both girls disliked school and had no friends.

After just a few months back in St. Peter, George obtained a one-year position at the National Lutheran Council, which oversaw mission work. The move took the Halls to Montclair, New Jersey, about twelve miles west of Manhattan. Camilla and Nan thrived in this urban environment, a true melting pot where they were surrounded by diversity and by children who had been born in other countries or who had traveled there. George continued to travel the world in this new position—to Holland, Germany, Finland, and many countries in Africa. This left Lorena and the girls alone, again.

When George's assignment ended, the Halls returned to Minnesota in 1958 so George could take a position as pastor of Arlington Hills Lutheran Church in St. Paul, just north of downtown. Camilla and Nan continued to flourish in a city. Arlington Hills was a large congregation with many children and youth programs, and all the Halls felt welcomed. The Halls would never live in a small town again. St. Peter, which twenty years before had seemed so bright and full of promise, now turned dark and cold with sad memories. Aside from travels and temporary appointments, George and Lorena would live in the Twin Cites and, later, Chicago for the rest of their lives. Camilla, too, would forever be an urban girl.

———

Pastors' time is not their own. They don't punch a time clock; they are always on call and always on display, always thinking about the people in their care. The job and the life are closely intertwined. George was lucky to find a compatible, supportive partner in Lorena, because being a pastor's spouse is a job by itself. As the pastor's wife at Arlington Hills, Lorena had stepped into a high-profile role. A pastor's wife was expected to be an equal partner in terms of leadership and hospitality. The previous pastor's wife had won many national awards for her work. George wrote of the tremendous pressure Lorena placed upon herself to live up to those expectations. "It was difficult for Lorena, not that the congregation expected her to be like [the previous pastor's wife] but within herself she felt she was not capable of doing the same."

While George was at Arlington Hills, the Lutheran World Federation asked him to return to Africa, this time for a six-month stint training African seminarians. George could not be away from a pastoral assignment for six months; he was expected to be present and to preach every Sunday. He longed for the flexibility he had once had when he taught at a college. So when he received an offer to work as a chaplain for the Lutheran Student Foundation at the University of Minnesota, he accepted. The position would mean working with students, which George had always enjoyed, and it would give him the flexibility to return to Africa. But it would be a step down, both in prestige and in pay. Still, he and Lorena decided to leave Arlington Hills after just two years, against the advice of friends and superiors. "It was an irrational decision similar to others we had made," he wrote.

It was at this time, around 1960, that the Halls moved to a house at 4532 Fremont Avenue in South Minneapolis. It was a neat, desirable neighborhood, just one block from Lake Harriet, part of the scenic chain of lakes in Minneapolis. They were within walking distance of Mount Olivet Lutheran Church, one of the largest Lutheran congregations in the Twin Cities metro area, where they would attend services. Washburn High School for Camilla and, later, Nan was about one mile away.

They got settled, George spent a few months working at the university, and then he went to Africa for six months. As in other times when George was preoccupied with work, Lorena managed life at home with Camilla and Nan. George says little about the times he left Lorena to be a single parent. That, too, is part of the duty of a pastor's spouse, though George was gone on extended trips more than most pastors. Lorena was apparently uncomplaining.

During these years, Camilla's two parents were present, yet not entirely. Her father's demanding jobs kept him busy. At Arlington Hills he was either at the church or meeting with parishioners, and at the University of Minnesota he met with students in the evenings after classes. When he was home, he was working, writing sermons, writing papers, reading, preoccupied with the problems of others. Lorena, at least for a time, felt intense pressure to play a public role as a pastor's wife. At the same time, she was the one who attended to the children and the housework. She could not afford to be distracted at home. When George was physically gone or emotionally unavailable, parenting tasks fell entirely to her.

And still there was Nan, who saw orthopedic specialists often and, owing to her limp, needed help getting around at home and at school. She experienced frequent pain. She struggled with high blood pressure and kidney problems. Nan's health demanded the bulk of George and Lorena's attention, and Camilla was often overshadowed. Camilla was healthy, strong, and independent. Perhaps her parents were grateful she didn't need a lot of attention. But just because she didn't clamor for their attention didn't mean she didn't crave it. Camilla learned at a young age to stay quiet, keep the peace, and not burden her already overtaxed, anxious, and worried parents. Once a fundamental aspect of one's character is formed at a young age, it proves difficult to recast.

CHAPTER 3

"It Was a Troubled Spring, Heavy with Grief"

DURING THE ADVENT SEASON OF 1962, Camilla was a senior at Washburn and Nan was a freshman. The sisters participated in the youth choir for an Advent concert at Mount Olivet, and the day of the concert Nan was not feeling well. The family had attended church in the morning and, after church, Nan walked with George to the car, parked a few minutes away. The day was cold, and Nan became chilled. At home, she went to bed to rest and warm up. By late afternoon she felt well enough to sing in the concert, but the next day she had developed a vicious cold. George knew a doctor in Minneapolis who had graduated from Gustavus, and the doctor made a house call to check on Nan. He listened to her chest, diagnosed lung congestion, and recommended they take Nan to the hospital. Once George got Nan settled in her hospital room, she asked him to get her some of her favorite cinnamon candy, which he did.

But soon her kidneys began to fail. She became gravely ill. A few days after her admission, on Saturday morning, George left to get cash for an advance payment for the hospital. At home, the laundry had piled up, so Camilla and Lorena went to a laundromat. Nan died alone.

"I sat by her bedside as her body cooled, and prayed," George wrote. "I contacted Lorena and Camilla at the laundromat in the middle of their wash. I arranged matters with the undertaker. At last we were together as a family about her bedside."

The funeral service was held just before Christmas at Mount Olivet, followed by a burial at Resurrection Cemetery in St. Peter. When George, Lorena, and Camilla returned to Minneapolis from the burial, they were greeted by something unexpected. Exhausted with grief, they had left the house dark and undecorated—Christmas had been the last thing on their minds during Nan's sudden illness and death. But as they pulled up to their house, they noticed a glow in the window. "The lights were on, [and] there was a beautiful Christmas tree and lights awaiting us. Our children's friends had somehow accomplished this surprise," George remembered.

Camilla and Nan were well liked at Washburn, so it's no wonder their peers did this good deed. To look at the yearbook from Camilla's senior year, one would never guess this young woman had just lost a sister and had lost two brothers years before. She was involved in a variety of activities—the literary journal, the newspaper, and theater. She played Wilson, the maid, in *The Barretts of Wimpole Street*, providing much comic relief. Camilla was voted "class clown" of the class of 1963. She was the funny one, the jolly one, the one who loved to laugh and make others laugh. Pictures from Camilla's yearbook all show her with a smile on her face.

Nan's absence meant the end of the impenetrable trio that was Lorena, Camilla, and Nan. A bond born out of their time in Tanganyika had continued after they returned to Minnesota. The three of them, against the world. While Lorena and Camilla maintained a loving relationship to the day Camilla died, something changed when Nan passed away. It was as if Lorena drew away. The change might have been subtle and hardly noticeable, but the effect was still there. After all, if three of your four children died, wouldn't you be bracing yourself for the death of the fourth? And when that happened, would distance lessen the heartbreak?

———

George was gone when Camilla was born. Lorena was about to burst with child, and she had a three-year-old and a four-year-old at home, yet George headed to Seattle for a week, having been asked to conduct Holy Week services for a congregation there. He was still gone when Camilla was born on March 24, the day before Palm Sunday.

And in early 1963, shortly after Nan died, George and Lorena left Camilla behind. George was called to serve at the newly formed Lutheran School of Theology in Maywood, Illinois, just west of downtown Chicago. Church leaders wanted him to lead Bible studies for laypeople who were going on mission work. George enjoyed working with students at the University of Minnesota, but he wrote that the work was "grueling," as he was on call at all hours to serve students' spiritual needs. "A new future in Chicago was inviting," he wrote.

A pattern emerges. Tragedy strikes, and George moves on. The boys died in St. Peter, and shortly after that the family left for Tanganyika. Nan died in Minneapolis, and shortly after that George took a job near Chicago. There always seemed to be something better on the horizon or a more exciting opportunity somewhere else. Or maybe George was trying to escape the reach of death's long, dark arm. Camilla would soon take this move straight from George's playbook.

When George took the job in Maywood, Camilla had just a few weeks left of her senior year. While George wouldn't officially start in his post until after Camilla was to graduate, he and Lorena spent the spring of 1963 preparing to move. They decided to keep the Fremont Avenue house and rent it out in the short term; the long-term plan was for Camilla to live there when she graduated from college.

While Camilla was finishing high school, throwing herself into her social life and activities, at home her parents had already moved on. Their attention was divided between their only living child and themselves, as they got ready to move to Illinois. Perhaps they thought Camilla was fine, just fine, as she had seemed to be all those years that Nan was sick. Now Camilla appeared well-adjusted; she was still funny, she still had lots of friends, she still took part in school activities. George and Lorena may have been thankful that they didn't have to take Camilla to a psychologist or psychiatrist or that they didn't have to deal with rebellious behavior. But not everything is as it seems. Sadness, and anger born out of that sadness, will always emerge.

———

It was Camilla's graduation day in 1963, and she was crying. She stood in the kitchen and slapped together a sandwich as she wept, while her tired parents watched.

"I'm your only child left," she said to George and Lorena. "The only one to make it to high school graduation! And this is how you treat me?" George and Lorena let Camilla speak her mind. The dam of midwestern reserve could no longer hold back Camilla's swelling emotions. Camilla wiped away her tears, took a deep breath, and quietly said, "I thought I would get more honor and respect today."

George and Lorena had started the day in northern Minnesota with a broken car. That weekend, they had gone to their North Shore cabin to open it for the spring and make needed repairs. They left the cabin the evening before graduation day, intending to drive through the night and get to Minneapolis in early morning. But on the road they collided with a deer, which bounced off the hood. The hood popped loose, flew up, and cracked the windshield. George pulled over and inspected the car; the radiator had broken and the water had escaped. They limped the car into the nearest town, found a house with a light on; the couple who lived there called a mechanic. The mechanic would arrive at daybreak. Meanwhile, George and Lorena tried to sleep in the back seat of the car. The next day, the mechanic found the necessary parts and tied the hood down, and George and Lorena were on their way. They arrived in Minneapolis just in time for the commencement ceremony.

"Everyone but not us was taking pictures," George wrote. "During the supper hour all the families had arranged for special dinners, but we did not know about this custom. We were tired from the night we had spent." Hence the sandwich in the kitchen and Camilla's tears. She saw all the care her friends' families had taken on this special day.

Camilla spoke bitterly and harshly, but truthfully. I don't know if this was a rare display of sadness on Camilla's part, but it was a rare mention of emotion in George's "I Remember Lorena." He recounts the entire scene in just one paragraph, squeezed between his typically mundane accounts of his work and travels. Why even mention it? He could have easily left it out. It mars what is otherwise an accounting of one man's good works and successes. In that one paragraph he's saying, *Here's where we made a mistake.* It reads as an atonement or a confession or an admission of guilt—or all three.

CHAPTER 4

Camilla Goes to College

MY FRIEND BECKY had a piece of good news for me one day. Becky was in my writing group and had read some of my early drafts about Camilla.

"A woman in my Monday morning coffee group went to college with Camilla. Her name is Frani Peterson. She'd be happy to talk to you," Becky said.

A real-live person who knew Camilla. These were hard to come by. Camilla was proving difficult to get to know—everyone who knew her well was dead. Most of her SLA comrades died with her. Her siblings were long gone. Her parents were gone by now, too. Lorena died in 1995 and George in 2000, less than one year after I first came across Camilla's story. How I wished I had found Camilla earlier, or recognized right away how much I would need George.

Camilla didn't even have close extended family members. As a family that moved frequently, the Halls never lived near George's or Lorena's siblings. Though Camilla had several cousins, she didn't know any of them well. It's hard for me to identify with this aspect of Camilla's life. If my immediate family were gone, people who wanted to learn more about me could choose from dozens of aunts, uncles, and cousins, as my dad had thirteen brothers and sisters, all of whom lived near us. We saw them often when we gathered for weddings, holidays, and funerals. I grew up knowing even my parents' aunts, uncles, and cousins and my cousins' other sets of grandparents, who treated me like their own.

So I started to cobble information together from whomever I could find, people who knew Camilla for small slices of her life because no one was alive who knew the whole Camilla. But I took comfort in realizing that such a person had never existed anyway. Once Camilla went to college, she drifted away from the people closest to her—her parents. And she became adept at keeping secrets from them.

———

Frani lived in a big, mission-style house built in 1913 in St. Peter, immaculately kept; the rooms looked like the ones styled for a home magazine rather than rooms in a house where people actually lived. Before we sat down to talk about Camilla, Frani gave me a tour of the grand house. A tornado had destroyed most of the house in 1998; that's why everything looked so new and white. She showed me the post-tornado addition and the way the house now sat crooked on its foundation; the space underneath the upstairs doors left an angled sliver of light.

She abruptly stopped in the kitchen. "Do you do feng shui?" she asked me. I shook my head. "I only know a little about it."

"This kitchen is just terrible. Look at this; there are five doorways." She pointed them out. "All the energy just leaks out," she said, waving her hands around.

With that, we slipped out of the kitchen and settled in the living room. Before I arrived she had prepared for my visit, pulling out her Gustavus Adolphus yearbook from her freshman year, 1963–64, along with several newspaper clips about Camilla and the SLA. She spread everything out on a glass coffee table. Frani admitted she hadn't known Camilla that well, yet she'd kept these articles for forty years. Like the former sheriff who kept the Wanted poster, Frani was one of many people who clung to this piece of the past, who was reluctant to let go of the connection with Camilla, no matter how tenuous.

———

When Frani and Camilla came to Gustavus in the fall of 1963, it might as well have still been the 1950s, especially in a small midwestern town like St. Peter, which would always be a few years behind the trends. In 1963 St. Peter was still in an era of poodle skirts, malt shops, sock hops, and boys staking claim to girls by giving them their fraternity pins. Of course there was some booze, or a rare instance of pot, but nothing like what would come later in the decade.

Frani, Camilla, and the other young women at the co-ed Gustavus campus were locked in their dorms by 9 p.m. The boys did not have a curfew. Frani said, "The powers that be determined that if there weren't girls [out and about], what were the boys going to do?"

At Gustavus, Camilla chose to conceal the darker shadows of her life. At eighteen years old, she already knew something about crafting a persona that would garner friends. Be the funny girl who keeps them laughing and they won't ask questions. Maybe this was something she picked up from George. Being a pastor demands, on some level, a bit of acting. George seemed natural at his job, but what of the times when he was struggling with his own problems yet people needed him? He had to be willing to listen and counsel at any time. George in public and George at home had to be two different people. Consider the way he moved on, quickly, from the deaths of his children.

Frani got to know Camilla in the dorm, Wahlstrom Hall. But she didn't even know her real name. Camilla went by "Candy," a nickname she used in high school. Frani wouldn't discover Camilla's real name until news about the SLA emerged in 1974.

In a locked-down Wahlstrom Hall, the girls could not help but spend a lot of time with each other. Their quarters were cramped; when the dorm was first built, it housed returning students from World War II, primarily sailors who knew a thing or two about close quarters. In Wahlstrom Hall, two girls lived in rooms that measured eight feet by ten feet. George recalled moving Camilla into her dorm; he called the rooms "cubby holes." "We were shocked and we drew Camilla aside and asked her if she wanted to stay or go back to Minneapolis and the University [of Minnesota]. She decided to stay," he wrote.

Camilla played the role of happy entertainer, a continuation from her high school days. Night after night, Camilla would pull out her bass ukulele and sing songs she had written, teaching the lyrics to the other girls. More than fifty years later, Frani remembered one song of Camilla's in particular: "Screen Door Summer Rockin' Chair Dreams." She tried to hum the tune. "It had a really good beat. So some of us who couldn't sing or play anything, we danced to it."

Frani admired Camilla's talent, her ability to write lyrics and sing and play. "I just got a kick out of her," Frani said.

———

Only one picture of Camilla appears in the 1963–64 Gustavus yearbook. This is odd, because she had been so active in high school activities. In the photograph, Camilla sits on the lawn, the middle person in a group of five: three women and two men. Frani said this is how class pictures were taken: alphabetically by last name with a group of people, as opposed to individual shots. Camilla's group was a hodgepodge of names, though, an *E*, two *H*'s, and two *S*'s.

Camilla wears a wraparound skirt and plaid blouse. She faces the camera with an assured smile, unlike the others, who, if they do smile, do so nervously. Of the group, Camilla looks the most confident. They are freshmen, just seventeen or eighteen years old—kids, really. The boys sport crew cuts and the girls have short, wavy hair. But even though Camilla is in the middle of the group, she's set apart. The boy and girl on the left appear to be almost touching, as do the boy and girl on the right. There's a lot of space between Camilla and the people on either side of her.

The photograph was taken the first week of school. Things would change for Camilla, and for the entire nation, as 1963 progressed.

———

Camilla ditched the sock-hop look after that first week. Frani remembered that Camilla gravitated toward the artsy students, who primarily wore black, and changed her wardrobe to match them. A change in outward appearance was the only acceptable way to proclaim a public identity. An inner identity that deviated from the norm—for example, identifying as gay or as nonreligious —could not be revealed, at least not in a place like Gustavus, and certainly not for Camilla. George had been gone from the campus for only five years, and most of the faculty and staff still knew him.

It's not clear when Camilla started to live as a lesbian. In letters to her parents throughout the 1960s, she occasionally mentions men that she dates, though knowing her later history I suspect this was just another act. Not until she met Patricia Soltysik in Berkeley in 1971 did she openly have a lesbian relationship. Even so, she kept that a secret from her parents—not difficult, since they were living half a continent away. But in 1963 at Gustavus, there was no chance that homosexuality would be acknowledged, much less accepted. Frani suspected there were lesbian relationships between some girls, though she couldn't say that about Camilla in particular. But in 1963, identifying someone as a lesbian wasn't even about sexuality. "It was just a boyish, mannish thing," Frani said. "The word 'gay' didn't exist."

Very few people at Gustavus knew the depths of grief Camilla had experienced as a result of her siblings' deaths. Frani didn't know anything about Camilla's family, though mutual friends hinted to Frani that sadness enveloped Camilla. Students who came from the Gustavus tradition knew the Hall family—for example, the daughter of Gustavus's longtime football coach, Lloyd Hollingsworth. The Hollingsworths were friends with the Halls, and their daughter Kay was privy to Camilla's family circumstances, but Kay didn't mention those facts to others—as if grief were a shameful secret.

"[Kay] didn't like to talk about Candy or the family situation because it was so tragic," Frani said. It wasn't until 1974, after Camilla's death, that Frani discovered Camilla's siblings had died as children.

Even the name "Candy" suggests a certain sweetness or frivolity. A "Candy" is a fun-loving girl, while a "Camilla" comes off as more mature and serious. Candy lived up to her nickname at Gustavus.

"She was a lot of fun, just very friendly," Frani said. "She was a big girl, stocky, not fat, and she had that big-girl laugh."

———

The freshmen who entered Gustavus in the fall of 1963 went home over Christmas break to a very different and bleaker world. President John F. Kennedy had been killed just before Thanksgiving, and now Lyndon Johnson was president. The next year was about to bring a major escalation of America's involvement in Vietnam. In that year, too, three civil rights workers would be murdered in Mississippi, and massive student protests at the University of California, Berkeley, would lead to the free speech movement.

In the spring of 1964, as all the Gustavus students went their separate ways for the summer, Frani and Kay and Camilla hugged each other and bid farewell. Frani and Kay returned to Gustavus in the fall; Camilla did not. She transferred to the University of Minnesota in Minneapolis.

It's no surprise that she started at Gustavus. After all, that was where George had taught for almost twenty years. Both the campus and the town were familiar to Camilla. While she had had happy times growing up in St. Peter, it also was where the family had lived when her brothers died. At Gustavus, she was less than a mile away from where Terry, Peter, and Nan were buried. I wonder if it was hard for Camilla to be in St. Peter alone. This was the last place where her family had been whole.

At the end of spring semester, Camilla packed her bags, stuffed them into her car, and left for her new home. At the University of Minnesota, she was now one of several thousand students instead of one of a few hundred. The public, secular environment may have appealed to her. Certainly at the U. of M. some students knew what "gay" was, knew that being a lesbian meant more than simply having an eclectic taste in clothing or boyish mannerisms.

The move from St. Peter to Minneapolis would be one of many in Camilla's short adult life. It was the beginning of a pattern of being unsettled, of always seeking the next new thing, always hoping that things would be better if she moved and tried something new.

———

In an application letter for a job after college, Camilla said that while she had enjoyed the close living quarters and companionship at Gustavus, she hadn't thought she "was getting as good an academic education as I had expected from the college and so I transferred to the University of Minnesota."

Camilla was an average student at the U. of M., where she majored in humanities. She graduated with a 2.5 GPA, just squeaking into the B range. She did best in classes related to theater and European history. But in other courses, such as art, she scored Cs and Ds, even earning an F in a basic sculpture class. Perhaps Camilla was a bright but not very dedicated student. But under the right direction she could be engaged. She took a theater class in the fall of 1964 and wrote to her parents, "My theater arts teacher is a very enjoyable lecturer and has a marvelously satiric and sarcastic wit (which I respect very highly). When I listen to him I feel more like I'm in a nightclub than in Scott Hall auditorium." She got a B in that class, while she complained about her philosophy professor in a class in which she received a C.

During her sophomore and junior years, Camilla lived at the Fremont Avenue property in Minneapolis that her parents still owned, and they were living outside Chicago. She lived in a furnished apartment above the garage, and renters occupied the house. "This was my first real experience with budgeting money and I was pleased with this independence. I prepared all my meals on a two-burner hotplate in my bathroom and washed my dishes in the bathtub," she wrote in her job application. By her senior year, though, she missed interaction with other students and moved to an apartment closer to campus.

Existing letters from her time at college do not suggest any type of political involvement. Camilla mostly kept her parents informed about her friends, the renters at the Fremont Avenue house, and her schoolwork. If she was active in the antiwar movement, she didn't say so. But she would become more openly involved in politics after she secured a job shortly after graduation in 1967 and entered the "real world" of full-time employment.

CHAPTER 5

Camilla Gets a Job

ON THANKSGIVING 1967, Camilla spent the day with her boss and coworkers. She was three months into her job as a welfare officer for St. Louis County in northern Minnesota.

Amid the food and camaraderie, Camilla's boss had something to say to her. "I'm pleased with your work with that thirteen-year-old girl," he told her. The young teen was pregnant, and the boss had assigned the tough case to Camilla because he admired her care and compassion with clients. "I doubt a more experienced caseworker could handle it as well as you have."

Camilla beamed. How good it felt to hear those words, to be trusted and highly regarded at work. She noted the conversation in a letter to her parents. "Let's hear it for me—yeah rah rah!"

Over the next few months, Camilla tried to persuade the girl to give the baby up for adoption. In that era, adoption was seen as the best option, and welfare offices were prepared to pull out all the stops to make it happen, though the methods seem cruel today. If the teen resisted the adoption path, Camilla would have the county attorney charge the seventeen-year-old father with carnal knowledge and the girl with immoral conduct. She told her parents she hoped it wouldn't come to that. "As I said, these would be the last resorts and won't be threatened until the last minute. It sounds mean I suppose, but it would be tragic to allow an eighth grader to keep a baby. I think I'll be able to convince her, but it's nice to know that I have some authority to fall back on in case she refuses."

The job at St. Louis County was Camilla's first job out of college. In August 1967 she moved to Duluth, Minnesota, a city situated at the southwestern tip of Lake Superior. Camilla felt a mixture of excitement and trepidation. She told her parents in a letter that the work sounded "tremendously challenging and scarey." She had asked college friends to write letters of recommendation for the job. One friend wrote, "While at school together and since then, I have seen her help numerous people with their problems. One of the reasons she is able to help people is because she likes them and understands them. She is not obsequious in dealing with people but is very open and direct."

As the months went on, Camilla's caseload grew. She had forty-nine clients in December and sixty-three in January. In Duluth, many people went on welfare during the winter months as the shipping industry slowed. She wrote to her parents of being overwhelmed and busy. Not only did she have to meet with clients both day and night depending on their schedules, but she also had to attend meetings and testify in court. "We prepare the cases for the county attorney and he presents them and gets all the credit. He takes care of questioning witnesses, but we provide him with all the information—we testify also," she complained.

But the teen pregnancy case seemed to occupy Camilla's attention; it was the only case she mentioned specifically and repeatedly in letters to her parents. In the middle of December she wrote: "I've been reading up on adolescent psychology for my 13-year-old pregnant girl and although she doesn't 'like' me anymore, I think I'm getting through to her and that's the important thing."

Despite the frustrations, Camilla had the opportunity to grow professionally. In March 1968, Camilla told her parents that she was looking forward to a symposium on unwed mothers, where she was going to be a discussion group leader. She also found ways to use her poetic and musical talents on the job. That month, the county kicked off a campaign to advertise the need for foster families, and Camilla wrote a song to be used in radio and television commercials. She conceived a syncopated calypso beat but was most proud of the lyrics:

> Do you have room in your home
> For homeless children—
> Room in your heart to love some more—
> Kids who need someone to guide them
> Kids who need someone beside them
> Kids who need the help only you can give
> Think how much you could help them
> If you'll just extend a welcome—
> Think of foster care

"Last I heard, they were also scheduling me to appear with other recruiters on local TV variety shows to sing the song and give the pitch," Camilla told her parents. "It should be a lot of fun, but I'm pretty nervous. If I do say so myself however, it's a darn good song to get across the idea. . . . Imagine my clients' reactions when they see their friendly caseworker on TV plunking a guitar and singing!"

Duluth was Camilla's first exposure to the realities of day-to-day living the poor experienced in the United States. Camilla had seen poverty firsthand while living in Africa and also on a visit to South America with her parents in 1964, but in the United States she lived in comfort as a member of the middle class.

From an economic perspective, Duluth was rough. "Gritty" would be a good word to describe the town in Camilla's time. Duluth sits on Lake Superior, which in terms of surface area is the largest freshwater lake in the world. The landscape looks like nothing else in the Midwest; it's more reminiscent of the Pacific Northwest or far northern New England, with rocky outcroppings along wind-whipped shores and immense tracts of pine, aspen, and birch. Scandinavian immigrants had settled here, attracted by forested vistas that looked much like the ones back home. Those immigrants worked in the timber industry, and immigrants from southeastern Europe worked in the iron ore mines. For decades, Lake Superior bustled with ships that took Minnesota lumber and iron ore to places all over the world, where it became furniture, paper, and steel. But by the 1960s, the mines and forests were all but stripped. Fewer goods came out of the region, and fewer goods meant fewer ships. Duluth, about 150 miles north of Minneapolis, was primarily a one-industry town; the weakened shipping industry sank the town's fortunes.

Camilla had been through Duluth several times during her youth as her family traveled to their Lake Superior cabin, another forty miles north of the city. In a letter to her parents shortly after she arrived in Duluth, she said she had always remembered it as dirty and old-fashioned. But now that she was living there, she saw how truly disadvantaged the town was. "The hill ghettoes reminded me of the favellas in Brazil (without the romance)." She found an apartment for seventy dollars per month in an old house that had been converted into a fourplex. She told her parents that she could have moved into a newer apartment building, but they wouldn't allow her to bring her cat, Keya. The massive mansions that lined Duluth's streets near the lake could be found just a few blocks to the north and east of Camilla's apartment. The rich and poor lived side by side, unlike in larger cities, whose segregation allowed the middle and upper classes to close their eyes to injustices if they wished. Camilla learned that many of her neighbors were receiving Aid to Families with Dependent Children (AFDC). She was curious as to how they would react if they found out she was a social worker for the county—she told her parents she did not want to be thought of as a spy.

But the bright spots about her job that Camilla enjoyed were not enough to outweigh her frustrations. She told her parents that morale in her department was low. Clients who wanted more money ignored caseworkers like Camilla and appealed directly to managers. Managers who did not want trouble issued illegal grants. "This makes me very angry both as a caseworker and as a taxpayer. The administration does not want anything to rock their boat so they give in rather than have the client go home irate."

At age twenty-three, Camilla began to see that though programs like AFDC worked on paper, reality was a different story. Her first year on the job, while not exactly a rude awakening, opened her eyes to the reality of human behavior. Here were the rules regarding what constituted welfare fraud, and Camilla, as a newbie, was prepared to follow those strictures. Coworkers frustrated her, because they let clients bend the rules.

"Somewhere along the line casework services failed for them and the caseworker let them get away with all sorts of stuff—this isn't good for the client or the agency, so I'm doing something about it. This aspect of my job has always bothered me, but I'm beginning to realize that we can't do therapy unless the client respects our position and our authority."

In October she wrote to George and Lorena, "Work steadily fluctuates between reward and despair, confidence and frustrations, success and failure. No two days are alike and this is both challenging and agonizing. I don't know if I'll be able to keep up the pace for more than a year, but I don't think that I could find a job I enjoy more right now. It's nice to feel useful and productive for a change."

She struggled to balance compassion with rules. To her parents she said, "I'm having a hard time keeping a professional distance from my clients— I'm human and I get emotionally involved. It's getting a little easier as I get more experienced because I'm beginning to realize that a good casework relationship requires both emotional involvement (<u>controlled</u> emotional involvement) and objectivity. I guess in a nutshell my job is to help the client realize and accomplish what is best for him <u>in the long run</u>. It's not as easy as it sounds."

When her idealism toward work wore off, Camilla turned toward politics. She was elected a delegate in her precinct to support Eugene McCarthy. A U.S. senator from Minnesota, McCarthy opposed the war in Vietnam. With U.S. involvement—and deaths—in Vietnam reaching unprecedented levels, people like Camilla saw McCarthy as the sole voice of reason. He was a rare politician who challenged the powerful machine of the Johnson administration and the Pentagon.

"DFL caucuses were this week and McCarthy did pretty well in Minneapolis, St. Paul and Duluth," Camilla wrote to her parents. "I was elected a delegate in my precinct to carry the McCarthy banner. It's a little risky tho because gov't employees are covered by the Hatch Act which states we can't actively campaign or be delegates. The county attorney encouraged me however and said he'd back me if there was any trouble (he's a delegate too and shouldn't be). Several other caseworkers are doing the same thing. So it should be interesting to see if anything comes of it. It seems to me that the Hatch Act is unconstitutional—maybe a test case would get it banned. We'll see what happens."

———

In June 1968, Camilla left Duluth and took a similar job in Minneapolis, for Hennepin County. Perhaps Camilla missed the hustle and bustle of Minneapolis, where she had lived for about seven years. That was the longest time she had lived in any one place. It was as good a home as any.

Hennepin County, as the state's most populous county, would have had the highest welfare caseload in the state. The work wouldn't have been easy, and if Camilla became frustrated at St. Louis County, the same was bound to happen in Hennepin County.

But she continued to charm coworkers. One, Jean Bigelow, spoke positively about Camilla when interviewed by a researcher a few years after Camilla's death: "[Camilla] was very witty; she was fun to be with; and she was very sympathetic and helpful. If you needed a favor or needed to talk, she was really very compassionate. And yet she also had very strong, kind of passionate, ideas."

A supervisor, Alan Carlson, said Camilla was always smiling. "I never once saw her depressed or disgruntled or cantankerous or in an ugly mood," he told the same researcher. "She seemed to have good rapport with other social workers. . . . There seemed to be a camaraderie in her relationship with other staff members. She was intelligent. She was interesting. She was talented. She was just the sort of person who seemed to relate pretty well with other people."

CHAPTER 6

A Turning Point

LIKE THE REST OF THE COUNTRY, Camilla witnessed the drama that unfolded at the Democratic National Convention (DNC) in Chicago in 1968. She watched on television as the antiwar faction broke storefront glass and smashed car windows and as police outfitted with gas masks, batons, and guns beat the protesters bloody. The war in Vietnam had come home.

Though just six years later Camilla would embrace her own brand of political violence, she did not support the DNC protesters. She wrote to her parents that the riots deflected attention away from what really mattered. "People have forgotten already (for 'practical' purposes such as the election) what happened at Chicago—not the hippies and yippies bit, but the fact that McCarthy and Kennedy ran away with all the primaries and had the popular support of the people (not with the machine obviously) and yet didn't get the nomination."

McCarthy proceeded with his candidacy and refused to endorse the party's candidate, fellow Minnesotan Hubert Humphrey. Camilla continued to support McCarthy, who stopped by his home state in October. Camilla was nearly starstruck. "Gee, he's handsome!" she wrote to her parents. She sat in the front row during his speech. "We even got to shake his hand!"

She grew impatient with people who called McCarthy a sore loser for not endorsing Humphrey. She criticized past McCarthy supporters who now backed Humphrey because he was the endorsed nominee. Where were their principles? she wondered. Would they blindly follow any endorsed candidate? "They gripe a little about the lesser of two or three evils, but they'll still play along with the machinery that is insulting their intelligence and judgment. As long as a party can continue to win elections and power with these tactics, they'll continue to use them."

She called the situation a "mis-use of democracy," adding, "We're always going to be denied a choice if we don't put our foot down and say NO. I'm campaigning for and voting for liberal legislators and local politicians, but I intend to vote NO for president. . . . In the next four years, we're going to take over the DFL [the Minnesota Democratic-Farmer-Labor Party]—we, the people."

Even though Camilla's anger and frustration were starting to bubble up, in many ways she remained the Camilla of years past—friendly, gregarious, and witty. One of Camilla's coworkers at Hennepin County, Bette Esbjornson, said everyone who met Camilla liked her. "When I first knew her she was really into the antiwar movement. It was interesting, because I had no opinion about it at all; and she really told me why I had to be against this terrible thing. . . . She was very honest, very deep-down honest, a really good person."

Camilla spent most of her free time in Minneapolis working on *The Silent Planet Speaks*, an underground newspaper. Camilla reported for, edited, laid out, and proofread the newspaper, which covered the peace movement. Her name never appeared on the masthead, though; the Hatch Act still forbade political activity by government employees who worked with federal money. She was involved in the Mobilization Committee to End the War in Vietnam, which sponsored a march with a good turnout—two blocks long. She participated in grape boycotts to support Cesar Chavez's National Farm Workers Association.

Bette remembered Camilla as politically active and vocal. "Camilla was always into revolution. . . . She went to several gatherings, not riots, but get-togethers protesting things. And she was sprayed with mace one time, and she wore contact lenses, so they really almost blinded her for a week.

That made her pretty angry too. . . . She wasn't into gun violence, just get-up-and-shout violence."

It makes sense that Camilla's letters to her parents became more political in 1968, one of the most tense and volatile election years the country had seen. "Very disappointed to watch Nixon win on the first ballot—Republicans are so consistently stupid. I hope the Democratic convention isn't so easy. Some say there will be a lot of trouble at it since it's the last vestige of hope for liberals." In the summer of 1968 she considered throwing her support behind Eldridge Cleaver, the minister of information for the Black Panther Party and presidential candidate of the Peace and Freedom Party. "Unfortunately, more often than not P&F people are too ivory tower-ish and alienate the middle class energetics. I've been to most of the plenary sessions and it doesn't seem too workable. They refuse to admit that you have to make your first main effort on the local level!"

She recommended that her parents read Cleaver's book, *Soul on Ice,* and also Dick Gregory's book *Write Me In!,* in which he discussed the Peace and Freedom Party. She also encouraged her parents to read the October 26, 1967, issue of *Ramparts* because of an interview with Huey Newton, and the fall 1968 issue of *Harper's,* which featured a report by Norman Mailer on the backstage activities at the DNC that year.

The letters make it clear that Camilla and George enjoyed rhetorical debate and political conversation. In many ways, Camilla was her father's daughter. George was a prolific thinker and writer, and he must have been pleased that his only surviving child not only took an interest in the larger world but also wanted to make a difference both in her job and in politics. In a letter written in September 1968, she provided feedback on an article her father had written about welfare. Camilla compared his article with works written by Max Weber, including *The Protestant Ethic and the Spirit of Capitalism.* Then she gave an articulate view of the welfare system. She praised Minnesota for being one of the most liberal welfare states at the time and criticized the southern states for ignoring the poverty problem. "The southern states react to poverty the same way they and Freeman reacted to hunger in America—they shut their eyes and say it simply does not exist."

It didn't take long for Camilla's frustration with her Hennepin County job to emerge much as it had in St. Louis County. While she had had a supportive supervisor in Duluth, that wasn't the case in Minneapolis. Camilla's performance reviews noted that she sometimes had a hard time accepting department policy.

"If she questioned, it was because she felt that policy needed changing. . . . If she was critical, it was for positive reasons not negative reasons," said Alan Carlson, a supervisor at the Hennepin County office but not Camilla's supervisor. When Camilla butted heads with her own manager, Delores Peck, she went to Carlson.

"I think that relates to Candy's maverickness," Carlson said. "She was a nice person, a very sweet person—Mrs. Peck—but I also think that anyone who gave her any kind of hard time in terms of questioning policy, would upset her."

By mid-1969 Camilla had worked in the welfare system for two years. It's not a job that someone with a high degree of empathy can keep for long. "And I think the reason she gave up her work was because it just got her down. She suffered with them so much," said Lorena of the clients Camilla worked with. "I think there were some rules that bothered her too. For example, you can't touch the client, you know. Well, you don't go around touching clients very much; but there are times when you should. . . . She differed with one of her supervisors about a number of things, I think."

Jean Bigelow said, "She never came off as an angry person. She would be intense about a case and frustrated sometimes in trying to help someone." She continued, "I think that it was sort of an underlying theme with her, the need to be in a helpful position. In fact, I think she entered social work with a lot of enthusiasm, almost too much idealistic enthusiasm. . . . She was really pretty disillusioned by it. I think she was 'riding' on her funny cynicism for a while."

Camilla grew restless, wondering if there was something better, both in terms of a job and a place to live. In the past six years she had moved from Minneapolis to St. Peter, back to Minneapolis, then to Duluth, and then to Minneapolis again. She was her father's daughter in this way, too. After leaving St. Peter, George didn't stay put for long. He, too, was always looking for new opportunities and places to fit in. He bounced from college teaching to mission work to preaching to chaplaincy and back to college teaching.

In March 1969, Camilla told her parents, "These days I'm getting my annual California fever and I want to just pick up and move. Going out there for a vacation isn't enough, but it's a start. I plan to have some job interviews while out there. If I weren't so conservative I'd close my eyes and jump—but I know I can't afford that right now." Sunny, bright places where she could have fun appealed to her. In the same letter she mentioned the possibility of a two-week visit to Mexico, where she would take guitar lessons. "Wouldn't that be a groovy vacation? I think I'll look into it some more."

By mid-1969 Bette Esbjornson and her husband, Dick, had moved to Los Angeles. Camilla visited them in June. The warmth and sun of California may have seemed enticing to Camilla, but more than once to her parents she mentioned the San Andreas Fault and the possibility of a major earthquake.

"It seems like San Andreas Fault is mentioned on every TV show that originates from the West Coast and it doesn't seem like such a joke anymore. One theory is that all the sin of America is concentrated in California and therefore as punishment it's going to drop off and be destroyed. I'm beginning to think I should keep my sins here in Minneapolis so as not to add to the sin quotient out there! Imagine my guilt feelings if I was the proverbial straw! Oh well, I'll just wait and see."

Bette and Dick persuaded Camilla to move to Los Angeles, which she did in early 1970, though plans had been in place for months before.

"I think she had done a lot of thinking before she came out here about what she was going to do when she got here," Bette said. "In fact, I know she did. She had it all planned out, because Camilla would plan these things out down to the letter. . . . She always planned everything out very well. She knew that she would come out there and try to be an artist."

Bigelow talked about Camilla's reasoning about her move. "She didn't present this trip to California in terms of an answer to everything; it was more like, 'It isn't here, and I'm seeking it.'"

PART II

Camilla Transformed

We want so much to make a movie of ourselves—our
adventures, our thoughts. On this trip we came up with the
opening scene: (background music we write, too) Camilla
walking across a field with a cigar box in her hands, then a
shot of me filming and me filming Camilla. Camilla trips,
box opens, and one butterfly escapes, and she quickly shuts
the box and recovers, walks out to a beautiful tree (in which
season? We haven't decided. Probably with foliage) and
she climbs up a ladder into the tree and opens her box and
beautiful butterflies flutter out and through the tree and
the scene continues, following them through the tree and
ending with one butterfly that has left the tree.

—Patricia "Mizmoon" Soltysik,
in a letter to her sister, 1972

CHAPTER 7

Camilla Moves to California

IN AUGUST 2016, I received an email from a woman named Cheryl Brooks.

"Dear Rachael Hanel," the email began. "I understand you would like to be in contact with anyone who knew Camilla Hall. She and I were best friends in her Los Angeles years, previous to her moving to Berkeley in the early 1970s." Cheryl went on to say she had been in touch with Camilla until just before the Hearst kidnapping, and that was the last time she had heard from her. "I would be glad to share my memories of those days," she wrote.

I'd kept a writing-focused blog since 2012, and occasionally I'd share updates on the progress of the Camilla manuscript. Camilla must have been on Cheryl's mind one day, and as she did an internet search, she came upon my work.

I was thrilled to hear from Cheryl. Finding people who knew Camilla more than forty years ago was proving difficult. Some of her friends whom I had contacted were reluctant to talk, vaguely paranoid about saying too much even about a bygone time.

Cheryl proved loquacious, a writer's dream. We arranged to talk by phone four days after she sent the initial email. She was what I expected in an artist: slightly loopy and prone to tangents, yet she exuded warmth and honesty. She seemed truly delighted to talk to someone about Camilla.

Cheryl told me she first met Camilla at one of the weekend art fairs that popped up around Los Angeles in the early 1970s. This particular fair was held in a large parking lot on La Cienega Boulevard, a popular thoroughfare for artists and art galleries. Around thirty artists would pay ten dollars for a space to display their works for sale.

Cheryl, a painter, was attracted to Camilla's whimsical line drawings. Cheryl was also struck by the sophisticated and intellectual work of another artist, David Russell. David, Cheryl, and Camilla grew close, showing every weekend on La Cienega, taking trips to San Diego, Pasadena, and Culver City for shows and displaying their work together in galleries.

For a while, the artist's life worked well for Camilla. In early 1971 she wrote to her parents of a five-day show in which she sold eight pictures and made $200. "That's the best I've ever done anywhere," she said. She planned a gallery show with Cheryl and David, and another gallery expressed interest in hosting her solo work. "So it looks like I'm on my way!" She sent work to a show in Chicago and planned to send work to a gallery in Atlanta as well.

Cheryl and Camilla spent time together not only on the weekends but during the week. They took printmaking classes. They smoked pot. They decided to become vegetarians, because all the vegetarians they knew seemed so ethereal and spiritual. But they were concerned about getting enough protein. So they ate three avocados a day. They made bread and slathered it with butter. Before they knew it, they had each gained ten pounds.

"She was a total delight," Cheryl said.

———

Camilla arrived in Los Angeles in March 1970, in Topanga specifically, where she lived with Bette and Dick Esbjornson. This was a big move for Camilla: it was her first time outside Minnesota on her own, and it was filled with both excitement and trepidation. Here was her chance for a complete break— from the Minnesota weather, from her emotionally draining work, from having to hide who she really was. She didn't have a job lined up; she just went. As George put it, "Friends who had moved to California urged her to follow, and in time she left Minnesota for the uncertain life of an artist in California." She was fitting into a place, into herself, leaving "Candy" behind and transforming into Camilla.

Camilla's parents noticed she seemed happier once she got to California. Lorena knew that Camilla had complained of stomach problems while working in Duluth and Minneapolis. But once she moved to Los Angeles, Camilla told her mother the pain had stopped.

———

It would be hard to find a place more the opposite of rural Minnesota than sunny, dusty, sprawling Los Angeles, a city teeming with life, even late at night. Warm sun, even in the winter. As Camilla wrote to her parents a month after she moved, "I still can't get over the weather here—it's absolutely perfect! I guess I never <u>really</u> realized before how much I've had to fight weather all my life. <u>Here</u> you don't even notice it—you take sunshine and 70–75 degrees for granted!"

People move away from Minnesota all the time. The assumption is that they leave because of the absence of warmth. But I think it's the absence of color that bothers people. Southern Minnesota's color in high summer consists mostly of shades of green—lawns, trees, corn, and soybeans, all essentially variations of the same color. It's lush, but monochrome. In California, though, the colors and plants are more exotic. Palm trees, and front-lawn bushes rich in yellows, purples, and fuchsias.

In Minnesota, the color lasts only about five months of the year. Leaves erupt on trees in late May, seemingly overnight, and by late October the leaves blaze fiery colors for just a couple of weeks and then fall away. By November and early December the landscape is a stark brown, if the snow hasn't already arrived. December through March, everything is painted in a coat of white. In late March and April, it's a muddy brown, dotted with pockets of dirty, melting snow.

Even before Camilla left Minnesota permanently, she'd had a taste of warmth—in the years as a missionary's child in Africa and on a visit to South America with her parents. That warmth probably got under her skin.

She spent almost a year in Duluth, which turned icy, cold, and dark in the winter. I can imagine what it felt like to a native Minnesotan to wake up in Los Angeles, stretch the arms and smile, and walk down the street, soaking in the light and color.

———

Camilla's art was distinctive. She created mostly line art in pencil or pen, the drawings whimsical and bubbly. The forms took on cartoonish or caricature-like proportions. Here's how George described his daughter's work: "Her art was unique, almost like Japanese Zen. She did not use a set up, or landscape scene or model to inspire her. Instead she put her pen to the paper not knowing what she would do and made a one-line drawing. Many were thrown away but she kept some. She placed these in frames and because they were small and rather inexpensive, they sold quite well."

After a time, Camilla moved out of Bette and Dick's house and into her own place on Sawtelle Boulevard, near the intersection of Venice Boulevard and Interstate 405. It was at about this time that Cheryl met Camilla. Camilla never mentioned Bette and Dick to Cheryl, and Cheryl never met them or any of Camilla's other friends. It was just their tight trio—Cheryl, David, and Camilla.

Camilla experienced ups and downs like many artists. By November her sales had slowed. But as she approached her one-year anniversary in Los Angeles, she remained excited and upbeat. "I've been out here for a year come March 3 and I'd say the 'Great Adventure' is just beginning! Hope I can hold out through the next few bumps!"

But the bumps soon became too many. By March, she had made plans to move to the Bay Area. She called February a "wretched" month for sales— only fifty dollars. "I've decided to try the market in San Francisco and will move up there in April or May," she wrote to her parents. "People that have shown up there feel it's a better place to be and that the tastes are more sophisticated—and my work is really becoming sophisticated, I feel . . . so it's worth a try."

A better place to be. Just as Camilla had thought Duluth would be better, then Minneapolis better, then Los Angeles better, now she thought the

Bay Area would give her what she was seeking, though what she wanted was always changing. In Minneapolis, it was a better job and also a bigger antiwar/peace community. In Los Angeles it was better weather and the chance to work as an artist. Now, in the Bay Area, it was a chance to make more money as an artist.

Cheryl told me Camilla's decision to leave Los Angeles came quickly. "I was kind of surprised. We were best buds and she just says, 'Well, I'm leaving town.' It was fast."

———

Camilla chose to live in Berkeley. She wrote to her parents: "After I saw Berkeley, I knew that I'd much rather live there than in San Francisco and I was lucky enough to find a 1 bedroom apartment about 6 blocks from campus.... I think the environment will be very stimulating and the 'vibrations' are just terrific. It's almost a world unto itself and is definitely a 'liberated zone.' They just elected 4 radicals to the city council, so it will be fun to see what happens." She told friends she liked Berkeley's "respected socialism." At this point Camilla seemed to still be embracing the gentle politics that characterized her time in Minnesota. She was more "Peter, Paul, and Mary" than radical. California friends remember her criticizing the more militant acts of some protesters.

The Bay Area's scenery might have looked familiar to Camilla, as it has much in common with Duluth's scenery: bodies of water so vast you can't see the other side, and the many steep hills rising sharply from the water. The waterfronts of San Francisco and Duluth are chilly; both are places to escape to when the heat and humidity of the interiors become too much to bear. As someone who enjoyed nature, Camilla probably noticed the similarities between the picturesque cities and their waters.

Her apartment was on Channing Way, just a block off the bustling commercial district of Shattuck Avenue, a couple of blocks from the elegant Depression-era Berkeley Public Library and a short walk from the UC Berkeley campus and from Telegraph Avenue, the famous hippie hangout that ran through town. That block of Channing Way was almost legendary in the way its residents came together. Neighbors worked in communal gardens, they drank coffee and tea in the local coffeehouses, and they held block parties. One lawn on the block sported a ten-foot-high red papier-mâché hand curled into a defiant fist. A burgeoning food co-op movement across the country found mass appeal in Berkeley, and Channing Way residents bought produce through a shop named the Food Conspiracy.

"It's really been an experience to be on my own again and being forced to meet new people," she told her parents in a June 1971 letter. "I had fallen into a really comfortable and friendly groove with Cheryl and David and found myself stagnating a bit—so this is an important move for me in many ways."

One of the first people Camilla met when she moved to her new apartment at 2021 Channing Way in May 1971 was her upstairs neighbor, twenty-one-year-old Patricia Soltysik. Pat had already lived there for three years. In her usual uniform of baggy harem pants and T-shirt or peasant blouse, Pat seemed to be the reigning queen of Channing Way, and in her disarming, engaging style, she quickly made Camilla feel welcomed. Even though at the time Pat was living with a man she had met at UC Berkeley, she and Camilla soon became lovers.

CHAPTER 8

Camilla and Mizmoon

A FEW MONTHS after Camilla moved to Berkeley, Camilla and Pat made a subtle declaration to others that they were a couple. One friend, who saw them at a Thanksgiving feast held for forty people, recounted, "They didn't come in and announce it to the group or anything, but they were holding hands and that's when they publicly wanted everyone to know. It was almost like an announcement, as if someone were to walk in and announce we're going to be married next year. On our block that was the way it was done. . . . When you first fall in love with someone, you walk with your arm around her or him or whatever or whoever it is. In this case it happened to be the two of them."

By the time Pat met Camilla, Camilla had been living on her own in California for one year. In that time she'd adjusted to a new version of herself and perhaps felt a new openness living half a continent away from her parents. Pat probably saw Camilla—who was five years older—as a wise sage, a strong, confident woman who embraced her sexuality. Camilla had had time to get a sense of herself, living in Duluth, Minneapolis, and Los Angeles, slightly reinventing herself each time she moved. To Pat, she could be a guide, a mentor, a teacher. Camilla, in turn, was probably charmed by Pat's outgoing personality, enthusiasm, and beauty.

Patricia "Mizmoon" Soltysik has suffered the same fate as Camilla—suspended in the time of her death in 1974, as if in amber, immortalized as a myth that only grows stronger. In the clichéd SLA story, Mizmoon is "angry" and "hardened." She's unfeeling, the one who lured Camilla into the army but then abandoned her emotionally. But as with Camilla, a step back provides a more nuanced view and reveals a complicated portrait of a complicated young woman. For Camilla, I rely on her father, her mother, and her friends speaking about her through the years. To best know Mizmoon, I turn to her brother, Fred Soltysik.

Fred wrote a book, *In Search of a Sister*, published in 1976 at the time of the Hearst trial. The immediacy lends the book a fresh, raw, and detailed look at Pat. Fred, much like George Hall, turned to writing in an attempt to reconcile someone he thought he knew with the media's narrative.

The media of 1974 liked to focus on Pat's attractiveness and popularity while she was a student at Goleta High School in California, which provided a dramatic contrast to the woman she became. She was indeed attractive and popular in high school, according to Fred. She was a beach bum, hanging out with friends near the ocean. She worked outside school, and she was a member of 4-H and of the Usherettes, a school service organization that comprised a who's who of the school's pretty and elite. She planned to become a lawyer.

But Pat's home life was troubled. Pat's mother was a Belgian war bride and her father a pharmacist. Fred reported that his mother said there had been "fourteen happy years" of marriage before things went sour. The Soltysiks had seven children; Fred was the oldest, and Pat the third in line. Fred recounted physical abuse at the hands of his father. At one point, Fred was literally kicked out of the house. When Pat was hospitalized while in high school for a ruptured appendix, her dad never went to see her. She wrote to Fred, "I guess, now that I practically died, he doesn't care too awfully much what happens to me, so all I'm going to ever bother him about is money." Pat's parents divorced shortly after her hospitalization. Pat would visit her dad at the hotel where he was living. "Hardly a meeting transpired without her crying afterward," Fred wrote.

Once in Berkeley, Pat searched for an identity, trying to figure out who she was and what she wanted. She lived with a fellow student, Gene McDaniels, for a couple of years. But after they broke up, she became more involved in the feminist movement and started to date women. She abandoned her plans to become a lawyer. She attended consciousness-raising sessions, in which women gathered to share their experiences, in hopes of increasing recognition of the many ways women were oppressed. According to Fred, "After attending Women's Caucus meetings and the International Women's Day, she began to formulate her 'new' identity for presentation to other women and circulated a series of mimeographed 'integration' papers to her fellow sisters."

———

In the early 1970s Berkeley was the place to be for a hippie, an outsider, a freak, a wannabe revolutionary. It was a mecca for radicals, peaceniks, and feminists, calling out to those who did not fit in anywhere else. Hair grew long on chins, heads, underarms, and legs. Women wore peasant tops and flowing skirts. Streets and coffee shops overflowed with people.

Even though the protest movement reached its zenith in 1968 and had died down in other parts of the country, Berkeley retained its countercultural flair well into the 1970s. The fervor of the New Left remained active and strong. John Bryan, a journalist living in the Bay Area, wrote in 1975, "Today Tele [Telegraph Avenue] is the last big 'hippie' scene left in America. . . . Its narrow sidewalks are always clogged with hundreds of lounging, doped-out drifters, radicals passing out the latest broadsides and proclamations, gawking tourists, students hurrying to class, and a whole fascinating bazaar of craftsmen who sell bangles, beads, belt buckles, ceramics, stained glass, and other bright and innovative handmades right on the pavement." Writers, artists, and liberal-minded faculty members helped make Berkeley an eclectic town, filled with international-cooking nights and foreign-film screenings.

While the main radical movement in Berkeley had started to fade by the early 1970s, the town became home to a group of white radicals who walled themselves off from the middle-class world. Berkeley became home to the largest group of "vintage" New Left radicals in the nation. The city seemed frozen in 1969, with people spouting Marxist and Maoist rhetoric and promoting militarism. "This Bay Left is a unique environment. What passes here for realism and mundane left politics is a never-never land, a cloister of nihilism in which there is often little or no distinction between sense and nonsense. Yet a public becomes inured even to this," wrote Vin McLellan and Paul Avery in the definitive book on the SLA, *The Voices of Guns,* published in 1977.

In October 1971, Camilla wrote to her parents about a trip she took with Pat. "Pat and I went camping and got hailed on, then rain, so we came home. But we had one good sunny warm day in the woods before that happened so I can't complain. She's going to Mexico for a few months in December. I sure will miss her; she's a wonderful friend."

In the summer of 1972, with the relationship still going strong, Camilla christened Pat with a new name, Mizmoon. Pat told her brother that she had been searching for a "me-name" for years. She wanted a name with rhythm, with meaning, one she enjoyed hearing and saying. The right name came along one night as she and Camilla were talking about poetry. That name was Mizmoon, which she went to court to claim legally. The name change came at around the same time she dropped out of UC Berkeley. When Fred wrote Mizmoon a letter asking why she had dropped out, she replied, "Sisters, none of us are free until we are all free."

George and Lorena visited Camilla several times in Berkeley and met Mizmoon, though Camilla was careful to define Mizmoon to them as a good friend, not as her lover. At this time, George was teaching about Eastern religions at DePaul University. For a few summers, he and Lorena traveled to Asia. They usually stopped to visit Camilla on the way. To a Lutheran theologian and his wife, Berkeley may have been a strange world, but Camilla appeared to be doing well. "We were concerned about the large number of young people who had come from afar to California with meager resources. On Telegraph Avenue they sold belts and trinkets to make some money; one sold poems written on any subject in a few minutes. We liked Candy's friends and she seemed to be doing well showing and selling her art with other artists on vacant parking lots in various locations on weekends." George reported that Camilla had adopted a vegetarian and health-food lifestyle and had "slimmed down beautifully."

George and Lorena usually stayed on the UC Berkeley campus, where George, as a visiting professor, had full privileges. One time they stayed in an apartment, house-sitting for a friend of Camilla. Below was a garage that had been converted into an apartment, where Mizmoon lived. George described Mizmoon (he writes "Miz Moon") as "Candy's best friend."

But sometime later in the summer of 1972, Mizmoon became restless, and she and Camilla ended their physical relationship. Camilla was planning a three-month trip to Europe in the fall of 1972, and the two talked about Mizmoon joining Camilla at some point. Camilla wanted more from the relationship and suggested an "experiment" to Mizmoon.

As Mizmoon wrote to her sister Sue, "The experiment is being lovers again, just for the six weeks before she splits for Europe. And if we dig it, I'll go visit/live with her in Greece or wherever. Our expectations then would be known before. She could look forward to a lover coming and not just our bizarre friendship. But, much as I want Camilla to be happy and get what she wants, I'm not into being her lover." She concluded the letter by saying, "I guess I'll tell her about the no-go on the experiment. I hate doing those kind of things."

It's not clear when that conversation took place, but in an August 1972 letter to George and Lorena, Camilla was upbeat and excited about her upcoming trip: "Went to a Greek tavern [in the Bay Area] and tried to dance some Greek dances . . . what fun!" Camilla also suggested the trip could lead to something more permanent. She had a friend who had lived in Greece for two years and who was going back to buy a farmhouse on one of the islands. "It started me thinking that if I saw something somewhere that was really out of sight, it might be a good idea to buy it if it was a real good deal. Then you could go there for your retirement or however long you wanted, and it would be constantly increasing in value if you ever wanted to sell it. We really should have a European base as well as American for our extensive interests, you know." In *The Voices of Guns,* McLellan and Avery quoted a friend of Camilla as saying, "She had expected to find a utopia [in Greece]."

Camilla and Mizmoon must have had some sort of contact while Camilla was in Europe. Fred visited his sister in January 1973, and she talked of going to Europe to meet Camilla. Mizmoon had been to Europe once before, and she wrote to Fred that she and Camilla thought about living in Greece, "maybe renting a villa on an island and just paint and write poetry. The men practically keep the women in iron underwear, but I loved it there. Takes a while to adjust, of course." But for unknown reasons, perhaps lack of money, ill health (Mizmoon had been ill, possibly with an STD, in January 1973), or a desire to stay in Berkeley, Mizmoon never went to Europe.

During that visit Fred's wife, Carol, noticed a marked change in Mizmoon's demeanor. Carol spent a few minutes talking alone with Mizmoon while Fred was in the kitchen making tea. After the visit, in the car, Carol told Fred that Mizmoon was talking about banding together with others to resist the system, to fight for change. Carol said, "It really sounded as if she'd been writing this all down or was trying it out loud to hear how it sounded."

Later that January, Camilla returned from Greece. She first stopped at her parents' house in Illinois to pick up some things she had left there, and Mizmoon met her in Denver so they could drive back to California together. Camilla sent a postcard to her parents on January 25 from Taos, New Mexico: "Howdy! Well, Mizmoon got to Denver safely and we're having a wonderful holiday crossing this beautiful and spacious scenery. I'm all well now and really feeling super—so nice to be with Mizmoon again." The postcard is signed "Mizmoon and Golden Mane," the latter a name Camilla had given herself. Mizmoon sent her family a postcard at the same time. "We plan to go to Europe together in one year," she wrote. Instead, one year later they would be plotting the Hearst kidnapping.

The two stopped in Berkeley and then headed down the coast to Santa Barbara to visit the Soltysiks. This was the first time the family had met Camilla. Fred said Camilla—who had brought drawings to hang in the house and played guitar—made his mother feel warm and happy. Mrs. Soltysik said Camilla and Mizmoon bounced around the house, giggling and smiling. "She noticed how natural Camilla was, how easily her face broke into that contagious grin." Mizmoon and Camilla had planned to spend a couple of days at a nearby hotel. But during the first night, Camilla left. Mizmoon showed up at the Soltysik house in the morning in tears. Mizmoon had never been one to be monogamous, and she and Camilla may have argued over Mizmoon's continuing relationship with a man named Chris Thompson.

But within a month, it would be another man, Donald DeFreeze, taking up Mizmoon's time. With him, Mizmoon would plan a revolution.

CHAPTER 9

The SLA Forms

FRED SOLTYSIK WROTE about the first time he met Donald DeFreeze, at his sister's Parker Street apartment in March 1973: "I remember planting a kiss, European style, on both sides of his face. I can't recall ever having greeted a stranger in America so warmly, nor can I be certain why, exactly, I was moved to do so . . . but I think it was rather that his certain, immediate gentleness moved me."

Mizmoon introduced DeFreeze as "Cin," short for Cinque Mtume, the Swahili name DeFreeze adopted in prison. DeFreeze had escaped from Soledad State Prison in California on March 5. "Escaped" isn't exactly the right word—he simply walked away. He had been assigned a job working on the boiler in a building near the prison's main gate. So when the guard dropped off DeFreeze at midnight and left him alone as he took the previous shift's inmate back to the main prison, DeFreeze walked out an open gate and climbed over a six-foot fence to what he thought was freedom.

———

DeFreeze had a long arrest record, but prior to 1970 he had spent very little time in jail. Again and again he was arrested, mostly for dealing illegal firearms, yet he was given nothing more than probation. It's widely believed that DeFreeze was a police informer, more useful to the cops out of jail than in. As Brad Schreiber writes in *Revolution's End: The Patty Hearst Kidnapping, Mind Control, and the Secret History of Donald DeFreeze and the SLA,* "The legal system accommodated him over and over, providing numerous chances to shift his behavior."

But he never made that shift and instead delved further into a life of crime. On November 15, 1969, police could no longer look away. That day, DeFreeze stole a woman's purse, pistol-whipped her, then took a $1,000 check made out in her name to a Bank of America branch in Los Angeles. He aroused suspicion by trying to cash the woman's check and fled when bank security guards closed in. He was met by police as soon as he left the bank. They exchanged gunfire. DeFreeze got off seven shots but didn't hit anyone. Police bullets grazed DeFreeze. He was found guilty and sentenced the next year to the California Medical Facility in Vacaville, where he was to undergo psychiatric evaluation. The prosecutor had written in his final report, "This person is a high-risk danger to society and . . . as soon as he is released from prison, he will return to his same violent career. It is my opinion, further, that this defendant will eventually kill someone."

Vacaville was the site of secret medical experiments conducted upon prisoners. The CIA had started to fund psychological research at Vacaville in the years before DeFreeze arrived, under the auspices of Operation CHAOS, which existed from 1967 to 1972 and was revealed in detail in the 1975 Rockefeller Report. Inmates who wanted to escape punishment for infractions were told they could instead "volunteer" for experiments and were subjected to electroshock therapy and drugs such as Anectine (succinylcholine chloride, which produces a drowning sensation, similar to waterboarding) and Prolixin (fluphenazine HCL, which causes pacing, restlessness, nausea, and blurred vision for up to two weeks).

It's unclear what, if any, drugs and treatments DeFreeze was exposed to in the two years he was at Vacaville. But even if he wasn't part of the experiments, he would have known inmates who had been subjected to such treatments. The mere knowledge that prison officials had these drugs at their disposal and used them as a form of bribery instilled fear among all prisoners: stay in line, or else.

One odd aspect of DeFreeze's stint at Vacaville was the length of time he stayed there. As a medical facility, Vacaville was a way station—a place for physically or mentally ill prisoners to get treatment before moving on to one of California's dozen other prisons. Most prisoners stayed there for a few weeks; ninety days was generally the upper limit. But DeFreeze, without any outward signs of serious illness, stayed at Vacaville for two years. It's as if someone wanted him to be there for a reason.

Something else odd was going on at Vacaville. Out of the many prison inmate organizations active there, the one DeFreeze was involved in—the Black Cultural Association (BCA)—had an outside coordinator, Colston Westbrook. At the time, Westbrook was teaching linguistics at UC Berkeley. Westbrook had been in Vietnam during the war, but in what capacity is unclear. The surface story is that he worked for Pacific Architects and Engineers (PA&E) from 1967 to 1969. PA&E is thought to have been a CIA cover in Saigon, possibly part of the CIA's Phoenix Program, which used various means to infiltrate the Viet Cong, including torture and murder.

When Westbrook returned from Vietnam, he was tapped by William Herrmann, an adviser to then California governor Ronald Reagan, to lead the BCA at Vacaville. Herrmann himself was Reagan's go-to guy on stopping and counteracting the leftist radical movement. According to Schreiber, the BCA was not merely the educational and self-improvement program for prisoners it touted itself to be. "In reality, it became a cover for an experimental project to explore the extent to which unstable or susceptible prisoners could be controlled for the purpose of infiltrating Bay Area radical groups."

DeFreeze was described by fellow inmates as "philosophical" and "introspective" in Vacaville, but not as a revolutionary. Perhaps he was just the type of pliable and easily manipulated person Westbrook was looking for. According to renowned conspiracy theorist Mae Brussell, "DeFreeze was told he would be a new black leader to replace Malcolm X and Martin Luther King [Jr.]."

If true, then the BCA was a spider web. Not only did DeFreeze walk into it, but so did several Bay Area radicals who later would form the SLA.

Willie Wolfe was the first future SLA member to participate in the BCA at Vacaville. Prison officials encouraged outside visitors, though that concept seems odd today. Wolfe first attended BCA meetings as part of an African American Studies class at UC Berkeley. Wolfe quickly befriended DeFreeze. Wolfe was only twenty years old, and impressionable. In DeFreeze, Westbrook found a prison insider to mold; in Wolfe he found a moldable counterpart on the outside. While Wolfe embraced revolutionary thought, nothing about him suggested a propensity toward violence. He was more theory than action. Chris Thompson, Mizmoon's lover, who also knew Wolfe, said no one respected Wolfe. "Willie was no leader. People wouldn't follow Willie Wolfe to the bathroom. He was a loser. He was just a rich white kid playing at politics. No one respected him."

But Westbrook encouraged and complimented Wolfe, perhaps sensing that he could orchestrate Wolfe's moves like a puppet master. On Westbrook's urging, Wolfe brought others to BCA meetings. Wolfe's housemate, Russell Little, went to BCA meetings accompanied by his girlfriend, Nancy Ling Perry. Bill and Emily Harris were also involved in prison politics. Once these additional radicals started to attend the meetings, the seeds that had been planted took root. A new radical leftist group was about to rise up.

When DeFreeze escaped, he went to Wolfe's and Little's house—which they dubbed Peking House—where they lived with others in a communal environment. All the residents at Peking House were hesitant to hide DeFreeze; they thought the place was too "hot," under surveillance because of the residents' radical connections. Little turned to Thompson for help. Thompson, in turn, thought of one person immediately: his girlfriend, Mizmoon Soltysik. Fresh from her breakup with Camilla, Mizmoon was far enough removed from known radicals in the Bay Area to escape suspicion. Thompson knew she was sympathetic to revolutionary causes and figured she'd probably be willing to house DeFreeze. He was right.

After Fred left Mizmoon's apartment in March 1973, her sister Sue stayed for a couple of days more. But she didn't get a chance to spend much time with Mizmoon.

The apartment was buzzing with activity. A few people came over for a film screening on the Mozambique guerrilla movement. After that, Mizmoon told Sue, "We're writing a serious document, our format and declaration." This struck Sue as strange, but she didn't ask further questions. Mizmoon was preoccupied, spending hours with DeFreeze typing documents in the bedroom. Mizmoon and DeFreeze took a short break to get ice cream with Sue. That was the only time the sisters spent together.

DeFreeze moved out of Mizmoon's apartment in April and into an East Oakland apartment. In June, she and DeFreeze moved into an apartment on East Seventeenth Street in Oakland. Mizmoon and DeFreeze, along with Wolfe and Little, made up the core members of the SLA that summer. Little then brought Perry and Joe Remiro, a Vietnam veteran, into the fold. Perry also moved into the East Seventeenth Street apartment.

DeFreeze was becoming increasingly unstable and paranoid. The gentle, quiet demeanor he displayed in prison was gone, replaced by a propensity toward violence. Those who believe DeFreeze was sent to infiltrate and discredit Bay Area radicals think he went rogue and truly embraced revolutionary zeal. Neither Westbrook nor anyone else was able to control him any longer. DeFreeze also constantly feared that someone would discover his earlier role as police informant. There was almost nothing worse than being known as a snitch on the East Bay streets. With that reputation, there'd be no way to raise money for the SLA and gain recruits.

On August 21, 1973, the SLA released its first document to the public. The document ends with "Therefore, we of the Symbionese Federation and The S.L.A. DO NOT under the rights of human beings submit to the murder, oppression and exploitation of our children and people and do under the rights granted to the people under The Declaration of Independance [sic] of The United States, do now by the rights of our children and people and by Force of Arms and with every drop of our blood, *Declare Revolutionary War* against The Fascist Capitalist Class, and all their agents of murder, oppression and exploitation."

The declaration was met with little fanfare or notice. Revolutionary groups popped up in the Bay Area with lots of talk but little action, and just as quickly disintegrated. The SLA was about to change that.

Two other people were involved in the SLA during this time but would quickly turn away from the destructive violence DeFreeze embraced. The involvement of Thero Wheeler and his girlfriend Mary Alice Siem pointed to troubles already brewing in the nascent organization.

Wheeler and DeFreeze knew each other from Vacaville. After DeFreeze escaped, Wheeler took the helm of Unisight, an offshoot of the BCA that DeFreeze had been leading.[1] The SLA's first coordinated action was to help Wheeler escape from Vacaville, which he did on August 2, 1973. The SLA saw in Wheeler a powerful recruiter. They could use his contacts and influence to find new members. But Wheeler was not interested. "I couldn't seriously recruit for him [Cinque] because he was off into suicide and bullshit. The people I knew just wouldn't accept the SLA."

Wheeler and Siem (along with her young child) stuck around for a few weeks. Siem apparently supported the SLA financially during this time. In a foreshadowing of what was to come, Siem, like Patty Hearst, was also a member of a wealthy, influential family: she was an heir to the Coggins lumber fortune. But Wheeler and DeFreeze continued to spar for leadership of the SLA, much as they had jockeyed for leadership of Unisight at Vacaville. Wheeler may have been an effective leader, but DeFreeze had already spent more than a year cultivating strong bonds with Wolfe, Perry, Soltysik, and the others. They looked up to him and trusted him.

In September, Wheeler and Siem moved out of the SLA apartment in Oakland. DeFreeze did not approve of this arrangement. Out of his sight, Wheeler and Siem would be difficult to control. DeFreeze and other SLA members went to Wheeler and Siem's apartment and a confrontation ensued, with guns drawn. Wheeler and Siem agreed to move back to the SLA apartment. But as soon as they could, under the pretext of grabbing belongings from the apartment they had just abandoned, they fled the SLA for

---

1. Unisight was created specifically for DeFreeze after he lost the election to be head of the BCA. Many of the future SLA members left the BCA and followed DeFreeze to Unisight.

good. "It [the SLA] didn't have nothing to do with reality, man, all it could do was get you killed," Wheeler said.

This was a blow to the SLA, not only psychologically but also financially, as their main source of funds was now gone. But they were apparently able to find money elsewhere, because they rented additional dwellings. Perry and Little moved into a house in Clayton, a suburb just northeast of Berkeley. Little also rented an apartment near the Oakland city hall, half a mile from the Oakland School District headquarters. Someone was supplying them with money, though it's not clear who. They may have had sympathetic allies among Bay Area revolutionaries—perhaps people who didn't want to openly join the SLA but who were willing to supply funds.

It's not clear exactly when in 1973 Mizmoon and Camilla reestablished their connection after their February breakup, but it could have been at around this time. The SLA desperately needed money, and Mizmoon knew that Camilla had a job. By the fall of 1973, no one in the SLA was working. Mizmoon had quit her janitorial job at the UC Berkeley library, and Perry had quit her work at a juice stand on Telegraph Avenue. Camilla was working for the East Bay Regional Park District as a park caretaker, and she also received regular checks from a securities fund. Her income between the job and the checks wasn't large, but it was more than the zero dollars the SLA was currently bringing in. Mizmoon, with a little sweet talk, knowing how much Camilla loved her, could have garnered Camilla's support, both financially and philosophically.

———

On November 6, 1973, the SLA announced its presence to the world with the biggest, boldest move it could imagine: assassination. They murdered Marcus Foster, the superintendent of Oakland Public Schools.

The SLA was a group all about promoting racial equality, a group in which many members had ties to prison associations made up mostly of black inmates, a group in which one member had been married to a black man, a group in which other members had had black lovers, a group that chose a black convict as its leader; it's hard to fathom that its first criminal act was the murder of a black man.

But the SLA had its reasons. The group targeted Foster because of his position on student identification cards. Foster was dogged by two issues in particular that some members of the public, and the SLA, seized on: a plan to require students to carry school-issued identification cards, and a plan to post police officers in school in an effort to curb violence and crime. Critics foresaw a slippery slope. They were concerned about rumors that Oakland police would carry shotguns in the schools and act as spies and that information on students could be fed into a national database to note troublesome behavior and remove problem kids from school. To the SLA and other opponents, this looked like a way to funnel troubled black youth directly into an already overcrowded and problematic California prison system.

On the night of November 6, three SLA members waited outside the Oakland School District offices. Foster and his assistant superintendent, Robert Blackburn, emerged from a side door after a school board meeting and headed to Blackburn's car. Blackburn noticed two men nearby, standing against the wall but partially hidden in the shadows. As Blackburn unlocked the passenger door for Foster and walked to the driver's side, the two men approached quickly and shot Foster. DeFreeze, who had been standing back, now came forward to shoot Blackburn. Blackburn managed to make it back to the building, despite his serious injuries. He continued to hear gunshots and saw muzzle flashes; Foster was still being hit.

Blackburn didn't clearly see the men, or what he thought were men. The identities of the three killers that day remain unknown, though Hearst testified at her trial that Bill and Emily Harris told her the three were DeFreeze, Mizmoon, and Perry, with Little and Remiro providing support at the scene in a backup car. However, when Little and Remiro were caught by police on January 10, 1974, after a routine traffic stop, they were immediately jailed as the suspected Foster assassins since a gun used in the crime was found in their possession. They were later tried and convicted on the murder charges.[2]

---

2. Little was retried in 1981 and acquitted in the Foster murder.

If the SLA was hoping for widespread support after the Foster murder, they didn't get it. Instead, the move was widely denounced. Any support the organization had hoped to get evaporated the moment Foster died. The SLA had isolated itself. But the group still believed it had a cause worth fighting for. They thought they could recruit enough people to raise an army and carry out their plans for a full-scale revolution. However, they managed to bring only a handful of new people into the fold. One was Camilla.

CHAPTER 10

Camilla Moves to Francisco Street

CAMILLA BRINGS the last of her possessions inside and sits down to rest. Keya purrs, rubs around Camilla's legs, and continues to explore this new space, a duplex on Berkeley's Francisco Street. The cat wanders back and forth, from kitchen to living room to bedroom and back to living room. She's seeking, like cats tend to do, a warm ray of sun. She spots it: a bright windowsill, sun shining through like a beacon. She hops up, curls into a ball, and settles in. A new home.

———

The Francisco Street duplex was a modest one-story bungalow on a street with similar one-story bungalows of the kind popular before World War II. It had dark brown shingles and shake siding and a small front yard. When I saw it in 2008, flowering vines climbed the walls, and it made me happy to think that Camilla, a plant lover and gardener, would have set out colorful plants on the front steps or in the window boxes. It looked like a perfect place to create a home, more than one could in an apartment. For the first time on her own, Camilla lived in a house.

Camilla moved here from Channing Way in September 1972. Francisco Street was much quieter than Channing Way, which was in the heart of

Berkeley's business district and near UC Berkeley and abuzz at all hours with foot and car traffic. Francisco Street (which runs parallel to Hearst Avenue) was just a few blocks north—a quiet, tree-lined residential street, with a clear view of the Berkeley hills rising to the east.

Camilla quickly got to know her neighbors. She helped organize a neighborhood association, complete with a newsletter and get-togethers. She spearheaded potlucks to try to draw more people into the gatherings. I don't know why Camilla moved, but she was twenty-seven years old when she settled on Francisco Street. Maybe she felt pressure to become "an adult," get a house, get a job, the type of things her parents did immediately after college. The Channing Way neighborhood stayed the same year after year, attracting college-aged residents, while Camilla grew older. On Francisco Street lived other young adults, families, and older people who moved in when the homes were first built and never moved away.

By this time, Camilla was continuing to morph into a healthier version of herself. She quit smoking, avoided meat, practiced karate, and hiked in the physically demanding California hills. Camilla wrote to her parents in April 1972 about getting a full-length mirror. It's a telling look into her state of mind and reveals a woman becoming more comfortable with herself. "I'm finally able to check out what a huge difference the weight loss has meant to my physical appearance—it's quite an adjustment still. My real body is emerging from all that fat and I find that it's an OK body with nice shapes and strong muscles. I guess I was always afraid I wasn't 'normal' and so I hid it with fat . . . but now I'm free and don't feel I have anything to hide—I'm just me, and I'm OK!"

———

In the spring of 1973, after Camilla returned from Europe and after she left Mizmoon in the middle of the night following their fight about Chris Thompson, she applied for a temporary job with the East Bay Regional Park District. Camilla was one of several women who obtained temp jobs, which were created because the park district, like many organizations, was pressured into hiring more women.

Camilla was assigned to Lake Temescal, an Oakland park that surrounded an oval lake in the shadow of the foothills just to the west. The park was a destination for residents throughout the Bay Area, who were lured by the sandy beach, wooded trails, and carefully tended flower gardens, an oasis in the middle of a city.

In the early 1970s, on sunny summer days, the young people of San Francisco would leave the cool dampness and fog at the edge of the Pacific Ocean and escape to Lake Temescal. The lake was just a twenty-minute drive from downtown San Francisco, but the Bay Area's microclimate made it seem like a whole new world. San Francisco would be shrouded in cool mist; at the same time, Lake Temescal would be gloriously sunny and warm, sometimes twenty degrees warmer, and the dry heat sank into skin thirsty for warmth. These young men and women, who mostly worked nights in the city's bars and restaurants, had all day to play and lounge.

When Camilla started work at Lake Temescal, she struck up a friendship with her boss, Eddie Collins, a longtime park employee. Lake Temescal was one of the smaller parks, and besides Camilla and Collins, there was only one other employee, an older man near retirement and in poor health who struggled to perform his job. At the time Collins was dubious about hiring a woman, but once he saw Camilla's work ethic and strength, he quickly changed his mind.

"She really was an incredible woman," Collins said when interviewed by McLellan and Avery for *The Voices of Guns*. Camilla eventually told him she was gay, and they both shared personal stories and talked about politics and landscaping. Collins may have served as a proxy father to Camilla, with her own father living half a continent away.

The job was a perfect fit for Camilla. Not only did she get to work outside, but the role involved dealing with the public, which suited her outgoing personality. The park was a busy place. Camilla was approachable, yet gentle and firm. She reminded people to follow the rules of the park, whether it was directing them to put their dogs on leashes or busting up teenage keg parties.

Collins was amazed at how she could enforce rules with ease. He remembered how she would approach teenagers drinking or smoking pot, many of whom were black, and after a few minutes they all would be laughing and the teenagers would be calling her "sister."

The park also had a small building that housed a co-op preschool, a place where parents volunteered a few hours a week. This meant that there were always small children around the park, and park workers like Camilla frequently talked to the children and taught them about the park's plants and wildlife.

Camilla's job working outside may have seemed to be a natural fit for a woman—to nurture, to plant, to arrange living things in an aesthetically pleasing manner. But her job at Lake Temescal was far more labor-intensive. She pruned trees, dug ditches, cleaned toilets, planted flowers, picked up litter, mowed the grass, emptied garbage cans, ran a chainsaw, fed wildlife, drove a truck. She even worked on plumbing and broken sprinkler heads. Plumbing was no problem; women have the strength to do it, Camilla told an audience in November 1973 as part of a panel on the future of jobs for women.

"This kind of work has been mystified," Camilla said. "To most people, manual work means man's work."

———

Later in 1973, Camilla embraced an activist role in her job. By September, the park district came under public scrutiny for its hiring practices. Camilla was one of eight female groundskeepers in the entire district, which employed 470 people that summer. Of the eight women, seven, including Camilla, were considered temporary and were to be laid off by September 30. She helped organize the female workers and served on a steering committee to advise the district on equal employment opportunities. She had a lot vested in this matter. Camilla had grown to love her job and the people she worked with. It gave her a sense of purpose and kept her busy. Without it, what would she do next?

Camilla wrote to her parents in a letter dated August 26, "I've been meeting regularly with some of the other women at the Park District to put pressure on the District to hire more women groundskeepers and open the doors of management promotions to women (there are no women higher on the 'scale' than clericals—management are <u>all</u> men!). Most of the women are not feminists (at least not <u>yet</u> . . . heh, heh) but they're angry at the way they've been discriminated against job-wise—and this is certainly a good place to start."

At a September 18 board meeting, the steering committee, union representative, and a representative from the Women's Action Training Center asked the park district to develop affirmative action policies and programs, to present the policy and plan to the board within a reasonable length of time, and to retain the seven female groundskeepers on a permanent basis. But the personnel director said there were no open permanent positions.

The board, however, was willing to write an affirmative action policy— though one of the board members, John Leavitt, hesitated. "If you are asking for complete fairness in employment practices, this is something the board will be very willing to give. However, if you are asking that the District discriminate against other groups of people, and perhaps even men, I am not certain the board could come to grips with that under those conditions." The board adopted a resolution that day to create an affirmative action program for presentation at the October 16 meeting.

Camilla also wrote in the August 26 letter, "Management claims the union does not, according to the current Memorandum of Understanding (contract), represent the temps for purposes of collective bargaining. A vast majority of temps have joined the union due to our organizing attempts, but management does not recognize us. So we've had to go to arbitration. Management has tried to drag this out hoping temp jobs would end and the problem would go away until next season again. We are waiting for the decision of the arbiter. I got to be excused from work to attend the arbitration because I'm on the steering committee. It was pretty interesting . . . but I can definitely see there are zillions of little paths to graft and corruption on both sides."

By the time of the October 16 meeting, Camilla and the other workers had been without jobs for more than two weeks. The laid-off workers and supporters crowded the room, buzzing with disappointment and resentment. The board had created an affirmative action policy, but one with no measurable goals or timetable for actually hiring women. The union representative called the board's policy "meaningless."

As the board members and speakers exchanged heated words, the crowd of women and supporters grew restless and audibly agitated. Board member Leavitt expressed his frustration: "Look, the point I'm trying to make is that the board is sympathetic to the women's cause. But, they can ruin that sympathy and position by their actions."

This comment was not well received. The crowd grew more raucous, with board members being shouted down. Eventually, the chairman threatened to adjourn the meeting. The crowd quieted enough to allow the board to approve the policy statement. The only woman on the board, Mary Lee Jefferds, made a second motion to set a tentative date for the implementation of an affirmative action program no later than November 15. The rest of the board and staff hesitated. The park district general manager said the staff was already overwhelmed, in the middle of working on both a master plan and a management study. Only three voted in favor of the motion; four votes were needed to pass.

In closing, a disappointed Jefferds said, "The motion's failure seems to me to be an indication of bad faith to the people and the public."

———

A couple of photographs of Camilla surfaced after she died. In the photos, Camilla appears to be at some type of work rally; she is wearing overalls and holding garden shears and she has a big smile on her face. She was in her element, around people, doing something, trying to make a positive change for herself and for other women, trying to make a difference. For that entire summer and into the fall, she didn't seem like someone who was plotting violent revolution. Unlike the other SLA members at the time, Camilla was working, not holed up in an apartment with an escaped convict writing manifestos. After her job ended, she appeared to throw herself into the union activism.

Camilla must have felt tremendous disappointment after the October 16 board meeting, at which it was clear not only that the women workers would not be hired back but also that the board was not interested in adopting an affirmative action policy at all. This disappointment happened at the same time Thero Wheeler and Mary Alice Siem left the SLA. The SLA had lost two key figures—one who they thought could help them recruit, and one who had money. If Mizmoon reached out to Camilla at this point, she couldn't have picked a more perfect time. With no job and no cause to work toward, Camilla was vulnerable.

CHAPTER 11

Camilla Joins the SLA

CAMILLA ENTERS SIEGLE'S GUN SHOP on a clear and bright Wednesday, January 2, 1974. The day is cool, with strong gusts coming in off the Pacific. As the last one to join the SLA, she has some catching up to do.

When she opens the door perhaps she triggers a bell that hangs above. The guy behind the counter looks up and within seconds sizes her up. To him, she doesn't look like typical gun-shop clientele, not that there is such a thing anyway. But he's come to expect a certain type of person to walk through the door, whether it's a biker dude, a survivalist, a hunter, a gang member. Siegle's has been open since World War II, and the relentless demand for guns in the United States is good for business. At this point, nearly half of all homes in the United States have guns.

But it's not too often that a woman comes into the shop, and even more unusual is a woman alone. Based on what he knows about guns and who buys them, he'd estimate maybe 10 percent of all women own a gun, and a lot of those women come into the shop with their guys, who persuade them to buy a pretty pistol. Every so often, one of those "feminists" will want a gun for protection. This blond chick, muscular and lean, with a confident swagger, looks like that type. She's not cheerleader pretty, not the type to get harassed walking down the street because she was showing a little leg or

The Hall family, around Christmas 1947. The children *(from left to right)*: Nan, Camilla, Peter, and Terry. This is the only known photograph of all four children together. NICOLLET COUNTY HISTORICAL SOCIETY.

Left: Camilla in the Hall home in St. Peter, Minnesota. *Right:* Camilla's graduation photograph in the Washburn High School 1963 yearbook.

COURTESY OF GUSTAVUS ADOLPHUS ARCHIVES.

Camilla *(center)* in her freshman year at Gustavus Adolphus College, 1963.

Camilla in front of her art at an outdoor art fair, around 1970. She left Minneapolis for Los Angeles that year in order to focus on her art.

A candid snapshot of Camilla at an outdoor art fair in Los Angeles, captured by her friend and fellow artist Cheryl Brooks.

I think
once in a while, when ~~I'm sure~~ I'm alone,
I call my name
and don't answer ... just to make sure

Hale

A line drawing with text by Camilla. Her work was called whimsical and Thurberesque.

"Chase."

"Drearia." COURTESY OF GUSTAVUS ADOLPHUS ARCHIVES.

"Adder Man Eve." ART IN THE AUTHOR'S POSSESSION.

Above: Patricia "Mizmoon" Soltysik. Camilla met Patricia when she first moved to Berkeley; Patricia lived in the same apartment building. Camilla later referred to Patricia as "Mizmoon" in a poem, and Patricia had her name legally changed. *Below:* George and Lorena Hall with Camilla and Mizmoon. The Halls knew that Camilla and Mizmoon were good friends, but Camilla never revealed to them the extent of the relationship.

Above: Camilla at a rally to support full-time jobs for female park workers in the East Bay Regional Park District in the fall of 1973. Camilla worked for the district in the summer, but ultimately all the women who worked in the parks that summer were let go. *Below:* A snapshot of Camilla and a young child.

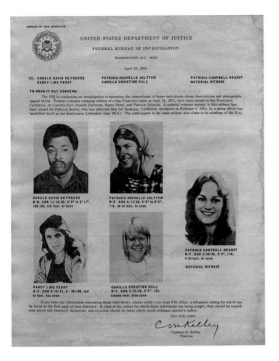

The FBI Wanted poster after the Hibernia Bank robbery on April 15, 1974.

POSTER IN THE AUTHOR'S POSSESSION.

Flames consume a small house in south-central Los Angeles, May 17, 1974, at the climax of an hour-long gun battle between police and a group believed to be members of the Symbionese Liberation Army. Five bodies were found inside after the flames subsided. AP PHOTO AND CAPTION. (Camilla's body is not included here; her body was discovered two days later.)

Camilla's grave, Resurrection Cemetery, St. Peter, Minnesota.

had full lips or nice breasts. She looked like the type of woman most guys would leave alone.

He asks what he can do for her. It's then that he notices something else that sets her apart from many people who come into the shop: she's happy. She smiles and laughs, her blue eyes twinkling behind her glasses. Sure, some people become elated at the prospect of a gun purchase, but most people here are all business. She's chatty and friendly, and he can't help but like her right away. She hardly seems like someone who has an impending sense of doom. She appears comfortable, even though she admits this is her first gun.

He asks Camilla, as he asks all newcomers, why she wants a gun.

———

Prior to Camilla's visit to the gun shop, her last documented appearance was on a women and work panel held in mid-November 1973. The panel was titled The Future of Jobs for Women, sponsored by the East Bay chapter of the National Organization for Women. "Some of the men challenged me to lift a 100-pound bag of fertilizer," Camilla is quoted as saying in a newspaper article, "and I told them, 'I'm no fool. Let's lift it together and it'll be easier.'" In other ways, she went about her daily business. She kept in touch with friends, and none of them reported any change in her behavior. She went to Illinois at Christmas to visit her parents.

So little is known about those six weeks between the panel discussion and the trip to Siegle's. At some point, Camilla made the decision to join the SLA. Emily Harris helps us pin down the time frame, telling a *New Times* reporter that Camilla didn't join the SLA until after the Foster murder on November 6— same as Emily and her husband, Bill Harris, as well as their friend Angela Atwood. Those four added to the core SLA that had been together throughout the summer: DeFreeze, Mizmoon, Wolfe, Perry, Little, and Remiro.

McLellan and Avery, in *The Voices of Guns,* suggest that Atwood was the last to join the SLA, moving in with the Harrises in early December. They based this reasoning on the fact that prison inmates familiar with SLA associates said they had never heard of Atwood. But no prisoners said they had heard of Camilla, either. McLellan and Avery do not speculate on how or when Camilla joined the SLA. It was as if she was a mystery these reporters could not solve, so they glossed over the information and figured no one would notice. Or care. Camilla is like a ghost, wafting into the midst of the SLA, no one knowing how she got there.

Of course Camilla doesn't tell the gun-shop clerk that she's buying a gun for the coming revolution. A more plausible reason Camilla can give for buying a gun is that she wants it for self-defense. She's a young woman in the mid-1970s in a city known for high crime rates.

For self-defense she has a lot of options, the guy tells her, but it all comes down to comfort. She's trim and lean, not big, so she's not going to want anything heavy or cumbersome. The gun needs to be easy to shoot, and fast. He tells her she can choose from many different pistols. There are big ones; there are small ones; there are ones in between. But he thinks he has something that will work especially well for her, one he sells to a lot of women. He shows Camilla a Mauser HSc that shoots .380 bullets. She buys it.

The Mauser is a solid workhorse of a handgun, the gun of choice for German officers in World War II. The majority of the Mausers manufactured during the war went to forces in the German army and navy and to police units. Production stopped after the war but began again in 1968. Camilla probably got a gun from that most recent batch, as North America was the primary market for the Mausers. The gun was compact, not super small but easy to conceal. The magazine held seven bullets, and the double-action trigger meant Camilla could shoot all seven bullets, one after another, before reloading.

A .380 bullet is smaller than the popular 9 mm, so there's less recoil. The 9 mm is heavier and fires at a higher velocity, she's told, which can be difficult to control since she's never handled a gun before. A 9 mm will pack more punch and can be more deadly, but if she can't shoot it straight or fast in the first place, it's not going to do her any good.

The Mauser isn't the type of gun you get if your primary goal is to kill people. There are many more effective models for that. A Mauser is good for self-defense, not for killing with intent.

Unless.

Unless Camilla plans to hollow out the bullets and lace them with cyanide, which was how the SLA killed Foster.

———

In November, Camilla is on the Future of Jobs for Women panel, talking about her work at Lake Temescal. At around the same time, Mizmoon—possibly the shooter in the Foster assassination—visits her brother Fred at the school where he's teaching fifth grade, the same elementary school she had attended.

She's also going to visit her mother while she's in town, but the primary purpose of her visit is to see her father. Even though they are somewhat estranged, she needs money, and he has it. She tells Fred that she's looking to get a job in a French restaurant and needs money for nice clothes.

Fred and Mizmoon's mother and sister all notice the drastic amount of weight she's lost since they last saw her in May. She also has a raging case of poison oak on her back and face. She tells them she's been dieting and exercising and doing a lot of camping. They'd only received sporadic letters and postcards over the last six months, none with a return address.

Ten days after the Foster murder, Mizmoon writes a letter to her mom. "When I'm in town [Berkeley] I stay with different friends—I met a really nice truck driver a few weeks ago and he wants me to drive cross country with him. . . . I feel so foot loose & tired of Berkeley. I may do that."

It's unclear whether this was true or simply something she made up to provide a story to cover up her radical activities. In the visit to Fred at the school, he brought up the Foster murder—only because he wanted to talk about current events, not because he had any inkling that Mizmoon was involved. Her end of the conversation shocked him. When he called the murder a "tragedy," Mizmoon responded: "Tragedy? The guy was in it with the pigs."

———

Nothing is known about Camilla's decision to join the SLA or about how she was invited into the group. All the others who became members of the SLA were already connected to one another. Camilla's only connection to the group was Mizmoon. But Camilla must have generated a strong feeling of trust among all the group members. Camilla was a lone wolf, so to speak, with only one person—Mizmoon—to vouch for her. How strong that bond must have been.

We do know that each prospective member was asked to read the documents that Mizmoon and DeFreeze had been producing throughout 1973, and they were questioned about their intent on joining. The SLA didn't let just anyone into its ranks, and its vetting process took time.[1] In *The Last SLA Statement*, Joe Remiro noted, "There were a lot of people who would have joined the SLA if we had approached them—people whom we met through the aboveground political work we were doing, but we knew they were flaky (they've proved it since our bust). The SLA would go to great pains to make sure someone's commitment was not based on romanticism or adventurism—we had talked about that a lot. You'd have to look a long way to find any more dedicated folks."

Emily Harris provides insight on why Camilla joined: "Because Camilla was a lesbian, I think a lot of women wonder why she would join a group like the SLA that was made up of men as well as women, but Camilla was not a separatist. She enjoyed working with women and she felt that the methods of the women's struggle had to be expanded. She didn't feel that working with men on that level would interfere with her lesbian–feminist ideas because she believed that women's oppression did not exist in isolation from the oppression of other people."

———

Camilla wasn't the only SLA associate to buy a gun at Siegle's. Joe Remiro bought his gun on August 17, 1973, Angela Atwood on November 7 (the day after the Foster murder, which contradicts the idea that she was the last to join), Bill Harris on November 27, and Mizmoon on November 28.

———

1. For example, Kathleen Soliah, a friend of Angela Atwood, was called "flaky" and was not invited into the group initially. Only after most of the group was killed on May 17, 1974, and the Harrises and Hearst desperately needed assistance was Soliah asked to help.

According to California law, Camilla had to wait five days before getting the gun. She bought it on January 2 and received it about a week later. In February, Camilla checked into the Chabot Gun Club's firing range in the hills of Oakland on three separate occasions. By the time Camilla went, the other SLA members had been taking target practice there for months. Records show that the SLA members usually showed up in pairs or groups—Nancy and Mizmoon; the Harrises, Nancy, and Mizmoon; Remiro and the Harrises. But the three times Camilla went to the range, she went by herself.

In the first days of 1974, the SLA coalesces. On January 1, the entire group is together at last and has a serious discussion about how to move forward. It's easy to view the group as a tight-knit family. Most everyone has known each other for months, and in some cases longer. Wolfe and DeFreeze go back a couple of years, as do Wolfe and Little. The Harrises and Atwood know each other from their undergraduate days at Indiana University. Camilla and Mizmoon are coming up on the three-year anniversary of their meeting. Fred wrote of his sister, "I had known for some time that Mizmoon's Berkeley friends had come to replace our own family."

What was it like for the entire SLA to finally come together? Bill Harris describes the first time he met SLA members. "I remember feeling a combination of excitement, anxiety and nervousness before we went into the house—you know, wondering what kind of people we'd be meeting. I half expected the SLA members to come on real heavy, but as we walked in from the garage they were all standing there smiling and they embraced each of us warmly. That was something I really hadn't expected. It was kind of like they had known me all along—like we were old friends."

In just a few short weeks, this group would spend every moment together, moving in and out of a series of increasingly cramped apartments as every FBI agent and police officer in the Bay Area sought them. If they were looking for a lightning-speed revolution, they were about to find it.

CHAPTER 12

The SLA Kidnaps Patty
February 4, 1974

CAMILLA'S FRIENDS thought it was strange when, in mid-February 1974, she told them she was moving to Palo Alto within days to take a gardening job. She was going to be a gardener at a private residence, living on the property in a refurbished carriage house. She said she wanted to pack lightly and wouldn't need much; the new living space was small. She'd be having a yard sale at 1353 Francisco Street on February 24 to get rid of her things. Some buyers that day offered Camilla IOUs, but she would take only cash. She said she didn't have her new address to give to them.

The next day, FBI agents showed up at the house. Patty Hearst had been missing for nearly three weeks, and they had just connected Camilla to Mizmoon, who was suspected in the kidnapping.

But Camilla was already gone. They were chasing a ghost, so close they could almost see her as she ran away.

On February 4, Camilla drives her blue Volkswagen Beetle slowly down Berkeley's Benvenue Avenue. She and her passenger pass by houses, trees, and fences lit by the full moon. They're just a few blocks away from the UC Berkeley campus; graduate students claim this section of Benvenue. The older houses are tightly packed together, shabby but affordable.

The car has been Camilla's trustworthy companion since her days in Minnesota. It's taken her through the plains and mountains and desert to the ocean. She drove it when she moved to California, drove it to see her parents in Illinois, drove it back to California. Many times, she drove it down to Los Angeles and back to the Bay Area. Sometimes she drove alone; sometimes she drove with Mizmoon by her side.

It's around 7 p.m., the evening chilly. Camilla steers the Volkswagen to the curb and parks directly across from 2603 Benvenue Avenue. The fourplex is boxy and square, sided with dark wooden shakes. Camilla eyes apartment Number 4, which is on the ground floor, left-hand side. She sees the sliding glass door, and against the light inside she can make out a couple of shapes moving around the apartment. One of those shapes is Patricia Campbell Hearst, a junior at UC Berkeley. The other shape is Steven Weed, Patty's fiancé and her former prep school teacher, now a graduate student in philosophy. The SLA's job tonight: to kidnap Patty.

In the prison reform movement that raged throughout California's dysfunctional penal system in the early 1970s, convicts bent on revolution had tossed around the idea of kidnapping a famous, wealthy person as a way to bring attention to their causes. The SLA had been born out of prison meetings, and almost all the future SLA members—with the exception of Camilla—had attended activist meetings with prisoner groups. Thero Wheeler, the SLA member who left the group in fear in October 1973, specifically named Patty Hearst as a potential kidnapping victim during one of those meetings.

A few people are walking on Benvenue despite the chill, students coming home from class, running errands, going out for a drink or two. A student-centered neighborhood is rarely quiet. If Camilla wants to remain completely hidden, if she doesn't want anyone to see her car, she's in the wrong place. She's hiding in the open.

Two women walking on the street keep glancing at the Volkswagen. They slow their pace, and it looks as if they're going to move toward the car. Camilla tenses. But the women pause, confer, and continue on their way.

The evening, instead of growing darker, brightens as the moon rises. The SLA had initially planned to kidnap Patty on January 7, the night of another almost full moon. But they didn't quite have their plan in place at that time. Did they think the light of a full moon would aid them? To make sure they didn't trip as they dragged their victim out of her home, or to be able to spot danger early? But the light is also going to work against them. The SLA will be able to see witnesses, will be able to warn them with gunshots, but witnesses will also be able to see them. The SLA soldiers will be in disguise, with wigs and theatrical makeup courtesy of their resident actress, Angela Atwood, but in the light witnesses will be able to easily identify builds and heights.

Camilla and her companion wait. Minutes go by, a half hour, an hour, now two hours. They've been given instructions from their SLA comrades: Wait for us. We'll come by with a car. We don't know exactly when, and we don't know what type of car, because we're going to steal one. When we arrive, things will move quickly. We'll get out of the car, approach the apartment, take care of Patty's fiancé, and grab her and go. If something goes wrong, you're our backup. Take care of business. You have to be prepared to shoot to defend us.

Camilla checks her gun. Magazine's in, extra magazine in her pocket.

But is she ready to shoot? She's had the gun only about three weeks. She hasn't yet been to the firing range. She's far less comfortable with her weapon than the others. They have been training for months. They've shown her how to load her weapon, how to aim, how to stand. But she's still so new to it. And the grip doesn't feel right. It doesn't fit her hand the way it should. It feels slippery and loose. She's fumbled it a few times.

Camilla's train of thought is broken by a knock at the window. She jumps and looks. Shit. The two women from before. Now they are at the car.

Play it cool, play it cool. Camilla hides the gun. Camilla has acted before; she can play a role.

She rolls down the window.

Is everything OK?, one of the women asks, peering inside. *We've noticed your car's been running for a couple of hours. Do you need something?*

Everything's cool, Camilla responds. She purposely lowers her voice a bit. *We're just waiting for some friends. We thought they'd be here by now. It's so chilly we wanted to keep the heat on.* She looks the women in the eyes, smiles and nods, hopes she's conveying a tone of finality.

All right, just wanted to check. The women walk away, but they look back one more time.

Camilla's heart pounds so loud she's sure her passenger can hear it. Her heart has little chance to recover, because now a green and white station wagon turns the corner and parks on the street in front of 2603 Benvenue. This is it.

———

One of the highest-profile kidnappings for ransom before Patty's occurred in Camilla's home state of Minnesota in 1972. Virginia Piper, the forty-nine-year-old wife of Harry "Bobby" Piper, a partner in the Piper, Jaffrey and Hopwood investment firm, was taken at gunpoint in broad daylight from her suburban Minneapolis home. The kidnappers demanded $1 million, which Bobby provided under the cover of darkness, driving to a designated drop-off point he reached only after following a series of written clues that had been left for him around Minneapolis. The kidnappers released Virginia shortly after; she had been chained to a tree in the Minnesota north woods for nearly two days.

The $1 million Piper ransom was the largest ransom ever paid in the United States, according to the FBI. Up until that moment, kidnapping children for ransom—which career criminals imagined was an easy way to obtain money—was not all that uncommon. The FBI annals were filled with such cases: the baby of famed aviator Charles Lindbergh; Bobby Greenlease, the son of a wealthy Kansas City car dealer; and George Weyerhaeuser, of the lumber family in Tacoma, Washington.

Patty's case was different: this was a political kidnapping, a bold statement on behalf of revolution. While political kidnappings were new to the United States, revolutionary groups around the world had used the tactic for years, not only to raise money but also to bring attention to their causes. The SLA took its inspiration from the revolutionary fervor springing up around the world. Che Guevara's National Liberation Army of Bolivia drew worldwide attention, but the SLA also studied lesser-known groups such as the Tupamaros in Uruguay. When the Uruguayan government clamped down on its people in the late 1960s, the Tupamaros took up arms. They distributed stolen food and money among Uruguay's poor. The group staged a series of political kidnappings, mostly of high-ranking government officials and businessmen. The kidnappings garnered widespread support among the people. Not only did the kidnappings reverse the power structure, but they also exposed the ineptitude of the police, who largely failed to locate and capture Tupamaros members. The SLA had a model to follow.

———

Shortly after the station wagon parks on the street, a white Chevy convertible arrives, parking in the driveway of Patty and Steven's apartment. Camilla and her passenger watch as the Chevy's three occupants—said to be DeFreeze, Bill Harris, and Atwood—get out of the car. Atwood knocks on the sliding glass door of apartment 4. Camilla sees Weed open it, and within moments, the two men behind Atwood burst through the door.

The minutes pass slowly, as if each second is mired in muck. Camilla rolls down the window to catch any sound from the apartment and again palms her gun. Her passenger does the same thing. Camilla hears a muffled racket, but so far no gunshots.

Camilla sees a few lights flicker on in other houses. If she can hear the commotion across the street, neighbors surely must be wondering what's going on. A couple of people step outside and look toward 2603 Benvenue. *Hurry up*, Camilla thinks. The noise will soon attract a crowd. In a moment there could be chaos—injuries, neighbors killed, SLA soldiers killed or arrested. But Camilla is prepared. Mentally prepared, even if not physically prepared where her gun is concerned.

Now she sees movement. Action. The two men have Patty. They have her! It worked! Camilla cannot believe her eyes. There's Patty, squirming and wiggling and screaming. She looks so small. Her thin robe has fallen off her shoulders, exposing her breasts. More people peek out their doors and windows. Now the SLA soldiers fire their guns. Neighbors under fire duck back inside.

The men open the trunk of the Chevy and shove Patty inside. They clamber into the car and speed away; someone in the car shoots out the window toward the houses. Camilla pulls away from the curb and quickly follows, as does the station wagon. She's now an accessory to a kidnapping. She has crossed a line: she's a criminal.

———

About a week after the kidnapping, Camilla visited her good friends Paul and Joyce Halverson to tell them about her move to Palo Alto. They were as surprised at this sudden move as her other friends were. They were even more surprised when Camilla tried to give them her major possessions, such as furniture and artwork. She even wanted to give them Keya, her cat. Joyce thought the request was odd, and with the Hearst kidnapping on everyone's minds, she told Camilla, "I'll bet you're going to join the SLA."

Camilla laughed. "No, Joyce," she said. "I know you wish I were, but I'm not."

A week later, Camilla visited Paul and Joyce again, this time to say good-bye. Again, Joyce mentioned the SLA. "Well, I'm glad you're not joining the SLA because you're too old for that kind of idealism."

Joyce remembers that Camilla didn't say anything in response. She just hugged her and Paul and went on her way.

———

For everyone in the three-car caravan, the kidnapping is a transformative moment. No one's life will ever be the same. As Camilla drives, she thinks through the possible outcomes. If the FBI locates Patty and the rest of the SLA, Camilla would be charged as an accessory to kidnapping. Maybe she would get some prison time. Or maybe she would become the prosecution's star witness, earning freedom in exchange for information. Still, she would always be "that woman" who helped kidnap Patty. It would be on her record, a burden to bear. What would her parents think? Their only child to live to adulthood, a criminal. Not just a petty criminal, but a criminal on the national stage. All of their parishioners would know the connection. How would George face his congregation?

But Camilla can't think that way. She must believe the kidnapping will succeed. The SLA is blazing a path toward real change. Patty's kidnapping will wake the masses from their hypnotized routines. In just a few days, the SLA will demand millions from Randolph Hearst, Patty's father. They will use the money to buy food for California's needy and hungry. Then the nation—even the world—will see how the poor can be served. They'll see that greed benefits only a few. That the poor can be fed, clothed, and sheltered with money already at hand. They will see. Camilla is part of something big. Something that will make her parents proud. They've worked all their lives toward social justice, but change has been slow. But here is Camilla's chance to make a big, bold statement.

———

A few blocks away from Benvenue, the Chevy convertible pulls over. Camilla guides the Volkswagen behind it and parks. The occupants of the convertible hustle out. They go to the trunk and grab Patty. Camilla waits in her Volkswagen, as she's been told. She's a lookout, a protector. It's her job to watch and listen, to be the eyes and ears for the others who are preoccupied with the physical exertion of the kidnapping.

Camilla sees one of her comrades lean into the Chevy's back seat. It looks as if she's talking to someone. It's the Chevy's owner. They stole the car, but Camilla hadn't thought they'd put the owner in the back and take him along for the ride.

The station wagon pulls up next to the Chevy. The Chevy's occupants—minus the rightful owner—throw Patty into the station wagon, jump into the car, and speed away. Camilla knows what to do. Just follow the station wagon.

———

On February 19, two weeks after the kidnapping, Camilla visited her former boss Eddie Collins at Lake Temescal. She found him working on one of the paths and gave him a big hug. She told him about the gardening job in Palo Alto and said she'd be making good money there.

They talked as they strolled around the park. Camilla actually brought up the Hearst kidnapping. It was what everyone was talking about, so it might have seemed strange if she didn't mention it. She specifically wanted to get Eddie's opinion on the food-distribution program that had just been announced. The SLA demanded $6 million in ransom from Patty's parents, Randolph and Catherine Hearst, and they planned to use the money to feed the poor in California—seventy dollars' worth of meat, fruits, and vegetables for each person who asked for it.[1] Some of the people for whom the food was intended didn't plan to take it; they didn't want food bought with ransom money while the young woman meant to be ransomed remained a hostage. Camilla told Eddie she thought it was a shame that not everyone was willing to take the food. She talked about how society had failed people living at the margins—people like her, people who were willing to work full-time but were denied the opportunity because of their gender. Still, her tone must have been conversational and warm, because Eddie was entirely surprised when he learned later that Camilla was involved in the kidnapping. He had never suspected a thing. Years later he would talk about Camilla with fondness, still baffled by her secret life.

———

Shortly after all the commotion on Benvenue, after the SLA and Patty are gone, police swarm the neighborhood. The woman who had approached the Volkswagen earlier tells a police officer her story. She cannot describe the passenger well. It was a woman, she says, but the hair looked odd and it

———

1. Randolph Hearst agreed to provide $2 million, $500,000 of his own money and $1.5 million from the Hearst Foundation. Anyone who asked for food was to be provided with it without needing to show a food-stamp card or other proof of low income. The first distribution, which occurred on February 22, was a complete disaster and devolved into rioting and chaos.

may have been a wig. A scarf partially covered the hair, making identification difficult, but it's possible it was Mizmoon.

But the driver—the driver stood out. The witness tells police the driver was an albino male. When a police sketch is drawn the next day based on the witness's account, the drawing looks remarkably like Camilla. She had probably worn her usual attire of baggy working-man's clothes. That, combined with an effect like a deeper voice, could let her pass for a man, and in moonlight, her fair hair and skin would look like alabaster.

———

Camilla follows the station wagon through the winding roads in the foothills east of Berkeley and Oakland. She knows they can't take the direct route from Berkeley to Daly City, a suburb just south of San Francisco where the safe house is located. The police may have already set up roadblocks on main thoroughfares leading out of Berkeley. So the team heads north and east, eventually turning around to head south. But the more time they spend on the road, the better the chance they might be stopped by police. Camilla is a diligent driver, eyes on the road, scanning the traffic for cop cars, paying close attention to posted speed limits. She's behind the wheel of her car. She's in control. She still has a chance to break away. She could take a left, take a right, slow down, speed up, whatever it takes to separate from the station wagon in front of her. She could completely foil this plan. All it would take is a quick turn.

But.

The woman next to her.

The woman in the trunk of the car ahead of her.

It's not up to Camilla anymore. Decisions are not for an individual to make. It's groupthink now.

CHAPTER 13

Camilla Slips Away

ON MARCH 6, 1974, two men in suits showed up at Cheryl Brooks's office in Los Angeles. They were from the FBI, and they had some questions about Camilla. "I was in total shock," Cheryl says. "I had no idea what was going on."

After they left, she immediately called the last phone number she had for Camilla. "A man answered the phone, and said she had left in the last month."

When the FBI visited Cheryl a second time, she didn't talk. She wanted to know what was going on, and she wanted to hear it from Camilla.

On March 1, Camilla walks into Central Bank on Berkeley's Shattuck Avenue. Nearly a month has passed since the Hearst kidnapping. Police and FBI agents are working almost nonstop to puzzle out this mysterious Symbionese Liberation Army who says it has Patty. FBI agents have already identified possible suspects, including Mizmoon.

If Camilla suspects she's under surveillance today, she doesn't show it. She doesn't wear a hat or sunglasses. She wears her regular attire of a T-shirt and baggy jeans. The only deviance from her usual appearance is that her hair, normally kept in a short, neat bob, is shaggier and longer than usual. She blends in with the busy foot traffic on the street. If she's being watched, no matter—she has no choice but to go to the bank. The SLA needs money, and money is what Camilla has. There's no other option; she has to take the risk.

She's been taking risks the past couple of weeks, living openly when everyone else has been in hiding. She's gone to the gun range to take target practice. The Chabot Gun Club is the same one that Bay Area police officers use. At the range, Camilla could have looked to either side of her and seen off-duty officers. Did any lingering glance from them cause her to tremble? And all the times she went to the gun range were after the kidnapping, when all officers in the Bay Area were on high alert. The unknown kidnappers were out there. The kidnappers had guns. They could be far away by now. Or they could be right here—San Francisco, San Mateo, Berkeley, or taking target practice next to them at the Chabot Gun Club in Oakland.

Camilla has used Central Bank since moving to Berkeley in 1971; it's just a couple of blocks from Channing Way. She's bound to run into familiar faces here, either fellow customers or, certainly, tellers. She knows the FBI is looking for her. She was forced underground in the past week, the last of the SLA members to go into hiding. But today she resurfaces, tasked with the job of getting money for the small group of eight, or nine if you count Patty.

But is she having doubts about this way of life? She's been a member of the SLA since the first of the year. She's with people who've committed violent crimes—they killed a man a few months before, and now they've kidnapped an American heiress. What would be next? This new life of Camilla's is one of hiding, one of running.

At the bank, she's alone. She's virtually free. There's nothing stopping her from walking into a police station. Right now, she could confess to a teller or a manager. But if she gave up her comrades, would they or their sympathizers find a way to target her? Or her parents? She can't bear the thought.

No, she's committed, more than ever. If she gives up, what message would that send to other would-be freedom fighters? That revolution isn't worth the fight anymore?

———

Directly across the street from Central Bank was the Berkeley office of the FBI, which had concentrated almost all of its Bay Area resources on finding the SLA and Patty. Agents had known about Camilla's connection to Mizmoon for about a week and had just missed her, showing up at her Francisco Street duplex one day after she moved out. The FBI had subpoenaed bank records in the Berkeley area looking for accounts held by SLA suspects. At Central Bank, two accounts popped up—those of Nancy Ling Perry and Camilla.

FBI Special Agent Charles Bates headed the Hearst investigation from his San Francisco headquarters. Now that he knew two SLA associates had accounts at Central Bank, he might have deduced they would need money to fund their mission. One or both of them would be coming to the bank. This was the biggest case of the year, the decade, maybe even the century. And here was a chance to break it wide open in Berkeley.

Agent Bates had a number of options. He could have posted agents at the bank, scanning faces, trying to identify Camilla or Nancy when they entered. He could have met with all the bank employees, some of whom had attended to Camilla and Nancy in the past. He could have told them, *If Camilla or Nancy arrives, delay them until agents can get there.*

Or, in the option that Agent Bates actually took, FBI agents in Berkeley casually mentioned to Fred Rowley, the bank manager, that Camilla and Nancy were customers. Some of the FBI agents already knew Rowley; they played handball together. So Rowley was simply told to keep his eyes open for the women. *Just give us a call if you see them, and we'll come on over and finish this thing.*

An Oakland police investigator, when he found out the FBI had narrowly missed Camilla, said, "This is typical of the way this case has been bungled from the start. The vaunted investigative resources of the FBI have been as effective as a Cub Scout troop."

———

Camilla walks into the bank and shakes herself off; it's a rainy, windy, raw day in the East Bay. She looks for the next available teller. She spots the familiar face of Patiah Lambert. Camilla strolls up to Lambert and they exchange hellos. Camilla is friendly and warm as usual, but Lambert thinks something's a little off, though it's hard to pinpoint exactly what. Camilla just seems a little nervous, a little fidgety. Maybe she glances back to the front door once or twice. Perhaps she shifts from foot to foot, or drums her fingers on the counter.

Camilla asks to withdraw the entirety of her account: $1,565 (approximately $9,000 in 2022). This type of request generally results in a few questions and comments—*Sorry to see you leave. Are you moving? Any big plans?* Camilla's request is no exception.

Lambert sees that a hold has been placed on Camilla's account. A note usually accompanies a hold—maybe fees haven't been paid or the account is overdrawn. But when Lambert looks at Camilla's hold, she doesn't see an explanation. Lambert figures it's a clerical error. Camilla has always been a good customer since she started banking at Central Bank. Still, an entire account withdrawal needs the approval of the operations manager.

I need to get a manager, Lambert tells Camilla. *Can you wait here, please?*

This small delay may be making Camilla nervous. What do the bankers know? For nearly a month, Camilla has managed to keep her involvement in the Hearst kidnapping a secret. Camilla has stayed aboveground longer than any other SLA member, still in contact with her friends and living at her duplex until just a few days ago. She is sure that no one suspects anything. But that could soon change.

Lambert returns. The operations manager has approved the withdrawal without question. Camilla sighs with relief and hopes her reaction doesn't betray the tension she feels. Lambert counts out the cash and hands the bundle to Camilla. She watches as Camilla stuffs the money into the pockets of her jeans, which Lambert thinks is odd. Camilla laughs and tells Lambert, *I'm a little nervous carrying all this cash around Berkeley.* The teller smiles and watches Camilla walk away, unnoticed by anyone, outside into the rain. With her went the best chance the FBI ever had to crack open the Hearst case. The next time Camilla enters a bank, she'll be carrying a gun.

CHAPTER 14

Camilla inside the SLA

PATTY HEARST WROTE A MEMOIR IN 1982, *Every Secret Thing*. She focuses on DeFreeze, whom she portrays as a crazy, domineering brute, and also directs her vitriol at Bill and Emily Harris. She only briefly mentions Camilla—known by her code name, Gabi—but each short mention adds up to a picture of a pitiful, solitary creature. Patty's book does nothing to help me understand why Camilla was in this group. In fact, it only suggests that she did not belong, that she was an outsider, never fully accepted: "Poor Gabi. She was like the cheese that stands alone at the end of the children's game 'The Farmer in the Dell.' Nobody wanted her. She was, in several ways, pathetic. She stood out in the group as a misfit, even more than I did. She was big, overweight, and awkward in comparison to the other women, and there was little, if anything, militant or combative in her bearing or demeanor. I considered her the most sensitive person in the group."

———

Camilla lived for 102 days after the kidnapping. Most of that time she spent in seclusion in tiny, dingy apartments with Patty and the other seven members of the SLA. They embraced a spirit of sharing and openness that dictated everything from toothbrushes (they all shared one) to bathroom policies (open door while using the toilet or bathing) to sexual relations (anyone could have sex with whomever they wanted, though it's highly likely it was not always consensual).

The SLA released several long, taped communiqués over those three-plus months, though Camilla spoke barely more than a minute out of all the hours of tape. The communiqués offered painstaking detail on SLA philosophy but said nothing about life inside the cell. In the tapes, the SLA made itself appear bigger than it was, like the cobra that was its emblem. Law enforcement officials had no idea what they were seeking. They didn't know how many people belonged to the SLA. Was this group of people who held Patty just one cell in an army of larger cells spread throughout the Bay Area, or the state of California, or even the nation?

Details about those 102 days emerged months, sometimes years, later. Officials picked up some clues after they stumbled across abandoned safe houses and sifted through the items the SLA had left behind. After September 1975, a clearer picture formed when Patty, the Harrises, and other SLA associates were captured. Patty's trial revealed more details, but they centered mostly on the issue of whether she had been brainwashed or had truly committed herself to the SLA.

To this day, we have only one account that claims to depict daily life within the group from February to May 1974, and that is Patty's *Every Secret Thing*, written three years after President Jimmy Carter commuted her prison sentence.

It is frustrating to go from George's memoir and Camilla's letters—from which I can reconstruct a fairly clear time line of Camilla's life—to having almost nothing about the last three months of her life, which was certainly the time when she underwent the most radical change. All I have are Patty's words, no doubt written to be self-serving and to clear her public image. But I think Patty would have little reason to lie about descriptions of where the SLA lived, life within the cell, and depictions of Camilla. I think, too, that George and Lorena must have hung onto Patty's words as much as I did, for they also had no idea what was going on during those three months. One thing Patty's book does do: it makes clear that Camilla is part of a group that descends into madness fostered by paranoia, isolation from the outside world, and constant talk of revolution, death, and martyrdom.

After the Kidnapping: Day 7

Camilla rings the doorbell at the apartment at 37 Northridge Drive in Daly City, a picturesque San Francisco suburb on the ocean. One of the SLA soldiers opens the door and greets Camilla warmly. The others come to the door and do the same—hugs, kisses, friendly words. Camilla has brought supplies. Food that can keep easily, staples such as bread and rice and boxed items that can fill a pantry. Perhaps she also brings ammunition and maybe some money. It's only been days since the kidnapping, and Camilla is still mobile. She can walk about outside, undisguised. She's the group's runner, a valuable member of the SLA.

The SLA comrades are riding a euphoria. They've successfully carried out a high-profile kidnapping and they revel in the fact that they are known across the country, even around the world. Patty as a hostage serves as a bargaining chip and allows the SLA to make grand demands. They float the idea of a prisoner exchange: Patty for Russ Little and Joe Remiro, who are jailed awaiting trial for the Foster murder. But that idea goes nowhere. They also issue tape-recorded communiqués to demand that Patty's father use his wealth to feed the poor. He agrees to donate $2 million, and the People in Need program is created to distribute the food. This is something Camilla can support: actual help for the poor. The SLA sees itself as real-life Robin Hoods.

At around this time Patty first meets Camilla, though Patty is still blindfolded so she only hears Camilla's voice. DeFreeze puffs up the SLA even to Patty, telling her that Camilla is joining them because she's been transferred from a supply unit to this combat team. The reality is that Camilla probably *was* the supply unit, and the "combat team" is the entirety of the SLA.

Of Camilla, Patty writes, "She had a soft, warm voice and seemed rather shy. . . . Of all the 'sisters' I seemed to have the least contact with Gabi. She seldom came to the closet to talk with me, which I attributed to her natural shyness. I could think of no other reason."

Day 25: March 1

Camilla empties her bank account. She's now fully underground, hiding with the SLA.

Besides failing to catch Camilla at Central Bank, the FBI makes other blunders. In mid-February, Bill Harris sent a letter to his mother in Indiana, routed first through a friend. He asked for money and included a stamped envelope addressed to a "Janet Cooper" at a post office box in Santa Clara. But he wrote the wrong zip code on the envelope. The FBI was monitoring his mother's mail, but agents did not think to verify the zip code. The letter ended up at the Santa Barbara post office. "Janet Cooper"—who may have been Emily Harris—kept calling the Santa Clara post office to see if the letter had arrived. Even though the FBI was physically staking out the post office, no one told employees to watch for any contact from a Janet Cooper.

In addition, Camilla sold her beloved Volkswagen Beetle to a dealership in late February, right before going underground. The FBI is actively seeking this car, since they know it was on the scene of Patty's kidnapping. Even though the car was sold to a woman who worked as a secretary in the San Francisco FBI office, agents haven't made the connection.

And when the SLA moves to an apartment on Golden Gate Avenue in San Francisco in mid-March, they are just twelve blocks from the FBI office, also located on Golden Gate.

Around Day 50

The SLA has been in its new safe house on Golden Gate Avenue for a few days. At this point, they let Patty take off the blindfold. She describes seeing Camilla for the first time: "On the left side was Gabi, who was noticeably heavyset and plain-looking, wearing glasses with thick lenses, her short straight hair dyed a peculiar shade of red."

It's odd that Patty would describe Camilla as "heavyset." Just a few months before, Camilla was going on long hikes, taking karate lessons, and whipping her body into shape. She had noticeably transformed her once-soft body into a lean physique through healthy eating and exercise. What had changed?

A clue comes from Patty's account of the daily rations within the cell. They eat a lot of starchy food that keeps well and is quick and easy to make: pancakes, potatoes, rice, bread, anything with flour. This food is cheap and supplies them with quick energy. A diet with few fruits and vegetables and high in carbs, combined with hardly ever leaving the safe house, could put pounds back on a woman who had carried extra pounds for most of her life.

Every Day

Camilla trains with military precision despite the cramped quarters. She and the other members perform calisthenics, wear combat boots, run from room to room, aim their rifles, pretend to shoot at targets, load magazines, clip ammo on and off their weapons, perform rollovers on the floor, say "bang-bang" and "rat-a-tat-tat" to simulate weapons fire. They hold combat drills every few days in preparation for an FBI raid they are sure is coming. In these combat drills, they follow each other in the small space, practice rounding corners while shooting and covering each other. Camilla wears a heavy backpack, a carbine in one hand, a handgun holstered on the hip, and does somersaults and comes up in a firing position. "The SLA would be ready to do battle with the pigs," Patty writes. They practice with knives, specifically how to slit throats.

Camilla helps take care of the weapons—fully automatic submachine guns, semiautomatics, single-action rifles, and handguns. She practices firing her weapon at life-sized human outlines tacked to the walls. She points and clicks unloaded guns at DeFreeze, Nancy, Mizmoon, whoever, at their heads and chests. She loads and unloads ammunition in the weapons and clips magazines in place with the goal of becoming faster. This training, for hours each day, may be honing her skills and making her a better shooter. Maybe.

Patty says Camilla has the most trouble with her weapon. "Gabi sort of lumbered about in an awkward crouch with a big shotgun." Patty calls Camilla "ungainly compared to all the others."

Day 58: April 3

A taped communiqué is sent to KPFA radio. This tape contains a bombshell: Patty has chosen to stay and fight with the SLA. She's adopted a new name, Tania, a name used by one of Che Guevara's comrades. A photograph of Patty as Tania accompanies the announcement. She stands in front of the

SLA's seven-headed cobra emblem, beret on her head, hardened gaze off to the side, automatic rifle pointed like she's ready to shoot.

Day 70: April 15

Camilla drives down San Francisco's Noriega Street in a green Ford LTD station wagon. In the car with her are DeFreeze, Patty, Mizmoon, and Nancy. They are going to rob the Sunset District branch of Hibernia Bank. Bill, Emily, Angela, and Willie sit in a red AMC Hornet Sportabout across the street from the bank. They are the lookout team, ready to shoot if the cops bust in while the robbery is in progress. Camilla illegally parks on Twenty-Second Street, just off Noriega, in a bus zone.

The five people in the station wagon grab their weapons and leave the vehicle. They are already wearing disguises, with two exceptions: DeFreeze and Patty. Mizmoon wears a scarf that covers her hair. Nancy wears a short black wig, and Camilla wears a curly black one. Patty, Nancy, and Camilla wear dark peacoats.

The surveillance camera shoots hundreds of still photographs, a few each second, and compiled together they form a choppy video. Though the video is silent, you can see DeFreeze and Nancy barking orders at the people in the bank, waving their guns as they speak. Patty aims her gun at customers who lie on the floor. Mizmoon, with lithe precision, vaults over the counter and starts to bag money. Camilla is mostly off camera, but Patty said in her trial that Camilla also gathered cash. DeFreeze checks his watch. He peers over the counter a couple of times to check on Mizmoon's progress. Patty checks her watch. Camilla strolls into camera range, walks past Patty, walks past DeFreeze. She stops briefly, turns to look over her shoulder at Mizmoon, her former girlfriend. She faces front again and walks forward. After a few steps, she looks behind her again. This time she can see Mizmoon, who again hops over the counter. When Camilla is sure that Mizmoon is safe, that she is coming, she resumes her calm, but quick, walk to the front door.

DeFreeze and Nancy shoot at two men at the bank's entrance during the getaway. One is hit in the hip, the other in the hand. The five robbers pile into the station wagon, the red Hornet just behind them. A few blocks away, they switch to cars planted there before the heist. They have taken $10,692.51 (approximately $62,000 in 2022 dollars). They drive off in the morning sun, with no one on their tails. It's been more than two months since they kidnapped Patty, and still they are ghosts.

The Remainder of April

The occasional freedom the SLA members had prior to the bank robbery has now evaporated. Before the robbery, members made excursions to get supplies or run errands. They donned elaborate disguises to leave the safe house. Angela, a former stage actress, had brought all types of makeup and brushes, and they also had a variety of clothes, wigs, hats, and scarves. But now their pictures are on Wanted posters all over town, all over the country. Until now Camilla's involvement was just speculation, based on her previous relationship with Mizmoon. But now she's solidly linked to the group. Everyone is looking for her as well as the others. The SLA doesn't want to risk going out in public, even in disguise.

Camilla has lived with the other eight for more than two months, with only rare chances to leave, to feel the sun on her skin. The sun is the reason Camilla moved to California, and now she doesn't even get to see it. The curtains are drawn tightly, even during the day. All nine people live in the tight quarters of a small apartment.

The psychological stress doesn't break the group. Instead, after April 15, Patty writes that they're more committed than ever. They increase the number and duration of combat and weapons drills and physical conditioning. But they feel the pressure of police closing in. The SLA plans to leave the Golden Gate apartment at the end of April. Over the past almost three months, the SLA accumulated diagrams, drawings, and plans, clothes and disguises, and books. They can't take all of it with them. They need to move lightly and quickly. Each person, including Camilla, will take only necessities on their next move: one disguise, a change of clothes, weapons, and ammunition. But what to do with all the extra things? They can't just throw them away; who knows where the FBI is nosing around? They try to flush paper bit by bit down the toilet after each use, but that hardly makes a dent in their cache. The night before they leave, they still have a lot to dispose of.

So they decide to fill the tub with water and dump in the papers. For extra assurance, they also throw in a half pound of cyanide crystals. Bill writes on the wall of the bathroom:

> Warning to the FBI, CIA, NSA, NSC, and CBS—There are a few clues in this bathroom. However, you will have to wait until they are dry. An additional word of caution: ½ (one half) lb. (pound) of cyanide (potassium cyanide) crystals have been added to this "home brew"—so pig, drink at your own risk. There are also many additional juicy SLA clues throughout this safehouse. However, remember that you are not bullet-proof either. Happy hunting, Charles.

The last line is a reference to the FBI's San Francisco chief Charles Bates. That's not the only mess they make. They leave food strewn all over the kitchen and turn over furniture. Any mess they can make, they do, as a way to thumb their noses at law enforcement. After a couple of days, a downstairs tenant notices swarms of cockroaches in her apartment. She tells the manager, who suspects they are coming from upstairs. He finds the debris in the abandoned apartment and informs the FBI. The media report that the SLA lives in squalor. To the public, the SLA is looking all the more crazy.

Early May

By now, the SLA safe houses are becoming more and more substandard. After the Golden Gate apartment, they move into a dilapidated duplex on Oakdale Avenue in the Hunters Point neighborhood, an old shipping bay in east San Francisco. Patty describes mounds of dust and cobwebs and an exterior that looks as if it hasn't been touched for months. But this space offers them more opportunities to increase their training. In a house, with no one above them or below them, they are free to run around at all hours, stomping their combat boots and clicking their guns.

By this time, the SLA has split itself into three teams, the intention being that each team would spread the SLA word and recruit additional soldiers. Camilla is originally placed on Bill's team with Patty. Bill is furious; for one thing, he thinks he should be with Emily. And second, he sees Camilla and

Patty as the weakest members, and he does not want them both. According to Patty, he said, "Our team would be crippled from the start. With Tania and Gabi, it couldn't work out. We're not strong enough to survive. They don't have the skills yet and I couldn't protect them both." DeFreeze caves to Bill's demands and trades Emily, who had been on his team, for Camilla. Camilla is now with DeFreeze and Angela. The teams bristle with rancor. Patty "hated" Bill and Emily, who she said excluded her from decisions. Mizmoon is on a team with Willie and Nancy, and according to Patty, Willie despises Mizmoon. And DeFreeze, no doubt, is displeased to have Camilla on his team.

After just a few days on Oakdale Avenue, the SLA feels squeezed. They start to feel claustrophobic, not only because of the small house but also because of the city itself, surrounded on three sides by water. They seek to get away from the pressure, to get away from the scenes of their crimes. In this high-crime neighborhood, police helicopters regularly provide backup to patrol squads and fly over every night. The SLA thinks the helicopters are homing in on them. A couple of the SLA soldiers are familiar with Los Angeles, including Camilla, so that's where they decide to go. A big city, with plenty of space to roam and get lost.

After three months in these cramped quarters, Camilla can't help but change. Without any outside influences, she's free to create her own reality, to see the world any way she wants to see it. She feeds off the paranoia of everyone else. In this world, revolution is imminent—no, it's actually starting. DeFreeze talks incessantly. He talks about antigovernment action occurring in cities all over the state and the nation. He talks constantly about death and dying for the cause. Camilla is ready to become a martyr. "Death filled the center room where we held our meetings every night," Patty writes.

They leave for Los Angeles on May 10. They drive three separate vehicles, each unit on its own. Camilla shares driving duties with DeFreeze and Angela. She's made this trip several times before, traveling to Los Angeles for art shows when she first moved to Berkeley, traveling back down with Mizmoon to visit the Soltysiks. To Camilla, even though the trips were just the year before, it must feel like a lifetime ago.

Days 96–101

The SLA ends up in Compton, an almost all-black neighborhood troubled by crime and poverty, situated in South Central Los Angeles. They find a safe house using a network of connections, friends of friends. This is the worst safe house yet. It's little more than a shack, with only two rooms and a kitchen. It has running water but no electricity or gas. They keep it dark inside, as usual, bringing their heavy drapes with them as they've done in all their moves. In this neighborhood, they have to be extra careful to stay hidden, to give the appearance that no one is living in the house at all. Not only are the cops their enemies, but so are their neighbors, who will regard white infiltrators with the utmost suspicion.

The group had probably already shown signs of collective psychosis before this point, but by the time they reach Los Angeles it's full blown, according to Patty. The group is more cut off than ever from the outside world. Each member suffers from battle fatigue. Death is no longer merely a concept; it's now a necessity. They fully expect it to come. Indeed, they invite death because the masses would be demoralized to see freedom fighters imprisoned. A more powerful message is a freedom fighter who is killed.

The cramped indoor training continues and intensifies. For the past few weeks, DeFreeze has assured them that the battle will begin in the summer. At that point they will reveal themselves and step into the outside world to recruit. Therefore, they must be more ready than ever to prepare for resistance.

For one drill, a door has been removed from its hinges and set sideways in a doorway. Everyone must run up and jump over the obstacle in full battle gear, carrying their guns. "Jump!" DeFreeze shouts as each soldier approaches. DeFreeze kicks anyone who hesitates for even a split second.

Camilla can't quite do it. She's not as nimble as the others and she stumbles. She's been kicked in the butt several times already, but DeFreeze gives her a final, fierce kick. She's filled with rage. "Who the hell do you think you are, kicking me like that? Don't you ever do that again!" DeFreeze gets in her face. "Well, what the fuck you going to do about it? Get your ass over that obstacle and keep running. . . . I'll kick you whenever I damn well please. Now, move!" Camilla backs down and does what she's told, big tears rolling down her face.

Day 102: The Last Day

At 2 a.m. on May 17, about fifteen hours before the shoot-out, Camilla and five of her SLA comrades arrived at a white stucco house at 1466 East Fifty-Fourth Street, hoping to find refuge. They chose this house because at 2 a.m., the lights were still on. In addition, a four-foot stone wall surrounded the property; it provided a natural shield.

They needed a new place to stay. The team of Bill, Emily, and Patty had left the day before to get supplies. At Mel's Sporting Goods in Inglewood, Bill decided to stuff a pair of socks into his jacket, even though he was paying for a variety of other items. A clerk noticed Bill's attempted theft, and as Bill and Emily walked out, the clerk confronted them just outside the front door. Bill took out his gun and scuffled with the clerk. Patty, who had been waiting in the van, saw the commotion and sprayed gunfire at the two men. No one was hit, Bill and Emily sprinted to the van, and the three escaped the scene. They abandoned the van and commandeered another vehicle. But they knew they had to lie low for a while; going back to the hideout would endanger the others. Meanwhile, those in the shack heard news reports of the debacle at the sporting goods store and decided to leave that house and find another.

When police located the abandoned van a short time later, they were in luck: a parking ticket remained inside, issued at the address of the shack. Police could now pinpoint the SLA to South Central Los Angeles. They descended on the area in plainclothes on May 17, and it wasn't long before they discovered the SLA at 1466 East Fifty-Fourth Street.

Visitors had been going to and from the house all day. The SLA didn't seem too concerned about keeping a low profile. Instead, they chatted with those who dropped by and even tried to recruit some of them into the now-sputtering army.

Two children who lived at 1466 East Fifty-Fourth came home after school to find strangers in their house, standing amid an arsenal of guns and ammunition. Their mother was passed out on a bed. The older child, eleven-year-old Timmy, knew something was wrong. He went down the street to get his grandma.

When the grandma, Mary Carr, arrived, she demanded to know why the SLA was there and asked them to leave. DeFreeze refused, so Carr took

Timmy but somehow left his brother, eight-year-old Tony, behind. Carr then informed police what she had seen at the house.

Carr's information pinpointed the SLA to an exact location. It was now about 5:30 p.m. The police would have to move quickly before dusk arrived.

Officers issued the first warning to the people inside the house at 5:44 p.m.: "Occupants of 1466 East Fifty-Fourth Street, this is the Los Angeles Police Department speaking. Come out with your hands up. Comply immediately and you will not be harmed." One minute passed with no response. The officer repeated the command.

Slowly, the front door opened. Police stood ready with their gas masks on, their guns cocked.

Little Tony emerged.

He stood on the front steps, frozen by the horrific-looking gas masks and guns in front of him. An officer darted to the steps and scooped Tony into his arms. It took Tony a few minutes to stop crying and describe to officers exactly who was in the house.

Police issued two more surrender commands. Official police reports indicate that eighteen surrender commands were eventually issued. When no one emerged, police threw tear gas cannisters through a window. A hail of gunfire from inside the house immediately descended on the officers. For minutes, shooting was continuous and deafening, broken only when officers had to stop and reload guns. Sometime around 6:40 p.m., something within the house caught fire and columns of thick, black smoke poured out the windows. It was over.

———

In the letter police said was found in the debris, Camilla appeared to tell her parents for the first time what she's involved in:

> Our support is from the people and will continue to grow with each victory as we prove to the American people that the revolution can indeed be successful. We intend to be around for quite a while to live and see the victories. I know you trust my sincerity even if you haven't come to agree with the course of action I have committed myself to.

I am young and strong and willing to dedicate my courage, intelligence, and love to the work. I really feel good about what I am doing and I want you to also.

Camilla's body, stuffed into a crawl space, went undiscovered for two days. Initial reports from the night of the shoot-out state that only five bodies had been found. As the identification process unfolded, people nationwide waited to hear whether Patty was among the dead. Who the others were was of little concern.

But back in Lincolnwood, Illinois, George and Lorena waited anxiously. They had known for about a month that their daughter was caught up in the SLA. Camilla's face appeared on an FBI Most Wanted poster, along with the faces of Patty and three others, after the April 15 bank robbery.

Throughout Saturday, May 18, the Halls let themselves feel cautiously optimistic, but still they worried because they hadn't heard from Camilla themselves. By the end of that night, police said only five bodies had been positively identified, and Camilla was not one of them.

The next day in church, the Halls received good wishes from members of their congregation.

"Sunday morning our church was jubilant as one and all expressed their joy and relief on our part," George wrote in "I Remember Lorena."

That evening, the Halls readied themselves to attend a concert in Evanston with their nephew and his wife. As they were about to leave home, the phone rang.

The coroner's voice echoed from two thousand miles away: Camilla's body had been found and positively identified. Their last living child was dead.

PART III

Camilla Revealed

There's a knock at the door; it's late at night. I open the door, and it's Camilla, looking distraught. I pull her inside, take her down into the basement to set her up to sleep, and we sit down together to talk. I ask her what's going on with her, why she's doing what she's doing. Is she all right? Does she need any food? But mostly why. I want to know why. And when she tries to talk to tell me why, either no sound comes out or it's electronically garbled so that I can't comprehend it. We can talk about anything else, and I can hear her speak; but when it gets to that—to why—the answers are always very frustrating. And I wake up shortly thereafter.

—an unidentified friend of Camilla,
describing a dream she had after Camilla's death

CHAPTER 15

Crumbs on the Trail

THE ARTIST CHUCK CLOSE uses a technique called gridding to create vivid, realistic paintings of faces—so realistic that it wasn't until recently I recognized they were not photographs. Close moved away from hyperrealism over the years and his grid became looser, more abstract. The result was a patchwork of individual small squares and rectangles. In some paintings, such as *Cindy (Smile)* (2013), the squares are a uniform, solid-color shape. In the case of *Self-Portrait Screenprint* (2012), each square and rectangle is filled with a colorful, geometric shape—circles, triangles, ovals. By themselves, each tile could be its own work. Close has said, "I want people to see what made the image. I like dropping crumbs along the trail like Hansel and Gretel."

———

How well can we know someone, even the person closest to us? Even if we have spent year upon year with that person, can we really know him or her completely? I hold shadows and secrets that I choose not to reveal. My husband is the one who knows me best, but even he cannot know the whole me. If people wanted to know the whole me, the best they could do would be to compare notes, triangulate the data, and create a portrait that way. The portrait may be clear, in the case of someone who lives an open life, or it may be fuzzy. Camilla's portrait is going to be abstract, built on a loose grid. But it's still a portrait.

Trying to ascertain Camilla's reasons for joining the SLA is like following crumbs on a trail. She dropped some crumbs—through her letters, her artwork, and her poetry—and so did those who knew her, like her parents and friends and to a lesser extent her comrades in the SLA. Crumbs can also be found by looking at the lives of women who made choices similar to Camilla's. But some crumbs are missing. They've been taken, they've disappeared, they've been destroyed. Some crumbs are misplaced, or have been moved off the trail, or appear to go in a different direction, or simply stop.

———

The media want simple answers in the aftermath of violence. Talking heads play a game that looks like *Jeopardy!*, one with clear questions and answers. What drives someone to fire a gun or plant a bomb? But a move toward violence has many root causes. Emotions like love, anger, and hate are complex. With that complexity, finding answers is not so much about determining one reason for violence as about looking at a whole life before the moment of violence and discerning where the scales tipped. A closer examination of Camilla's life reveals her progression toward more radical ideas, enough to concern her parents the last time they saw her, at Christmas 1973.

I've accumulated materials related to Camilla's life over the years. I've acquired documents here and letters there. Old Hall family pictures show up on sites such as Wikipedia, Find a Grave, or Ancestry. I've read Camilla's poems and I've seen copies of her art. I've read book after book about the SLA, which rarely mention Camilla but at least give me a background on that time and place. I took a research trip to the Bay Area, where I snapped photos, got a feel for the places Camilla lived and worked and visited, and gathered newspaper articles.

I worried I didn't have enough. But once I sat down to write and laid it all out before me, I realized I had plenty of data. Incremental progress while writing and researching is almost too infinitesimally small to measure, and

I couldn't see all that I had. It's not like building a house, where you can see beams, walls, and a roof emerge during the process.

Only Camilla can tell me the one true story about herself. But absent that, I think I've come close. Her voice comes through her letters, her poems, her artwork. George speaks through "I Remember Lorena." And in one important source, the Halls speak at length, as do Camilla's friends, revealing valuable insights into her actions. Leave it to a Jungian analyst to give us an educated perspective into Camilla's state of mind. It's as if Camilla herself sat on a therapist's couch and talked.

———

I first met Harvey Honig over Thanksgiving weekend 2014. I had read and reread his 1978 dissertation "A Psychobiographical Study of Camilla Hall" many times over the years, dating back to 1999 when I found it in the collection of George Hall's documents at Gustavus. I had emailed Harvey over the years and had spoken to him by phone, but I had yet to meet him.

He lived in an older house on the east side of Madison, Wisconsin, where he'd been in private practice as a psychologist since 1979. I drove down Washington Avenue, turned right, then left, and easily found Harvey's house on a corner. It had already been snowing for a couple of weeks, though this was a relatively warm day, temps climbing into the forties. The snow on the road was turning to slush.

I walked up a few steps to Harvey's front door. It was opened by a slight man, with a neatly trimmed beard, who greeted me warmly. I was instantly at ease. If I ever needed to visit a psychologist, I thought, I would want someone with Harvey's quiet, gentle demeanor.

To my surprise, Harvey still had most of the documents he had used when writing the dissertation nearly forty years before. He kept them in a couple of small boxes, which he had brought out to his dining room table. He had copies of letters from Camilla that George and Lorena gave to him. I already had some of those letters, but others were new to me. With them, I could reconstruct a fairly solid time line of Camilla's life from 1964 to mid-1973, from her early college years, her years in Duluth and Minneapolis, and her years in Los Angeles and finally Berkeley.

I find that once people come across Camilla's story, they don't forget her. Harvey is no exception. Like me, he was drawn into the Hall story through media reports. While living as a young man, around Camilla's age, in Chicago, he tracked the news of the SLA as events happened. He was teaching adolescent psychology to adult learners who were in their midtwenties, and he found that the SLA captured their attention. "There was a tremendous fascination with the events and personalities of [the SLA], and a need for some kind of explanation, some context of meaning, which I shared," Harvey wrote in the beginning of his dissertation.

The local Chicago media focused on Camilla and on Emily Harris, whose family also lived in the Chicago area. "What we heard of these two seemed only to add to the curiosity: two women from good families, both seemingly well liked and well adjusted, and in Camilla's case the daughter of a Lutheran minister," Harvey wrote. After the May 1974 shoot-out, the coroner's office in Los Angeles attempted to pull together a psychological study of the victims. But the task was overwhelming, complete data were unavailable, and the parents of the victims were skeptical and worried about what the results might look like. The report was abandoned.

Harvey remained interested in the psychology of the SLA as a doctoral student at Loyola University. He decided to focus on just one individual rather than the whole of the SLA. George and Lorena were willing to talk to him, and they thought he could help them understand her motivation in joining the SLA. They wanted answers, someone to help them figure out the mystery of their daughter. It's why they talked to Harvey, it's why they talked to Susan O'Brien, a high school classmate of Camilla's who thought of writing a book, it's why they talked to newspaper reporters, and it's why, just before his death in 2000, George agreed to let me quote from his documents at Gustavus. The Halls were probably too close to the story, only able to see the little pixels that made up Camilla's larger portrait. But perhaps others could gather enough information—ovals, rectangles, and squares of color—to create the long-range view in which a clear picture begins to emerge.

CHAPTER 16

The Missing Letters

SOMETIME IN LATE FEBRUARY OR EARLY MARCH 1974, George and Lorena gathered all the letters Camilla wrote to them over the years—dozens of letters spanning the previous decade, from when Camilla first went to college. Camilla was a prolific letter writer, as Lorena had noted: "She wrote home much more than I ever wrote to my family when I was in college."

The couple set aside time between Lorena's job as a social worker and George's pastoral duties to go through each letter, one by one. It must have taken them hours. In their house in Lincolnwood, Illinois, on Keating Avenue, just a few doors down from St. John's Lutheran Church, where George was the pastor, they read their daughter's letters.

It's impossible to glance quickly through letters we keep. We keep them for a reason: they are treasures, their words the symbols of our relationship with the writer. We read them and let the words sink in, let them spark our memories, and reflect upon them. Letters freeze moments of time that otherwise pass all too swiftly.

I'm sure George and Lorena took their time with Camilla's letters, able to see all at once their daughter's evolution from college girl to California artist to nascent radical. Ten years of thought compressed into pen and paper. After they had read through them all, they probably had a better understanding of Camilla than they had ever had before. Things that previously hadn't made sense perhaps became clearer. The letters may have provided answers to questions they had about the past few months, when Camilla was acting more mysteriously and sounded more discouraged about the state of the world. And with that, having more answers and more clarity, George and Lorena destroyed Camilla's most recent letters.

The FBI was on to Camilla in late February, when they visited her Francisco Street house one day after she had left. They just missed her when she withdrew her money from Central Bank on March 1. Now, agents were watching George and Lorena in Lincolnwood on the chance Camilla might visit her parents. The Halls were scared.

They had a right to be suspicious about the FBI and its tactics. By 1971 word had leaked out about COINTELPRO, the illegal FBI program that had been targeting left-wing activists and "subversive" organizations since 1956 in an effort to undermine movements on the left. Fred Hampton, the leader of the Illinois chapter of the Black Panther Party, was killed in his Chicago apartment in December 1969 via an FBI plot. The Halls, living in the Chicago area, surely would have noted the headlines after his murder. Government interference in leftist politics knew no bounds, and that may have concerned George and Lorena.

Lorena told Harvey in an interview, "For a while the FBI was coming around awfully close. We didn't know what they might do. We didn't know whether they would demand to see her letters or whether they would come in unannounced while we weren't here. We just didn't know what they would be able to do. And we were frightened, because she did speak out a great deal. We could understand many of the things she said, because we felt rather strong about some of these things ourselves."

The Halls destroyed any letter they thought could have heightened FBI suspicion that Camilla was more than a mere acquaintance of the SLA. The FBI had tied Camilla to Mizmoon, a suspect in the Hearst kidnapping and the Foster murder, though they couldn't pin any crime or nefarious activity on Camilla—yet. The Halls must have thought Camilla didn't need to look any worse than she already did in the eyes of the FBI. So: gone were letters with revolutionary rhetoric, anything that hinted at anger or a propensity for using violence to solve the nation's problems. They kept only the most cheerful and sanguine letters. The result is a significant gap between what we know of Camilla in her own words and the very different way she was living during the last few months of her life.

I have copies of about fifty of Camilla's letters that survive. They are notable for their lack of revolutionary content. In these letters, Camilla gives no hint of violence, and when she does express political thought it's not unlike that expressed by the majority of her generation. Because of this gap, it can look as if Camilla wandered into the SLA only because she desired to be near Mizmoon. It can appear that she had no strong political feelings of her own, that she was sucked into the SLA only for love, like a puppy that will follow its master anywhere. It's an easy narrative that makes for eye-catching headlines, a lurid "lesbian love" pulp storyline for the 1970s.

That narrative still prevails, even among those who look more closely at the SLA. Jeffrey Toobin, a former *New Yorker* writer, wrote to me while he was doing research for his book *American Heiress*. While Toobin would give the story a fresh perspective, I still cringed at the thought of yet another story about the SLA in which Patty steals the show. Patty's domination almost assures us that the rest of the SLA associates will fall into the shadows again and will have the same old stories told about them. Toobin, too, reiterated to me the prescribed narrative about Camilla: "I am much more of the view that Mizmoon wrecked Camilla's life—that Camilla only got mixed up with that crazy crew because she was in love with Mizmoon and was still pursuing her. Absent that relationship, I [don't] think there would have been any way that Camilla would have gotten mixed up with violence."

Mizmoon *was* Camilla's entry into the SLA—everyone in the SLA had a point of contact. Willie Wolfe was drawn in through meetings at the Vacaville prison, and through him others—Mizmoon, Joe Remiro, and Russ Little—became involved. The Harrises were drawn in through Wolfe and Remiro, and they brought along Angela Atwood. The group was tightly knit, with connections flowing every which way. It's true that Camilla was an outlier who probably didn't know the rest of the group before joining. But to say Camilla was the only one motivated by love, by fear of being alone, by fear of abandonment, while all the others were the true revolutionaries, is dismissive. Russ Little said in *The Last SLA Statement* that they tried to ferret out the "flakes" or those who wanted in for less-than-revolutionary reasons, including adventure or romanticism. Camilla must have convinced not only Mizmoon but also the rest of them that she believed in revolution, too. And if we had the letters that George and Lorena destroyed, we might be able to see that.

Thanks to Harvey, we know that Camilla was changing her rhetoric more than the existing letters suggest. He pointedly asked Lorena about the gap: "I'm perplexed too because from what I've seen so far of her letters, I couldn't pick up the anger or the hatred that is usually there somewhat underneath the surface and along with the positive motivation."

That's when Lorena told him, "Well, we have destroyed some of her letters."

"Well, it helps to know that fact," Honig said, "because it was almost like there was something missing between the last letter and where she'd been before. So you could see more of that change in her letters?"

Lorena: "Yes. I wish now I hadn't destroyed them, but I was worried."

George and Lorena must have felt Camilla slipping away as they destroyed her words, like sand escaping through a closed fist. All the promise, all the hope, the bright future ahead of her, now in danger. I wonder if the Halls thought the odds were in their favor—that they would not lose yet another child, their last surviving child, after already watching three die. The odds that they would grow into old age having outlived all four of their children must have seemed astronomical. As they read through the letters, I wonder if George and Lorena had a sinking feeling that they would never see their last remaining child again.

They destroyed her words in an attempt to save her. If her words made her a suspect in revolution, and if the FBI was intent on destroying home-grown revolution, would the FBI stop at anything less than destroying Camilla and the rest of them? Even Patty understood the deadly power of law enforcement. As she said in a taped communiqué after her kidnapping, "I'm sure that Mr. Bates [Charles Bates of the FBI] understands that if the FBI has to come in and get me out by force that they won't have time to decide who not to kill. They'll just have to kill everyone. I don't particularly want to die that way."

CHAPTER 17

"A Perfect, Loving Daughter"

FOR SEVERAL YEARS early on in my research, I had only a dozen or so of Camilla's letters to her parents. I made copies of a few letters housed at the Gustavus archives, and Harvey included five in his dissertation. All told, they spottily covered the years 1967 to 1973. But when I met Harvey in 2014, he turned over two manila envelopes with copies of forty-five letters, from 1964 to 1973. Some of them duplicated letters I had already seen, but others were new to me. When he handed over the envelopes, it was like the passing of a torch. It was my chance to make something out of all this. I felt like I had found a buried treasure after fifteen years of searching. The letters do not date past September 1973. Still, reading them in order, in one long sitting, revealed to me a new side of Camilla.

The letters I had all these years were mostly upbeat, full of details about Camilla's jobs, her art, her many moves, and her travel. These are the ones the Halls kept, which perhaps explains why they are overwhelmingly positive. In his dissertation, Harvey writes (and underlines for emphasis), "These letters are <u>too good to be true!</u>" In the early letters, while Camilla is in college, she is slightly critical of others (notably the family who rented the Hall's Fremont Avenue house in Minneapolis). But then, Harvey observes, "After that, we have a perfect, loving daughter, who is never angry with her parents, always understanding, never demanding, and seems to communicate on a level of genuine intimacy. She also almost never has anything negative to say about her own life, and never reflects any depression or loneliness. There is a lot of chatter about the minutiae of life, like a description of a block party or a camping trip, etc. It almost sounds like a series of letters to a close college friend."

The only negativity she expresses is directed at national politics, and those references are brief. "The personal images are all positive, and there is almost [an] unreal quality in the juxtaposition of some of the innocent chatter from someone who in the final [letter] was involved with a group plotting to kill Marcus Foster and kidnap Patty Hearst."

Harvey is right. There's no mistaking the overwhelming positivity. But when I read through all the letters, in order, something more emerges from between the lines. Something a little sadder, a little more forlorn.

———

Camilla repeatedly tells her parents how much she misses them. Letters from the summer of 1967 are especially pleading. This was the summer after Camilla's graduation from the University of Minnesota, when she had secured the social worker job in Duluth. She enters the adult world of work and moves to a new city. From the letters, I infer that George and Lorena were traveling, perhaps on another extended mission trip. If so, it was probably difficult for them to maintain consistent contact with their daughter.

In a July 7 letter, Camilla signs off: "I miss you both very much! I hope you're having a good time. Write when you can."

Just a week later, on July 13, again: "Write when you can. If you can't, call," and she lists the phone number, which she had also included at the end of the July 7 letter.

On September 19: "Write when you can."

October 9: "Well, write when you have a spare minute."

October 25: "Glad you liked the mums. It was my way of saying I miss you and thank you for calling." At the end of the letter: "Write again when you can."

In December of that year, Camilla often mentions a Christmas visit. From December 8: "I'm really excited to be coming to Chicago—only 3 more weeks!"

December 16: "Can't wait to see you guys again."

December 30: "Well, thank you again for another wonderful Christmas."

The exhortations to "write when you can" almost sound like a chastisement for not writing, perhaps a passive–aggressive criticism embedded in the pleas.

George and Lorena no doubt were busy that summer, as they always were. They tended to throw themselves into their work, perhaps as a way to stay busy and ward off the grief of losing three children. Lorena went to work, too, after Camilla left home. She completed her own training as a social worker, perhaps inspired by her daughter. Lorena was a caseworker in suburban Chicago, generally working with immigrant families, and she learned Vietnamese in order to communicate with her clients. At this point, visits and phone calls with their only child probably had to be carefully arranged around work schedules. I wonder how many times Camilla had proposed a visit only to be told the timing wasn't right.

George and Lorena come across as emotionally unavailable. I don't think it was intentional. I think they loved her very much. But I also see them as a bit obtuse. As their only surviving child, the one who made it to adulthood, surely Camilla deserved extra warmth and attention. They probably saw Camilla as outwardly independent and strong-willed, and they may have been proud of her for those qualities.

I ran this theory past Harvey. Though he talked to George more than Lorena, he did sit down with both of them. The loss of a child affects any mother, much less three losses within a dozen years. "I think she was emotionally devasted and somewhat withdrew. I don't think she was always that available," Harvey surmised. Did she fear becoming too close to her last surviving child? Did she fear that once she got close, Camilla would be taken away, too? There's a constant push–pull in the relationship: a desire to be close, but also a fear of closeness.

———

To get a better understanding of the Hall family dynamics, I read journal articles about sibling loss. Typical parental roles described in the articles echo what I know about the Halls. Fathers were described as calm and stoic, in accordance with gender roles at the time. They saved their displays of grief for private times. In the company of others they gave the pretense of functioning, but they were often dazed, distant, and preoccupied, not really hearing what was being said to them. Mothers tended to be "severely withdrawn, preoccupied, and depressed." They blamed themselves and experienced guilt over what they saw as their shortcomings as mothers who could not protect their children.

Where Camilla and her parents diverge from typical grief response is in how the parents treated their daughter. When a child dies, the typical parental response is to fiercely protect the other children, hover over them, keep them close. But the Halls were willing to have Camilla out of sight. After her high school graduation, just a few months after Nan's death, Camilla would never live near her parents again. They kept in touch primarily through letters and occasional phone calls and visits. The children in one study were often immature and fearful, feeling small in a world that seemed big and dangerous. This was not how Camilla portrayed herself.

But other studies acknowledge a more unusual parental response. A successful child who consistently avoids danger can lessen the parents' feelings of responsibility, write Robert Krell and Leslie Rabkin in "The Effects of Sibling Death on the Surviving Child: A Family Perspective." It isn't uncommon to see parents unconsciously pushing their children away. Even while being protective in some ways, "parents may simultaneously withdraw or lessen their emotional ties to the child, as if in preparation for the eventuality of another loss."

In Camilla's surviving letters, she only rarely mentions her siblings. In summer 1969, Camilla was still living in Minneapolis but contemplating a move to Los Angeles. Maybe that was prompting her to think of family and distance and relationships. In a July 14 letter, she tells her parents the story of a high school classmate who got married, moved west, but then had a schizophrenic breakdown and ended up in a sanitarium. Camilla says they traced the illness to "an over dependent relationship between her and her mother—and moving away from home was just too much for her." Camilla then writes, "You know, I often think back and realize how easy it would have been for the three of us to become over dependent on each other after Nan died and how difficult it must have been for you to 'let go' of me when we drove down to St. Peter to move me into the dorm. And yet you did—and I'll always be grateful for that."

And in a March 26, 1969, letter, Camilla sends her mother encouraging words as Lorena was applying for a job as a social worker: "Add to these beautiful qualities your varied life experiences dealing with all sorts of people of different nationalities, languages, backgrounds, etc., the strength you have had to have to carry you through losing two sons and a daughter and your constant appreciation of the problems other people have and their difficulties in overcoming them, and your constant appreciation of other people's potentials and attempts at actualizing them—all of these combine to make you a very valuable person in any helping process."

Harvey offered his own assessment of the letters in his dissertation, but he also sought another opinion. He sent Camilla's letters to Dr. Lee Roloff, an expert in analyzing written communication such as poetry and letters, at the time a Northwestern University professor. Roloff read through all of Camilla's letters on two separate occasions. Roloff noted, "In a psychological sense she was never free, never felt free, and only gave a sense of freedom in her shared fantasies." Those fantasies, he said, involved a search for an Eden. "Always she suggests to her parents that other places are more alluring, more attractive, more suitable . . . for her than where she is," he said. "This obviously becomes a critical factor in the development of her personality[,] for the 'revolution' will eventually create the Eden that she became radicalized to."

Roloff's assessment reminds me of George as well. He, too, was restless, taking new opportunities offered to him. He went into his first job at Gustavus thinking he would be there for the rest of his life. Instead, the deaths of his children seemed to precipitate a need to keep moving. He bounced from mission worker to missionary trainer to big-congregation pastor to university chaplain to small-congregation pastor back to university professor. He was an itinerant traveler, taking several trips to Africa, South America, and Asia.

George may have been looking for his own Eden. Was he ever satisfied? Did he pass down that yearning to his remaining child?

———

It's the letters, I think, that more than anything create the empathy I feel for Camilla. The letters convey her humor, her tenderness, her love for her parents. I never see a cold, calculating woman bent on murder and destruction.

It's the Camilla in the letters with whom I identify. I have felt the search for an Eden, wondering about the greener grass on the other side. I may not write out the fantasies in epistolary form as Camilla did, but they're in my head. I wonder about a different line of work, checking out job boards even though I'm in a steady, secure, fulfilling job. I wonder about different places I'd love to live—England, Colorado, the Bay Area. Even as I sit in my beautiful home with my attentive husband and sweet dogs, content and happy, still I'm nagged by a feeling that there's an idyll out there that I haven't found.

I have felt the push–pull of parental relationships that run warm and cool, relationships that may go for weeks without contact. The desire to be outwardly independent, but at the same time the wish to be a child again with someone to take care of me. I left home shortly after I graduated from high school. College wasn't to start for a couple of months. I probably would have stayed at home until the fall, but grief and sadness of the preceding three years had caused tension between my mom and me. It was just the two of us; my older brother and sister had been out of the house for years and had lives of their own.

I felt strong and independent, and in many ways I was. Mom saw me as independent, and I wanted to live up to that expectation. And how does an independent child act? Not needy. Not complaining. She does things for herself. I was excited to put my high school years behind me and move on to a new phase of my life. But I never stopped wanting my mom and my dad. I never stopped feeling the intense sadness at the ways my life had changed.

I wonder if Camilla wanted to not contribute to her parents' worry and burdens, since they were already dealing with so much. My mom was working through her own loss of a life partner. One reason I didn't want to talk about my feelings was not because I didn't think she cared, because she did, very much, but because I didn't want to burden her with worry that would couple with her own. To this day I don't want to worry her. My reports to her are like Camilla's reports to her parents: upbeat and positive. Work is fine; David is fine; my dogs are fine. Here's what I'm doing to stay busy; here's what I have coming up. It's a sanitized report, devoid of anything negative. I don't tell her my periodic struggles with David or with life in general. I don't tell her when I'm not feeling well. I don't tell her if I'm waiting for results from a mole biopsy or mammogram. I've always thought if I had a health issue, as long as it was treatable, I probably wouldn't say anything. If it's all going to turn out OK, why cause unnecessary worry?

On the surface of her letters, Camilla comes across as independent, adventurous, and happy—a well-adjusted daughter any parent would be proud of. But then that neediness intrudes and I wonder if she was masking a deeper pull for her parents.

Harvey thinks so. He sees Camilla as "split" emotionally. She wanted to be close to her parents, but she may have felt suffocated and so wanted to get away. She was burdened, unconsciously, by being the sole survivor. As such, she had a desire to please her parents, to be the "perfect" child they deserved after experiencing such tragedy. When the pressure became too much, then she wanted to get away. But once away, she desired a close relationship.

"Part of her was really attached to her family and wanted to be the center of it," Harvey told me. "That was real. But there was another part where she wanted her own life apart from them."

CHAPTER 18

The Last Christmas

SOMETHING WASN'T QUITE RIGHT when George and Lorena last saw Camilla, which was during the Christmas holiday of 1973.

"We just felt there was something different about her," Lorena told Harvey. "She seemed older; she didn't quite have her sparkle. Oh, we had fun and laughed and all that; but there was something, an undercurrent there. We couldn't figure it out. It bothered me a little; but we just couldn't bring ourselves to open it up, you know. . . . We thought it was just something she had to work out. And at that point, I don't think anything we could have said would have made any difference. Apparently, plans were already under way for going underground. She didn't discuss them with us, and we didn't ask any questions."

George's memory of that Christmas was still clear when he sat down to write "I Remember Lorena" twenty years later:

Everything was normal but we sensed an apocalyptic mood common in the West that a great depression was coming, banks failing, civil unrest and war. She was dressed like a gardener, manlike clothes and work shoes . . . a great contrast with usual church attire in Lincolnwood. She received a long distance call from California that seemed to increase a sense of urgency. Before she left the car at O'Hare for the plane, she spoke ominously of future events. I did not worry about it at the time for I attributed it to difficult times her age group was experiencing all over the West with unemployment, the incident of the poor man's park [People's Park] in Berkeley and uncertainty about her application to be re-employed for the coming season in the city parks where she had been involved in a threatened strike.

In early 1974, Camilla stayed in touch with her parents as usual, through letters and phone calls. They all talked by phone after the Hearst kidnapping; George and Lorena were concerned that it had happened in the city where Camilla lived. "She assured us . . . that she was all right," George wrote.

By mid-February Camilla was telling her friends about her plans to move to Palo Alto to work as a gardener. She also told her parents this story. They, like her friends, thought this sudden move was strange and uncharacteristic, since they knew their daughter usually made careful plans. This sounded too rash.

"We didn't quite understand that, what she was going to do there and why she didn't know where she was going to live," Lorena told Harvey. "We just couldn't bring ourselves to press it, though. There are certain levels on which you can't communicate even though you're the best of friends in other ways. And we just had a feeling like that. So often my husband says, 'Oh, if I had only just asked her what's going on, what's wrong; let's talk about it.' But we didn't. I don't know that it would have done any good."

———

Many people will read the preceding paragraph and wonder why George and Lorena didn't press Camilla. If they had asked her one simple question, maybe she would have opened up. Maybe Camilla would have seen the concern in her parents' eyes and their warmth would have melted her resolve. Getting out of the SLA at that point might have been tricky, even dangerous, but perhaps they could have figured out a way to make it work.

But I understand George and Lorena's reluctance to pry. I do not find fault in their silence. This type of reticence rings true to me. I see it play out often here in the Midwest, especially in families who have their roots, like the Halls, in the stoic northern European countries of Germany, Norway, and Sweden. These cultures value independence and making your own way through life. You are expected to manage problems on your own.

The Halls did not let negative emotions intrude. Going back into the family's history, this pattern appears again and again. George's dad suffered the death of his first wife and child. Lorena's dad had an accident that caused him to lose his vision, which ended his career as a journalist. But he adapted and became a business owner and craftsman. Losses were expected, but they were not to be dwelt upon. "There was tragedy, but there was little time wasted on self-pity or despair," Harvey observed.

Lorena had a sister who was diagnosed with terminal cancer but let her family know only toward the very end of her life. Harvey noted, "These are . . . problems to be borne individually, in silence. This is in many ways an admirable attitude, particularly for an earlier generation, but it does have its costs."

———

After my dad died when I was fifteen years old, no one inquired into my thoughts and feelings. My family, like the Halls, wasn't the type to ask probing questions. As long as you appeared well adjusted on the surface, others assumed you were fine. After Dad died, I did well in school, had a lot of friends, and participated in activities like plays and marching band. And I truly felt happy, but only as long as I pushed down the deep sadness inside. My family never talked about Dad. We didn't talk about his life, we didn't reminisce over good memories, we didn't bask in the love he left behind. We didn't talk about his death and what a massive impact it had on all of us.

Mom and Dad had a hands-off style of parenting, one common in the 1970s and 1980s when kids were kids, adults were adults, and we all moved in separate spheres. I spent long summer days on my own, entertaining myself, getting together with my parents at evening meals. Mom continued this style after Dad died, becoming even more hands-off as she took a night job. I could go days without seeing her while I was in high school.

At the end of my senior year, I received flowers from my boyfriend, John—the first time I had ever received flowers. I hadn't told Mom about

John, partly because the relationship was still developing and I wasn't sure where it was going. But when I got the flowers—red roses—I was elated. I brought them home and put them on the mantle, front and center. Mom never asked where they came from.

There's a fear behind asking. If you ask, you might get answers you don't like. Answers that crack open real, and difficult, emotions. For people not accustomed to that rawness, the prospect of revelations can be terrifying. The status quo of keeping up appearances, of maintaining ignorance, is much easier to manage, at least in the short term.

So why not ask a simple question about flowers? Mom suspected I was spending time with John, whom she worked with on the night shift. She was not impressed with his long hair and his affinity for marijuana. She may have guessed the flowers came from him, but asking about them could have resulted in a confrontation, a release of emotion, maybe even an all-out fight between mother and strong-minded teenage daughter. Perhaps it was better just to leave things alone.

Why not ask a simple question about how Dad's death affected us? Maybe there was a fear that opening those feelings would lead to an emotional breakdown. We already had to forge a new way of life; we didn't also need to fear that expressing emotions might land one of us in a psychiatric ward or on a therapist's couch. It was easier just to leave things alone as long as everyone appeared to be doing well.

Why not simply ask Camilla what was going on? What might have been opened if George and Lorena had asked why she seemed depressed and anxious? Why might George and Lorena have been reluctant to do so?

———

Camilla's letters to George and Lorena reveal tremendous love. She cherishes them, she misses them, she treasures visits and phone calls. But surely the situation was more complicated than that, as so many parent–child relationships are.

One of the more telling and intriguing insights about Camilla's relationship with her parents, particularly with her father, comes from one of Camilla's close friends. This insight is rare because few of Camilla's friends ever met her parents. The trio of George, Lorena, and Camilla existed mostly in isolation, with almost no one—no other family, no close friends—around to witness their relationship as adults.

The insight comes from Bette Esbjornson, with whom Camilla lived in Los Angeles for a few months and whom Harvey interviewed for his dissertation. Bette met George and Lorena once, when they visited Camilla. Bette described George as I have pictured him: upbeat, personable, and talkative, someone able to spin captivating stories.

But Camilla would get angry with George when he would "treat her like a child," Bette told Harvey. Bette couldn't quite understand that reaction, because from what she could see, George was kind and treated Camilla like a fellow adult. "But maybe she didn't see it that way," Bette said.

I find it hard to believe that George would coddle Camilla or assume she didn't know how to live on her own when she'd been doing it for years, though I can imagine George feeling a need to be protective of his only surviving child. Perhaps Camilla felt smothered by that protectiveness, even though physically she was two thousand miles away from her parents. The protectiveness may have been so subtle that others could not see it. Bette contended that George did not know the full extent of Camilla's thoughts toward him and that, had he known, he would have taken steps to address her feelings.

Bette said Camilla had a "love–hate" relationship with her father. She loved her mother very much but saw her as weak compared to her father. George had achieved professional success; he was good at his job. When your skills are in demand, it can be easy to think that you're doing something right, that your way of thinking is the best. Camilla was strong-willed, as was her father. It's easy to see that they might clash.

And if Camilla had rejected religion, as Bette contended, she may have placed some of her negative feelings on George. Church and God and Christianity had always been woven closely into the fabric of his life. Of course he would defend them if challenged. "And he was always so right," Bette said. "He was always the professor." George came off as all-knowing, as if he had all the answers and he was always right. That irritated Camilla, Bette contended.

Harvey saw another side of George, and he told Bette so. "My feeling about him is that he is much less certain about any answers. Not that he's not still Christian; but part of this [Camilla's death] has really touched some deep spot in him that doesn't know the answers anymore," Harvey said.

"Oh, Camilla would be very happy to hear that," Bette responded.

———

Maybe George and Lorena sensed some of Camilla's anger when she visited them that last Christmas. If they did, I can understand why they might have been hesitant to pry or to say anything that would constitute criticism. Maybe they feared driving Camilla away and losing their remaining child. They were always so supportive of their daughter. I think that throughout Camilla's adult life they were hesitant to confront her or criticize her. She held a powerful, though unspoken, bargaining chip: she was their last child. They didn't dare do or say anything that might damage that relationship. Stay positive, stay upbeat, stay supportive. Maybe everything would be all right, and Camilla would work through whatever problems she had on her own.

CHAPTER 19

The Sole Survivor

CAMILLA WROTE A POEM to Mizmoon in July 1971:

"Sister,"
that's what your button said
the first time I met you—
and I believed you
and now I feel it too—
sister...
Thank you.

———

To me, the most striking part of Camilla's remarkable life, in which there were many arresting events, is the deaths of all her siblings. And then Camilla dies, in such a horrific manner, leaving George and Lorena as members of an extremely rare population: parents of multiple children who have all preceded them in death. I know of only one other example personally, a gentleman in Waseca, Minnesota, whose six children and wife were killed in a car–train accident in 1959. My parents mowed the cemetery where the Zimmermans are buried, and I often stood in front of the twenty-four-foot-long gravestone and tried to wrap my mind around the depths of Jim Zimmerman's tragedy. A death in the family forces you to redefine yourself. Jim Zimmerman somehow had to cope with having a full house one day and an entirely empty house the next. From husband and father to single man, all in a matter of hours.

The Halls had to redefine themselves as a family not once, not twice, but three times. Camilla was three years old when Terry died unexpectedly and quickly. Peter died as the result of a longer illness when Camilla was five. Camilla was seventeen when Nan died, again after a slow decline in health. After the two boys died, Camilla was no longer a "little sister," only a big sister. After Nan died, she was no longer a sister. Camilla's new role was that of sole survivor.

Harvey spends quite a few pages in his dissertation contemplating the impact the siblings' deaths might have had on Camilla and the family. "No family, no matter how religious or how integrated, can go through blows of this kind without experiencing some anger, depression, and despair," Harvey writes.

But the Halls did not express those feelings freely. George, Lorena, and Camilla hardly mentioned the deaths in writing. When I visited the Lincolnwood neighborhood where George and Lorena had lived for years, I talked to a couple—Al and June, the only ones left on the block who had lived there since the 1970s—who had known George and Lorena as friendly neighbors, people you talk to across the street but don't socialize with. Though they'd been acquainted with the Halls for several years, George and Lorena never mentioned their children who had died. Suffering was done in private, in the shadows.

Harvey references Carl Jung, who theorized extensively about the shadow and persona. Unlike the true self, or ego, the persona is what we portray to the world. Shadows are the aspects of our personalities that we hide. For a minister, the persona is critical. George had to display a carefully crafted persona to his congregation and to others he worked with. Good ministers must be emotionally stable. They take on others' burdens while their own burdens are borne alone. Ministers' spouses play a similar role, for their emotional states reflect on their spouses. Lorena recognized this and set high standards for herself. As George put it in his memoir, Lorena placed tremendous pressure on herself to excel in the public role of minister's wife. Ministers' children, too, reflect on them. How successfully ministers head their own families can determine how successfully they can lead their church families. Camilla did not escape the pressure to keep up a stable outward appearance. And the more one feels pressure to live up to outside expectations, the deeper the shadow side is, Harvey writes. George and Lorena would have developed deep shadows because of their public roles. Camilla would have developed a deep shadow side to counteract the unconscious expectations her parents had for her to be a model child.

"It is not that Reverend Hall is a man who hides behind his role or that he is unaware of his humanity. Nevertheless, he and Mrs. Hall are people with powerful, though quiet, personae, and this is one thing that Camilla at times needed to fight against in search of her own identity," writes Harvey.

Harvey likes the Jungian term "unconscious anger," which surfaces in both his dissertation and in conversations he's had with me. Though the Halls didn't seem to address their anger over the loss of their children, it still pervaded family dynamics. They may have been angry at God, at the doctors, at the hospitals, or at themselves for failing to protect their children. This anger settled over the family like a ghostly fog. While adults may be more or less adept at corralling anger, children are not. Camilla was the only child left to absorb the fog of anger. According to Harvey, Camilla internalized it, learning by example to keep it hidden. But she couldn't release her anger toward her parents because they were always loving and caring. So she had to find other outlets for it. She had warm relationships with friends, so she couldn't lash out at them. She might have been angry and might not have wanted to believe in a God who would let young children die, but out of respect for George she kept her views on religion quiet.

Children who experience the death of a sibling can become distrustful of anyone who was supposed to take care of the sibling—the medical establishment, parents, or God. Almost as strong as the children's distrust of doctors and hospitals is "the child's confusion about God's portrayal as benevolent," write Albert Cain, Irene Fast, and Mary E. Erickson in the 1964 article "Children's Disturbed Reactions to the Death of a Sibling." Children who lost siblings wondered why God would take them away. Some even saw God as a "murderer" and grew fearful of God's power.

"Since she could not believe in a God who was running an unfair world that could allow children to die, she was compelled to believe in an all-powerful establishment which controls everything, but in a very unfair and destructive way," Harvey writes. Camilla could turn her anger toward a large, faceless government that was making poor choices—sending kids to war, ignoring inner cities, and focusing on profit over people.

The deaths that forced the family's redefinition many times influenced the path of Camilla's life; how could they not? But to what degree is impossible to say. I'm not a psychologist. Camilla is dead. Even if we could get Camilla into a therapist's chair, would she be able to articulate the effect? This territory is fraught with psychological minefields, ghosts of dead children, and complicated family relationships. But if I had to guess, the sibling deaths may have been one of the most influential of the factors responsible for the path Camilla took. It was my experience with my father's death when I was fifteen years old that set me on a new course.

———

When my dad died, I experienced the swift, harsh change a family loss brings. I made some radical decisions that I know I would not have made had Dad been alive. Shortly after I turned nineteen, I became engaged to David. We married eight months later, when I was still nineteen. That version of myself was not someone my friends knew; I barely recognized her. I had hardly dated in high school. I was a budding feminist, recoiling at the notion of traditional marriage embodied by the previous generation. I was not going to be a housewife, I was not going to work in a factory, I most certainly was not going to have children.

Before David, before Dad died, I had my life all planned out. I was going to be a journalist; my goal was to start my life in the big city of Minneapolis. I would work hard and play hard. I was going to be single and on the town, a *Sex and the City* Carrie Bradshaw before she was invented. I would travel and have grand adventures. I would live in the best part of the city amid other young, urban professionals.

I was off to a good professional start. As a freshman at the University of Minnesota, I secured a writing position at the student newspaper, the *Minnesota Daily*, a rare feat for a first-year student. When I left the *Daily* at the end of the school year, with plans to transfer to a smaller university in Mankato and get married, my editor sent me an email asking me to reconsider.

But no way. I was drawn not only to David but also to his family, which in many ways looked like my own from years before: a dad, a mom, three children, and a loving and cherished grandmother. Nearby aunts, uncles, and cousins. A life that revolved around hard work, family, and church.

After Dad died, it was as if my family fractured. My mom, sister, brother, and I all retreated into our separate spheres of grief, finding ways to cope as individuals. I didn't realize how much I had missed family closeness until I met David. I couldn't wait to get it back. I didn't want to wait until I finished college, I didn't want to wait until I secured a job, and I didn't want to wait until after I had had my own adult life experiences and seen more of the world. I had to start this new life, right now.

I went after my replacement family with gusto and got the prize. I was lucky because they made me feel safe and secure. If I hadn't found them, I know I would have continued to seek out some type of family. But would I have always been making smart choices? I was searching for something. I just happened to find it early, and I happened to find the right thing.

On the surface, it's easy to assume that Camilla joined the SLA because it represented a replacement for her siblings. Camilla might have viewed the members, many of them women, as siblings. In this era of burgeoning new wave feminism, women commonly referred to each other as "sister" as a way to proclaim a familial bond.

———

A number of studies address sibling loss and the effects on surviving children, though this area of grief studies is not as well documented as, say, studies about parental loss or spousal death. The journal articles I read eerily echoed what I already knew about Camilla and even offer plausible theories that might explain some of her actions.

Harvey homes in on the theory of "survivor guilt." Robert Jay Lifton coined the term after talking with survivors of mass killings such as the Holocaust and the bombing of Hiroshima. But he noted that this guilt also can occur in smaller units, such as families. The fundamental question in a case of survivor guilt is, *Why did I live while others died?* A survivor can look at the situation two ways: She has lived because something bigger and grander is waiting for her. She is now responsible for doing the living of those who died and must make the most of it. Or, on the other hand, she cannot understand what has made her special. She doesn't see the forces of fate or faith that led her to this position. She doesn't feel worthier than the others who have died, and she doesn't feel worthy of living. For a lone remaining child like Camilla, there's tremendous pressure to embody the potential of all the other children. I can understand why Camilla would feel the pressure to please her parents and not want to disappoint them, even though I don't find any evidence that they placed pressure upon Camilla.

For someone with a strong belief in God, like George, only God has answers to questions about life and death, about survival. The human mind does not have to trouble itself with questions of *Why me?* or *Why not me?* But Camilla did not have the same faith, and at an early age she started to ask questions and express doubts toward religion.

Lifton says, "For the survivor can never, inwardly, simply conclude that it was logical and right for him, and not others, to survive."

Not only did Camilla have to contend with survivor guilt on the family level, but she was also of a generation that faced death from many frightening angles. The Cold War, with its threat of annihilation by the Soviets, in which bomb drills were conducted in schools; the Cuban Missile Crisis, occurring in Camilla's senior year of high school, just two months before Nan's death. The world was a dark and scary place. To someone like Camilla, every day of survival perhaps seemed like dumb luck, luck that was bound to run out at some point. She saw, more than most of her peers, that the possibility of early death was very real.

One study of sibling loss states, "The children, of course, had a generally heightened awareness and fear of death, feeling it could strike at any moment, and at his other siblings or parents as well as himself. Notions of their parents' invulnerability, all-powerfulness and especially of their parents' strength as protectors, came crashing."

In a 1966 study titled "Children's Reactions to Sibling Death," R. Rogers found children's reactions are influenced by sibling order, and guilt feelings may be exacerbated if a younger sibling dies. "The older child seems overwhelmed with guilt because his wishes that the younger child would disappear have come true." Lorena told Harvey that when Camilla was young, she sometimes struggled with feelings of jealously toward Nan; Nan's health problems received so much attention both from within and outside the family. Lorena said, "She did have this problem of being somewhat jealous of her younger sister. She perhaps didn't realize that a handicapped child needs special attention; and it was only natural that she should be resentful. There were difficult times."

Cain, Fast, and Erickson write that the primary reaction in surviving children was guilt, which in some cases lasted years. "They insisted they should enjoy nothing, and deserved only the worst." These children also expressed a death wish: "Some had suicidal thoughts and impulses, said they deserved to die, wanted to die—this also being motivated by a wish to join the dead sibling." Growing up and growing older meant "death was constantly imminent." Overall, a sibling death can mark the beginning of a child's "existential anxiety," according to Helen Rosen and Harriette L. Cohen, authors of "Children's Reaction to Sibling Loss."

Sibling deaths also caused confusing thoughts about the relationship between illness and death. A very small child might think that any illness, even a cold or a stomach virus, could result in death. More than one study notes that children who have lost siblings exaggerate minor illnesses. They believe they would die as their siblings had. In around 40 percent of the studied cases, the children displayed prolonged and pronounced reactions to having symptoms similar to those that had killed their siblings.

Harvey interviewed an unidentified friend who said Camilla was ill in late 1972 or early 1973 with a kidney or bladder infection. She apparently had been taking medications to treat it, but they didn't seem to be working and Camilla didn't like the side effects. Instead, Camilla turned to natural remedies such as garlic tea. The friend, whom I will call "Linda," said her parents were doctors who didn't believe in homeopathic remedies, and she could not convince Camilla to see a medical doctor.

Out of this comes Linda's "off-the-wall" theory about why Camilla became involved in the SLA. In her theory, the kidney or bladder infection was actually more serious, a disease related to the kidney troubles that had killed Camilla's brother, Peter, and sister Nan. And the reason the traditional pills weren't working was because the illness was incurable and fatal.

"That puts a whole new light on it. If I can assume that she knew she was going to die, then I can make the leap, the mental leap, that it takes to turn that person into a suicidal personality," Linda said.

But, referring to the SLA's suspicion that they would meet sure death, Harvey asked, Why choose that method of suicide?

"Because it was handy," Linda said. That was "the only thing I can imagine; because she was too logical, too rational, a person to think that they would succeed. You don't get together with six, eight, ten people and plan on using automatic weapons against the powers that be and expect to overthrow the world. It's just not going to happen. I cannot believe for a minute that they believed it. Maybe one or two of them were crazy enough to believe that; but Camilla wasn't crazy."

And if Camilla had been suicidal, it was because she was facing her own imminent mortality, according to Linda. Even though Camilla took great care of her body at this time, that could have been a sign of a final preparation. "You know you are going to die very soon, and now's the time to get your body in perfect shape and enjoy the end of it. The alternative is to lie in bed and die. So, the opposite of that is to take ten-mile hikes and do push-ups, the opposite of passively accepting the inevitable."

Linda admitted that she could have misread Camilla. Maybe she overlooked a radical change because she didn't want to believe it. "I don't accept that, but it is a possibility." Or perhaps Camilla was trying to protect her by withholding the truth. "So, rather than lose our friendship, she misrepresented her perspective. Yes, that's possible." But Linda had problems with that explanation, too.

"Either she was lying to me from the beginning or else she changed at some point. I'm opting for the second possibility, that she changed later for whatever reason. . . . But the important thing is why did she change, not that she was making things up for me. What made her change? That's what I can't reconcile. . . . I thought I understood Camilla Hall, her basic sense of reality was very humane, life-enhancing, very warm, loving and hopeful. But the politics she ended up with was very inhuman, very unwarm, unloving and very hopeless. And to make that drastic a change in such a short period of time, is inconceivable unless there is an intervening factor like her approaching death."

Harvey took this conversation and speculated about it. In his dissertation, he says there are data that support the theory that Camilla worried about death. He considers that Camilla may have suffered from unexpressed depression. But outwardly, even in those final months, she was full of life and energy and expressed some hope for the future. Perhaps, Harvey says, her kidney problems created a sense of urgency, a desire to act quickly to make changes. "Camilla certainly had reason to fear death from her kidney problems in light of her siblings' history, and there is ample evidence of her preoccupation with death in her conversation with friends and her parents during those final months."

———

I will cradle you
in my woman hips
kiss you
with my woman lips,
fold you to my heart and sing:
     Sister woman,
     you are a joy to me.

CHAPTER 20

"She Was a Pacifist"

SHORTLY AFTER THE KIDNAPPING of Patty Hearst, Camilla visited Linda in Berkeley. Camilla was still aboveground, not yet connected to the crime. Harvey interviewed Linda for his dissertation, and she told him that she and Camilla had talked about the kidnapping; it was what everyone was talking about in the Bay Area. Linda told Camilla it was a "useless, ridiculous revolutionary tactic. This is not the way to change the world."

And Camilla agreed.

Both Linda and Camilla called the SLA actions "crazy." They both believed the SLA members were hopelessly divided against themselves. And they both thought it would be only a matter of weeks before the FBI wiped them out.

Through all of this, Camilla appeared to be the same old Camilla that Linda had known. Not only did Linda know Camilla in Berkeley, but she and Camilla had been high school classmates at Washburn High. She had no reason to believe anything was amiss.

Linda told Harvey she didn't think Camilla was lying—Linda truly felt that Camilla had thought the kidnapping was a poor decision. Linda wondered whether Camilla might have had misgivings about the SLA at that point and wanted to bounce ideas off a friend. Was there one small opening in that conversation, one pause, where Camilla was about to spill it all?

But Linda imagined that Camilla was committed. "You don't go to a gun range and practice firing weapons with a group of people intent on getting good at it, without the intention of using them. And for her to make that leap from the politics that I thought she was at, requires some incredible intervening factor. And it's not naivete. And it's not a love affair."

Camilla was guarded with her parents, at least in her letters. But with friends and coworkers, people with whom she spent the most time, she was either more open or found it harder to mask frustrations and disappointments— feelings she hardly ever expressed to her parents. Camilla conveyed the same upbeat attitude toward most friends, though a darker, more fatalistic side sometimes showed through.

Transcripts of four interviews with her friends and coworkers appear in Harvey's dissertation. He interviewed two of Camilla's coworkers at Hennepin County, Jean Bigelow and Alan Carlson. He also interviewed Linda as well as Bette Esbjornson, who had worked with Camilla in Hennepin County and who had been Camilla's roommate in Los Angeles.

Through these friends' accounts, the portrait of Camilla becomes clearer. In many ways, their descriptions of her are remarkably consistent. Almost all describe her as funny, warm, and personable. But while some of them were shocked by the news that Camilla was part of the SLA, a couple of them claimed they could see seeds of radical thought, anger, and even violence. It's as if Camilla carefully crafted a persona for each friend.

Most of Camilla's friends said she was the least likely person they could imagine to get involved in a group like the SLA. This is different from what friends and family said of Mizmoon; Mizmoon's radical change occurred before their very eyes in 1973. And different from Nancy Ling Perry, whose involvement in prison visits and whose friendship with Russ Little and Joe Remiro placed her in the vanguard of Berkeley's increasingly radical revolutionary movement. Camilla kept different aspects of her life compartmentalized, circles of friends who did not intersect.

Although Jean and Alan weren't necessarily connected socially to Camilla, they got along with her and came to know her after spending hours together each week at the Hennepin County welfare office in Minneapolis in 1968–69. Alan remembered Camilla as a pleasant person who always had a smile on her face. "She was intelligent. She was interesting. She was talented," he said. If she had a darker or depressed side, he never saw hints of it.

Jean called Camilla "very witty" and "very sympathetic and helpful" and "really very compassionate." Jean's use of the word "very" when describing Camilla suggested she wanted to emphasize Camilla's good qualities, perhaps to make up for the one-sided media portrayals of Camilla as a hardened, radical terrorist. Jean worried that public understanding of the SLA was shaped largely by the media, which focused on the violence and neglected some of the foundational fundamental beliefs of the group—the more intellectual and emotional foundations.

Harvey asked Jean whether Camilla was ever angry. Jean didn't use that word to describe Camilla, but Camilla was unable to hide every negative emotion. Instead, Jean used words like "intense" and "frustrated" to define Camilla's personality when cases at work didn't resolve as she had hoped. Jean saw Camilla as frank, direct, and confrontational, perhaps a hint of what was to come, especially four years later when Camilla fought for women's employment in the park district. Again, Jean used the word "very": Camilla had "very strong, kind of passionate, ideas."

Once Jean and Alan learned about Camilla's involvement with the SLA, they did not agree as to how much she may have truly embraced the ideology. On one hand, they understood her decision. But after talking more about it, they thought her actions were uncharacteristic.

Alan said he was surprised when he saw the news about Camilla. He did not doubt that she believed in the cause, "But at the same time, it kind of bothers me that maybe she got 'hooked' on the thing." She was an intelligent person, he said; at some point she must have realized she was stuck. "I'd be willing to bet that if I could have gotten to her before the police, she'd say: 'I'm in this thing, and I don't know how the hell to get out of it. I know this is going to end up tragic, but I don't know what to do about it.'"

Upon that, Harvey asked Alan, "She was aware of what the consequences would be?"

Alan responded, "Sure. She was too bright not to figure out how this thing was going to end up. . . . I can see where she could have gotten into it, but I bet her 'wheels were spinning' on how to get out of it gracefully. It obviously would have been a very difficult thing to do."

Jean was less surprised than Alan that Camilla was part of the SLA. She said she thought Camilla would gravitate toward the communal aspects of the SLA, such as the camaraderie and closeness. But the level of violence the SLA embraced struck her as antithetical to Camilla's beliefs. "Yet she had that streak of logical dedication, which I could see simply as an extension of her feelings. And logically if you couldn't make people change, then maybe this would be an approach."

When, after the shoot-out, Jean talked to others who also knew Camilla, they said they thought Camilla must have "flipped out" or lost her mind. That explanation was too simple for Jean. "As long as she had gone that way, she did so for reasons which also made her empathetic, sympathetic and underdog-oriented." In other words, the same reasons why she was so good at her job and why she felt for her welfare cases so deeply.

Jean said Camilla was the type of person who would have had to agree with the SLA not only on an intellectual level but also on an emotional level. But Jean couldn't tell which part initially drew Camilla in—the ideology, or the emotional connection to Mizmoon. "I'm sure that her complete dedication would be greatly influenced by her ties to the person; but also, if she had not had such an influential tie with that person, she might not have become so involved. She wasn't just an intellectual being," Jean said.

Alan had a hard time believing that Camilla agreed with the SLA's violence. "She was a pacifist, and to go this route is a little bit out of character." But Jean saw the SLA as lining up with Camilla's beliefs. "If you find that you cannot change the system, you can't help people without taking methods like this, you have to set your priorities about what is more important to you. To be a pacifist would be secondary to the need to help people."

Friends, family, and coworkers overwhelmingly described Camilla in a positive light after her death. Harvey wondered if that was due to the "halo effect"—a reason why eulogies and obituaries can be so glowing. But both Alan and Jean said that they would see Camilla in the same way whether she was alive or dead and that her radicalism and violent death didn't affect their attitudes toward her.

Jean said, "I guess I think of her as being tremendously self-demanding, very hard on herself, crushingly so. And so, needing to be carried along in part of a bigger philosophical movement would explain and justify her actions."

———

Camilla's friends spoke with an intense longing, wishing that things had ended differently, that they could have been the ones to save her. The desperation almost jumps off the page when I read Harvey's interview transcripts. The words are there in black and white, in an old typewriter font, simple and clean. But strung together, the words are anything but simple. Alan portrayed himself as a savior if only he could have reached Camilla. Linda said as much, too. "I would be willing to commit a felony to find out why the heck she had done this, what had changed her so and try to pull her out of it," she said.

Linda knew Camilla as someone whom everyone liked. Like Jean, Linda used the word "very" to emphasize Camilla's qualities. Camilla was not just warm; she was "very warm." Not just generous, but "very generous." Not just loving, but "very loving."

She also remembered a Camilla who was in great shape, which ran contrary to media reports that forever portrayed her as heavyset. Camilla and Linda went on a hike in the northern California woods, camped overnight, and hiked back the next day. "She was in tremendous good shape; it just didn't phase her at all. But, it practically destroyed me to walk ten miles out, sleep overnight, and walk ten miles back."

This Camilla was a gentle woman who, instead of poisoning snails in her garden, collected them at night in a burlap bag and released them at Lake Temescal. Linda could not reconcile this person with the one who wielded a gun in a bank robbery and helped kidnap Patty Hearst. "It is a puzzle," Linda said. She continued, "The FBI man asked me if I thought she could handle a gun. Could and would are two different things."

Linda told Harvey about a dream she had after Camilla was killed: "When she comes to the door, she's not distraught, she's exhausted. She's very tired, malnourished, dirty and obviously has been through a lot; but she's also happy, smiling and at peace. She's very calm, not frantic or hysterical; I'm the one who's frantic, hysterical. I'm trying to get her in out of the street lights, to hide her in the basement."

In the dream, Camilla is calm, direct, and sincere. She has an explanation for what has happened, but her friend cannot understand because Camilla's words are garbled. Camilla knows what happened; she knows why she got involved. But those who cared about her are left without a clue.

Linda even went so far as to hope that there were two Camillas, that the real one was safe and sound, that "there are really two different people, that Camilla is down in Palo Alto somewhere gardening, and that somebody who looked just like her did these things. That's not really a theory; it's just a wish."

Linda did not see evidence that Camilla possessed radical political thoughts. She had never seen her express anger except in general ways toward President Richard Nixon and the politics of the time. She did not see any "intense hostility in Camilla." Linda saw Camilla become passionate about politics when it became personal. When Camilla helped organize the female park workers, Linda said, "that was something thrilling for her."

Linda dismissed many explanations about Camilla that were thrown around after the shoot-out. For one thing, she said it was not depression that led Camilla into the SLA. Linda never saw Camilla depressed except after her breakup with Mizmoon, but even that was an intense and localized depression and passed quickly. "It did not permeate her life," she said. Nor was it love that drew her in, which has always been the most touted explanation, even all these years later.

"The first theories from newspaper writers were that she was a crazy radical, like they were all crazy radicals; and you could write them off as human beings. . . . Then, they started writing about each one of their personalities and trying to delve in some superficial newspaper reporter–type way. More than one report came to the conclusion that Pat [Mizmoon] drew her siren-like into this. I just can't buy that," Linda said.

Linda had met Mizmoon a few times but didn't think she was sociable. "She was a distant person, hard to get to know, a very private kind of person, kind of dark and glowering. . . . I never felt threatened by her or anything; but she didn't want to get close to me. I would come over, the two of them would be there, and Pat would leave shortly."

There had to be more to Camilla's involvement in the SLA than just Pat, Linda thought: "I can't buy that for the love of one person she would turn all of her politics inside out; and would go to an extreme that is clearly suicidal; lose her intelligent, rational ability to judge what's going on; and fall head-over-heels into this thing because she wanted to be near someone. That she would change her life and her personal integrity for the sake of a love, that someone else wouldn't have her unless she changed, I can't accept that."

Harvey asked whether Camilla could have been more radical and angrier than she portrayed herself. It's possible, Linda conceded. But Camilla wasn't one to lie or hide her true feelings and thoughts from her friends. "I suspect that up until a certain point, she was telling the truth to me," she said. Linda suspected Camilla didn't truly embrace violence until she entered the SLA. When the SLA communiqués were released, Linda could not make that connection between them and Camilla's thinking. "I can't see an iota of Camilla in all the writings of the SLA so prolifically printed everywhere," she said.

But there was one friend who disagreed.

CHAPTER 21

"I'm Not Surprised"

AFTER A FEW MONTHS of sharing a house with Bette and Dick Esbjornson in Los Angeles, Camilla prepared to move out. The relationship among the three had been strained for a while. Camilla had landed at Bette and Dick's when she first moved to Los Angeles. They were all great friends in those early months together, but then something changed, and Bette never knew quite what it was.

Like many of Camilla's friends, Bette sat down for an interview with Harvey. She didn't offer many details on the split between her and Camilla; she said only that Camilla thought Bette had taken something of hers, and Bette was hurt. Then Camilla moved out.

"She was going someplace else; she was evolving out of my interests," Bette told Harvey. She said Camilla was becoming more of an artist and wanted to be with artistic friends, such as Cheryl Brooks. But when Bette mulled over Camilla's decision to leave, she wondered if Camilla was already transforming into a person determined to cut ties with people from her previous life.

Bette knew about Camilla's pattern with friendships; it was something they had discussed in their frequent one-on-one talks. "She said that when she left one place she would leave those people behind." Bette quoted

Camilla as saying, "I don't try to maintain that relationship. I just leave those people where they are; and if I come back and they're still there, that's great."

Most friends expressed surprise upon learning about Camilla's fate with the SLA. But Bette insisted that she had seen flashes of anger from Camilla years before. In the interview with Harvey, Bette's answers to his questions are assured and pointed; she puts forth her own armchair psychological analysis of Camilla. It's hard to know if Bette simply wants to be the contrarian, the person who claims to have been able to accurately read someone and anticipate future intentions. When the shadow side of someone we thought we knew well is revealed, there's always someone who confidently says, *I saw that coming*. But in her defense, Bette spent more time with Camilla as an adult than anyone else Harvey interviewed, so maybe her insights and theories are the most accurate read we have of Camilla during this time.

When they worked together at Hennepin County, Bette noticed Camilla's strong opinions. Bette was older than Camilla by a few years, and she said that antiwar and civil rights issues didn't resonate as strongly with her as they did for people Camilla's age. Bette said Camilla had helped her think differently about the Vietnam War.

Those first months in California, Bette described herself and Camilla as "really close friends." They shared not only a home but also intimate conversations that ranged from politics to relationships to their pasts. Bette appeared to be in an excellent position to see all sides of Camilla. Bette said that people generally did not see Camilla's anger, especially back in Minnesota. "She hid it too well."

Yet Bette spoke warmly of Camilla, like everyone else, calling her "very feeling, thinking, seeking," "very, very tender hearted," and "very honest, very deep-down honest, a really good person." She said, "Everybody who met her liked her. Everyone liked her," and added, "It's weird how she changed."

Bette did not necessarily think Camilla suddenly changed or became a new person when she moved to Los Angeles. More likely, whatever had lain dormant in Camilla was brought to life in a new environment. When a person moves to California, Bette said, "a funny thing happens. . . . It happens to everybody. They become more of whoever they are."

Like Linda, Bette also discounted the notion that Camilla joined the SLA only to be near Mizmoon. "I think she knew exactly what she was getting into," Bette said.

Bette thought Camilla carefully weighed the pros and cons of joining. Camilla was a woman who did not make decisions hastily and who methodically planned her moves. Why should her decision to join the SLA be any different? But still, Bette was dumbfounded when she discovered the truth.

"Yes, I just couldn't believe it," she told Harvey. "But then again, I guess I could." Unlike Linda, who did not see Camilla in any of the SLA's rhetoric, Bette did. Bette said the language and phrasing of the SLA communiqués sounded much like the angry Camilla she knew. She wasn't surprised that Camilla became involved in something radical and political, but that Camilla would embrace violence came as a shock.

Harvey told Bette that she was the first person he interviewed who mentioned seeing Camilla's anger.

"Oh, I'm not surprised," she said in response.

"I've been pursuing it, because I was sure it was there," Harvey said.

"Yes. Why wouldn't it be there? How could it not be there?" Bette asked.

Harvey said that the personality test Camilla took when she started at the University of Minnesota (the Minnesota Multiphasic Personality Inventory, MMPI) revealed an odd, placid equanimity that suggested she may have been hiding strong emotions.

But if you believe Bette, Camilla did not hide her anger when she moved to California. Bette said Camilla's political views only became more "twisted."

One personal experience deeply affected Camilla, Bette said. For years, Camilla had not been paying the federal excise tax on her telephone bill, a surcharge used to fund the war effort. Bette said officials from the Treasury Department tracked down Camilla and took twenty-five dollars she owed out of her bank account, plus another twenty-five dollars for a service charge.

"And she was outraged!" Bette said. "She was so angry. I think that really screwed her up that the government could have such ultimate power over her, that they could touch her personally like that."

Once Camilla was in Los Angeles, the naive hope she had felt seemed to have disappeared. In Minnesota, Camilla had been an idealist. She worked within the county welfare system and believed that the government could provide for its citizens. It could help teenage mothers. It could help those who needed food assistance. Camilla believed that the government would respond to the will of the people, especially during the politically volatile year of 1968, when protesters turned out in droves. She believed then that the government would listen to people, recognize its mistakes, and change its ways. But it didn't. "If you can't [effect change] by talking and pleading with them and demonstrating, then you keep going until you do get their attention," Bette said. She said Camilla saw that violence needed to be part of the revolution, but more "get-up-and-shout violence," not gun violence.

Bette thought that Camilla had reached the end of her rope in Berkeley. She had realized that nothing was going to change. "She couldn't get along in the world she was living in, because her thinking was all screwed up. And she couldn't understand why nobody could understand her. That's just a theory that I've evolved," Bette said.

CHAPTER 22

Camilla Reveals Herself

IN ONE OF CAMILLA'S LINE DRAWINGS, a nude woman sits with her back straight against a wall, one knee up, the other leg extended. The woman sports shoulder-length hair and glasses. I wonder if it's a self-portrait, if this is how Camilla saw herself. The words that accompany the drawing say, "Once in a while, when I think I'm alone, I call my name and don't answer . . . just to make sure."

Camilla's letters to her parents rarely showed emotion, and she mostly kept her frustrations and anger hidden from friends, so it's only when I take a closer look at her art and poetry that I get a glimpse into her psyche. I can see a glimmer of her shadow side in the letters, but it's so fleeting that it took me several years of rereading the letters to see how much she loved her parents, and how her upbeat chatter may have masked loneliness. In her poetry, she's not afraid to be direct and strident. It's as if in the lines of her poems she can be her true self, as if she can tell people what to do. Camilla frequently uses the imperative, silently commanding others:

Please don't say no
Until you know . . .

And don't say yes
If it's just a guess.

A poem from March 1971 ends:

Look in the mirror,
      When you least expect it
            And you will see it
Too.

Reading only her letters, it can be easy to see Camilla as always happy and well adjusted, which makes her entry into the SLA so bizarre to a casual observer. But her art and poetry reveal deep love and deep disappointment. Her creative work shows both lightness and darkness. And two poems written by Mizmoon to Camilla reveal a new perspective on their relationship. I see things about Camilla that I hadn't seen before.

After Camilla's death, her parents collected some of her drawings and had them made into greeting cards. All of these drawings are pen and ink, though Camilla also worked in other media. The drawings are varied; some are deceptively simple and show just one or two figures, while others are busier. Some are whimsical, such as the drawing of four figures on bicycles. The figures seem happy, traveling at a fast pace. The one woman in the group has hair flowing almost straight back. Like many other female figures in Camilla's drawings, the woman is nude.

One of the more detailed drawings has a signpost that says:

DREARIA
Here, there, and everywhere
2 miles

In the drawing, all the figures are on beds that appear to have wheels—perhaps hospital beds? The faces have slashes that denote closed eyes, and they appear to be wearing pajamas. Are they dead? Did they die of boredom? Are they sleeping away a dreary day? One bed is tethered to a horse-like creature, and two other horse-like creatures are located on the bottom left. Four clouds punctuate the upper half of the drawing, suggesting that the horses and the people on the beds are floating in a suspended state of sleep or death.

Some of the humans throughout the drawings are gender neutral. One shows a reclining figure. Or are there two people? It's hard to tell. Either it's one person hugging him- or herself, or it's two people in an embrace. Only the buttocks and hands are readily identifiable; there's a suggestion of a leg, a hip, and a head (or two).

All the dated drawings are signed "Hall '71." Camilla moved to Berkeley in May 1971, and it's unknown whether these drawings were done before or after her arrival. One drawing shows two women holding hands across a space. There appear to be doors and steps, perhaps leading up to an apartment. It's not a stretch to think this might be Camilla and Mizmoon.

Camilla also created paintings full of bright color. It's in these paintings, rather than in the line drawings, that the figures are menacing and angry. In one painting, a purple-faced figure—almost monster-like, with a curved, spiny back—leers at a smaller figure it holds in its hand. The mouth spreads wide in a yellow-toothed grin. The figure looks like it's about to devour the smaller being.

Camilla's art evolved while she lived in California. Bette Esbjornson noticed the change. "When she first started doing her little drawings, they were fun and their meaning was obvious," Bette told Harvey. "But they kept getting more and more obscure. If I didn't understand the meaning of her drawings, she would get really angry with me. . . . It got to the point where it became senseless to talk to her about artwork anymore, because she was off in some other head from me."

What can art reveal about a person? Harvey was interested in this question, so he enlisted an art therapist to view about forty slides of Camilla's work. He didn't tell the therapist, Abby Calisch, the artist's identity, only that it was completed by a nonhospitalized twenty-nine-year-old female.

Calisch called the artist "skilled." A few characteristics stood out to her. The eyes of the figures are prominent, and some of the subjects are a combination of animal and human forms. Some pieces are playful and childlike; others are more sinister and ominous. Camilla at times was direct in the work, while at other times her art was hazier and flowing. Many of the pieces feature two figures. Sometimes male/female figures blend in terms of gender; sometimes there's a large figure and tiny figure.

Calisch's analysis supports Harvey's assertion that Camilla struggled with competing personas. "[Calisch's] impression was of a person with two distinct parts: one was playful, childlike, 'floaty,' lyrical in a specific, defined way. The other was a very controlled, powerful, aggressive, possibly critical person," Harvey wrote. One particular series seems to have come out of a place of depression or anguish, and Calisch surmised the artist had problems with male relationships, or relationships in general. But Calisch "experienced her as someone she would probably like, with a lot of capacity to integrate feelings, and a lot of drive and motivation to accomplish things. Camilla seemed pretty well integrated in terms of her ability to function, but there was some concern about the images of watchfulness verging on paranoia, and the critical, suspicious side."

Harvey also showed the slides to another art therapist, Linda Cohen, to get a second opinion. Cohen also noted the dual nature of the personality, but she saw darker overtones in the works than did Calisch. Cohen noted that many of the characters were posed defensively, and overall she felt that the artist was expressing a negative self-image in the works.

———

When Camilla moved to California, she made a big leap in leaving her day job to work full-time as an artist. She was able to support herself for a little more than a year, but when she moved to Berkeley she focused more on supporting herself with gardening and landscaping work.

Camilla seemed happiest when working as an artist. Letters to her parents during her college years are filled with grumblings about tests and professors. The two years she spent working in county welfare offices were rewarding in some ways but were ultimately challenging and frustrating. But while living as an artist, her letters overflowed with positive energy. Everything seemed to point to an exciting future: a new, warm place to live; a focus on art; and meaningful relationships.

But by 1973, artistic expression seemed to disappear from Camilla's life. She did not mention art anymore in letters to her parents, whereas in the preceding years almost every letter contained details about art fairs, art classes, and gallery shows. The last mention of a gallery show was in February 1973, in Los Angeles. She left a budding career, and for what?

In the summer and fall of 1972, as her relationship with Mizmoon waned, Camilla started to turn more attention to herself. She took karate lessons and often went camping. She may have viewed her body as a work of art, sculpting it into something lean and strong. She prepared for her European travels and spent the last part of 1972 and the early part of 1973 out of the country.

Her breakup with Mizmoon in early 1973 would have been a perfect time to return to art, it would seem, and maybe Camilla did for a brief time. But that spring she started work at Lake Temescal. Perhaps the job left her little time or motivation to continue creating art. Maybe she felt she was at a crossroads with her artistic career, doing all she could at the moment with her line drawings and not knowing where to go next. Maybe she just wanted a break—from art, from Mizmoon.

Camilla broke up with Mizmoon in February 1973, and they reunited later in the year, though it's not clear when. But once they got back together, Camilla's time may have been filled with revolutionary discussions at Peking House or taken up by reading books such as William H. Hinton's *Fanshen: A Documentary of Revolution in a Chinese Village* (1966) and Frantz Fanon's *The Wretched of the Earth* (1961), required reading for any wannabe revolutionary.

I wonder if Camilla started to see her art as frivolous, as unimportant, given everything going on in the world. Maybe she saw it as a juvenile pursuit; now was the time to grow up. Camilla was the oldest member of the SLA. Yet did she look at Mizmoon, five years younger, and admire her dedication to revolution? Mizmoon stayed busy throughout 1973, creating SLA manifestos with DeFreeze and Perry. Revolution was a full-time job, and everything she did had to support that. Reading books, watching documentaries, endless conversations at places like Peking House, running, hiking, gun training—who had time for art?

The unidentified friend who spoke to Harvey said, "The other time I saw her in a kind of depression was when she decided to give up drawing and to get down to the practical reality of making a living. But that was not a depression so much as a frustration."

———

In addition to the two envelopes of photocopied letters, Harvey also passed to me an envelope containing photocopies of twenty of Camilla's poems. As with the letters, I had seen some of these poems before. Harvey had reprinted a few of them in his dissertation, and one was in the collection of papers George Hall had left to the Gustavus archives. But while the poems I had seen before were transcribed and typed out, the poems in the envelope were written in Camilla's hand. I can almost feel her putting pen to paper. The poems emit a rawness and make her seem more real. Camilla's handwriting is cursive, but not as traditionally taught. She puts her own spin on how each letter of the alphabet should look. Her handwriting is on the small side, but neat and easily readable. It's more angular than round, the letters straight up and down, no slant.

If I knew nothing else about Camilla and only read her poems, I would see a woman who loves deeply. A woman wounded by love. A woman who gets excited, discouraged, and excited again about relationships. A woman who is carefully observing others. A confident woman who imagines herself telling people what to do and what to think. At times a funny, witty woman, at other times a sad woman.

I scour the poems for clues, as I do when I read her letters or look at her art. The poems were written between 1967 and 1972. When I arrange them chronologically, they reveal an arc of moods. They start with the high of a relationship, then dive down into a series of darker poems that coincide with her time in Los Angeles, then they lift up again when she moves to Berkeley and meets Mizmoon.

I read the poems as autobiographical, though that's an assumption on my part, or perhaps a wish. From what I've learned about Camilla, I don't see her as someone who could hide her feelings and emotions in her art, or as someone willing to adopt a separate narrator persona.

The collection also contains two poems not written by Camilla, presumably written by Mizmoon. They offer insight into their relationship not seen before.

———

Camilla's poems speak of relationships, both with Mizmoon and with others. Aside from Mizmoon, the subjects of her poems are not only unnamed but also genderless.

In "Naked," from September 1969, while Camilla was still living in Minneapolis, the narrator sits on a "lumpy" mattress on the floor with another person. They drink tea, share their favorite poems, and discuss the meaning of life. The narrator loves "the beauty of your power at rest . . . peaceful strength." It's a short poem, only a few lines, but the word "naked" starts a line twice, as if to emphasize the fact, reiterate it into being, commit it to memory. But with whom is she sitting on the lumpy mattress? The poem provides no physical description, not even a gender. The person is naked, but we can't even envision gender, age, or race.

Some poems are light, but others are darker. They're a lot like Camilla's drawings, which, despite the whimsical curves and caricatures, can come off as menacing and dark.

One poem from January 1971 is almost apocalyptic and contains nearly direct references from the books of Psalms and Revelation.

> . . . INTO THE VALLEY OF
> (THE SHADOW OF) DEATH
> RODE THE SIX HUNDRED.
> >   many for you; some
> >   much more for you two.
> THAT'S the same
> as
> lonely.

But in a couple of months, the poems are more hopeful. In March 1971 Camilla is planning to leave Los Angeles for the Bay Area:

I've got to move on;
Begin again
The search I left off

And my favorite, also from March, oozes confidence, power, strength—I'm rooting for the narrator:

Others have gone
                    (especially you)
and I won't be left
again.

Hurray!
It's my turn soon—
can you feel me coming?

Camilla's love life before Mizmoon is mysterious. About whom is she writing? The poems of 1970 don't necessarily reference romance, but they suggest dark feelings toward another person—could it be Bette? A July 1971 poem reflects on a relationship that seemed to go beyond platonic. By this time, Camilla was living on Channing Way in Berkeley. She had met Mizmoon but they were still just friends—the relationship would bloom later that year. The July 1971 poem speaks of a relationship that's already over:

it's hard not to want you—
even in my memory
    (where I thought I'd be safe)
I keep dragging you out
        past old times & old friends
        odds & ends of yesterdays
that just won't go away.

it's hard not to want you—
harder not to tell you
harder still & hard enough
to fill that part of me
that just cannot forget.

The two poems not written by Camilla presumably come from Mizmoon; they are signed with a "P" or "P.S."—Pat Soltysik.

The poems are steeped in infatuation—those heady first days, weeks, maybe even months, of romance. That time when you're willing to drop all commitments, all plans, all the things you work so hard for in order to spend every moment with that person. The moment when you lose your mind. You can't get enough of your new love. You want to drink them in, inhale them, enter them, and never part.

Let it be known:
That P.S., who for
Sometime now, has been
Preparing to leave for
MEXICO
Is no longer going—
Due to having in the
Meanwhile fallen and
Jumped deeply in
　　LOVE.
　　　　　　　　P [with a heart drawn]

Mizmoon's handwriting is neat and classic. A perfect capital *L*, whose like I haven't seen since I learned cursive in third grade. The small *r*, written with the precise angles as is taught. The penmanship almost looks like that of a schoolchild who has practiced writing the letters over and over.

And the birthday poem to Camilla, probably written in March 1972, overflows with love and excitement:

happy birthday!!
Camilla *Sister* Women!!
happy birthday
    Golden Mane!
(I'm hurryin'!!)
Lots & Lots & Tons
    Of LOVE yes!
L*O*V*E
    Da <u>big</u> P.

By that point in March, Camilla and Mizmoon had been together since Thanksgiving. Four months into their relationship, Mizmoon still professes love for Camilla.

The two poems help answer some enduring questions regarding the relationship between Camilla and Mizmoon. According to the media story, the two women had a relationship and when it fell apart, Camilla was always pining for her former lover. There's a sense that the pairing was unequal, that Camilla was suffering from a case of unrequited love.

But the poems speak of the love Mizmoon felt for Camilla. That deep love is confirmed by Mizmoon's brother, Fred, who wrote that Mizmoon was devastated when Camilla left her in mid-February 1973. A couple of weeks later, Mizmoon agreed to harbor DeFreeze, who had just walked away from prison. Shortly afterward, Mizmoon and DeFreeze began to write out SLA philosophy. Camilla may have been drawn into the SLA through Mizmoon, but did Mizmoon throw herself into the SLA because of the breakup? As a way to take her mind off Camilla? Consider this: maybe Mizmoon was the one pining for her former lover and thinking of ways to win her back. How would that change the narrative? What if Camilla was the one with the power?

———

In addition to the letters Harvey sent Roloff, the professor who specializes in therapeutic analysis of writing, he also sent Camilla's poems.

The professor sees Camilla's poems as descriptive in feeling but generally lacking imagery. But when Camilla does draft images out of words, the visuals appear suddenly, quickly, and violently. "They <u>erupt</u> from the page," Roloff writes (emphasis his). He discerns that the writer is someone who suffers from depression but is trying to hide it, whether consciously or subconsciously.

Roloff focuses on two poems. In one poem from 1972, Camilla writes about her cat, Keya, soaking in the sunshine. The sunshine in the poem is powerful and life-giving, sustaining the plants Camilla has placed in the window. In the last stanza Camilla writes:

> Ah yes, Keya shares her sunshine with the plants—
> basking, side by side, in the window.
> And when it gets too crowded
> > (no room to unfold)
> > > she bites them.

Roloff sees the powerful sun as masculine. The cat moves through the plants that have been nurtured by the sun, but suddenly fights back and attacks them because they have encroached on her space. Of this, Roloff writes, "I would not be at all surprised that she possessed enormous latent hostility at/for her father, but because of his 'powerful sun quality' could not consciously confront him."

The other poem is the only one that Camilla gives a title: "Reflections on a Pimple: Pore Little Me," written in 1969. In its entirety, it reads:

> When I get sad & feeling grim
> I just climb inside my skin.
> But it's so thin from living in
> I break out on my chin.

I see wit and a clever play on words, but Roloff sees something darker. He says this poem "is the clearest expression of her psychological state that you are going to find in the poems. . . . She makes her position perfectly clear." She's basically stating that she's a blemish, Roloff contends. He continues, "What kind of blemish was she? On herself? This is a very strange reflexiveness and narcissism. On her family? This is more credible. The shadow side of her personality never found adequate form of expression as far as I can determine."

Roloff also comments on the physical structure of the poems. The poems themselves are usually short, as are the lines. There's plenty of negative space; the poems have room to breathe. In a sense, they feel incomplete; there's more being said in between the lines. The poems don't follow conventional forms or rules and convey a sense of freedom and flow.

In his dissertation, Harvey wrote that he was surprised by Roloff's analysis, in which Camilla comes across as negative, depressed, and lacking self-confidence. Roloff did not read the letters and poems blindly; he knew who Camilla was and how she died, so Harvey didn't rule out the possibility of undue influence on the analysis. But as Harvey thought more about Camilla's writing, he saw that the letters and poems aligned with what was revealed in her artwork and the MMPI personality test—both of which suggested a darkness that she hid well.

Harvey wrote, "The lines themselves reflect such a positive persona, that the space almost necessitates, by contrast, an emphasis on that shadow personality which is not directly revealed. At any rate, Camilla seems to reveal herself again as a more complex personality than she revealed to her friends and her family, and perhaps more complex than she fully realized herself."

CHAPTER 23

A Parallel Story

Our faction of the SDS was excessive in its attempts to stifle
and kill certain tendencies. Nevertheless, Diana was always
sensitive to human feelings and needs. . . . Weatherman lost
many people who wanted to retain that sensitivity. It became an organization of those who were either cold in the
first place or who had found a way to conceal their gentility.
Unfortunately, repression is the method of killing a character-
istic. Diana managed to hang on to her beautiful sensitivity for
an incredibly long time.

—a friend of Diana Oughton, writing to her
parents after her death in 1970

FOUR YEARS BEFORE CAMILLA WAS KILLED by Los Angeles police,
twenty-eight-year-old Diana Oughton died in a townhouse explosion in
New York City. She was building a bomb with four other members of
the Weatherman—a radical offshoot of the Students for a Democratic
Society—when their attempt went awry.

In March 1970, Camilla would have just been settling into her new life in
Los Angeles. She doesn't mention the Weatherman in any surviving letters.

She may have seen media reports and she may have talked about it with her friends, but at that time there's no indication that Camilla was inspired by violent activism, especially the type that would result in bodily harm or death. The world of the Weatherman was far away; Camilla was probably enjoying her first late-winter season without bone-chilling cold and snow, making her art, soaking up the sun's every ray with pleasure. But had Camilla taken time to read more about Diana, she would have found a young woman whose life closely paralleled her own in many ways, and perhaps she could have caught a glimpse into the dark future that awaited her.

I have to approach Camilla from many angles in order to create a robust picture. I have her own words, words from her parents, words from her friends. But still, those words don't answer questions about Camilla's motivation for joining the SLA. It can be worth a step back to see if other women like Camilla can help me understand her.

The Weatherman (later known as Weather Underground), like the Symbionese Liberation Army that came after it, dedicated itself to violent revolution. Its members admired Che Guevara, Fidel Castro, and the Vietcong. They saw it as a moral imperative to fight the violence of the United States with violence.

A United Press International journalist, Thomas Powers, wrote a book about Diana in 1971 titled *Diana: The Making of a Terrorist*. In the book, he's asking the same question of Diana that I'm asking of Camilla: What's behind the transformation of a midwestern girl from activist to domestic terrorist? I thought the book might offer me clues.

———

Diana was born in 1942, three years before Camilla. She grew up privileged, her parents of a much higher social status than the Halls. Diana's father, James Oughton, was a banker and restaurateur in Dwight, Illinois, about eighty miles southwest of Chicago, and later served in the state legislature. Her mother, Jane Boyce Oughton, stayed home and played the part of socialite, supportive wife, and mother. Diana came from a long line of high-status and wealthy forebears: Her great-grandfather William D. Boyce founded the Boy Scouts of America. Diana was the oldest of three girls, who were raised in part by a nanny/housekeeper. Open fields surrounded the Oughtons' large house, and a fountain graced the estate. In photographs, her home looks like an English countryside manor.

Diana's path followed what was expected for a child of privilege in the 1950s. In tenth grade, she left Dwight to attend the Madeira School, an all-female boarding school in McLean, Virginia. Her schoolmates were daughters of prominent businessmen and Washington elites. Diana's world was one of debutante balls, silver tea sets, and training for the skills needed to succeed in the upper classes of the future. Before graduation, she applied to all of the Seven Sisters colleges and was accepted into each one. She chose Bryn Mawr, outside Philadelphia.

Bryn Mawr was a place where a student could remain sheltered from the realities of the world. It is easy to see how a young woman like Diana could be sheltered by her family, by teachers at Madeira, and by teachers and peers at Bryn Mawr. How easy it would be to continue that sheltered life for as long as she lived.

Diana stepped out of the confines of Bryn Mawr in her senior year, when she took a job tutoring children in Philadelphia's inner city. Here Diana got her first glimpse of "the real world." It was 1962. The idealistic, postwar world of Diana's parents still prevailed. Kennedy's Camelot hadn't yet crumbled. But society's cracks were beginning to show themselves even to the privileged. Diana could hardly believe that many of the children she tutored couldn't read, even though they were in seventh grade.

Diana wanted to learn more. She read *Black Like Me* by John Howard Griffin, in which he documented his time in the South disguised as a black man. The book achieved incredible popularity, especially among white high school and college students in the early 1960s. For many, it was their first realization of the magnitude of the racial disparity in the United States. Besides tutoring inner-city youth, Diana also worked in voter registration in Cambridge, Maryland. Griffin's book, Diana's own experiences, and the burgeoning school desegregation issue all combined to help her see there was more beyond her small-town perspective cultivated in Dwight. Her tunnel vision started to expand.

But that happens to many of us during our college years. College is supposed to be enlightening. Students from small towns the world over flock to campuses in larger cities. They meet a variety of people representing all races, sexualities, and political leanings. But why does one student grow up to be a concerned citizen, someone who volunteers time and donates money to good causes, while another student becomes a bomb maker intent on overthrowing the government?

Perhaps one difference is that most of us become distracted: we find love or get married or throw ourselves into our first jobs or dedicate ourselves to running marathons or having babies. We surround ourselves with friends doing the same thing. But people like Diana and Camilla only became more embroiled in the moment.

———

When she graduated from Bryn Mawr, Diana was "worldly" and well-rounded in the Ivy League sense. She had traveled internationally, like Camilla. Diana majored in German and spent her junior year in Munich. After graduation, Diana did not settle into the path that had been prescribed for her; she was more adrift than her classmates. The majority of her peers went on to graduate school, got married, or headed for exciting careers in New York City. Diana had a serious boyfriend while in college, a football player from Princeton who wanted to marry her. Good Bryn Mawr girls married their Princeton football-player boyfriends. But something inside Diana bristled at the thought of being a wife, and she turned down his proposal. She left college with a nagging thought that there was something more out there, that life was more than diamond rings and luncheons and white picket fences. That life was more than Dwight, more than the life her parents led. Her friends and family were aware of her thought process but didn't give it much credence. If anything, they saw Diana as a "do-gooder" headed toward a career in social work. If she wanted to help people and save the world, her friends and family thought, she'd do so through accepted channels.

Like Camilla, Diana gained firsthand knowledge of developing nations and their struggles. After graduation, Diana joined the Voluntary International Service Assignment (VISA), a program administered by the

American Friends Service Committee. She was assigned to Guatemala and spent 1963 through 1965 in Chichicastenango. According to Powers, Diana didn't have any strong feelings of wanting to save the world when she joined VISA; she joined a bit out of boredom and having no other plans. This, too, could have been another notch in the belt of a good Ivy League girl. The Peace Corps had just launched, and thousands of idealistic, wealthy youth joined the organization.

But Diana underwent a radical shift while in Guatemala. She saw her privilege as a cause for embarrassment. She lived as simply as possible, in a spartan apartment, eating meals that villagers ate. A dissonance emerged, and from that, a new self. She was surrounded by friends in Guatemala, both fellow Americans and those from there, who told her that her work was only delaying the inevitable revolution in the country. Individuals like Diana could help villagers learn to read or institute the best farming practices, but vast inequalities between rich and poor existed because of the social system and the few ruling families who grabbed all the wealth for themselves. Might the same be said of the United States? Diana began to reject capitalism and saw the benefits of socialism. American aid in Guatemala ended up in the hands of the wealthy. Diana became angry at what she saw as U.S. interference. She also became impatient. She was just a helper in a long, historical chain of helpers, dating back to missionaries hundreds of years earlier. Long after she was gone from the earth, there would be another line of helpers behind her. But that wasn't enough. She wanted to be the one to enact change, and she wanted to do it now.

———

When Diana returned to the United States in 1965, she moved to Ann Arbor to enroll in a master's of education program at the University of Michigan. Ann Arbor was the birthplace of the Students for a Democratic Society (SDS), which began in 1962. By the time Diana arrived, the group still existed but remained mostly as an intellectual exercise—lots of talking about what needed to change, but little action.

In the summer of 1966, Diana returned to Guatemala for a visit. There, she met with guerrilla leaders of the Fuerzas Armadas Rebeldes (FAR), who were taking action to improve the lives of the poor. Their actions included kidnapping the wives and children of the business and political elite and holding them for ransom. They used the ransom money to pay for their revolutionary activities.

When she returned to Ann Arbor that fall, Diana worked in a progressive experimental school called Children's Community School (CCS). There she met Bill Ayers—an SDS leader—and they fell in love. At the time, Ayers was at the forefront of a new, more radical SDS that later became the Weatherman.

Diana's work at CCS, much like her work in Guatemala and Camilla's work in social services, was all done as part of a legitimate system designed to help others, whether they be third-world farmers, young children, or unwed mothers. Camilla worked within the system for about two years before she burned out; Diana lasted a bit longer between her VISA service and teaching at the school. But both grew frustrated with the slow pace of change, red tape, bureaucracy, and corruption. CCS had closed by 1968, leaving Diana and Bill adrift and looking for something new to work on.

———

Diana's transformation did not occur only in the mind; it also took physical form. The difference between two pictures of Diana, taken thirteen years apart, is striking. Camilla transformed her body, too, eating a vegetarian diet, learning karate, and going for long hikes.

Diana, pictured in 1956 at age fourteen, looks every bit the all-American, midwestern girl from an upper-crust family that she was. Her blond hair is made up in a stylish bob, a wave of bangs framing her face. She wears a black scooped-neck dress and a string of dainty pearls around her neck. The picture was taken before she left her Illinois home in tenth grade for the Madeira prep school. Maybe it's just the style of the time, but she looks much older in the picture, nineteen or twenty.

Diana's mug shot from 1969 could not look more different. It was taken after her arrest during Chicago's Days of Rage demonstration, her hair short but shaggy. She still wears black, but it's either a T-shirt or a sweater, close around her neck. No earrings or necklace. She stares straight ahead at the camera, mouth set neutrally—no smile, but no scowl, either. No visible emotion. Her eyes really stand out. You hear people described as looking "cold" or "hard," but it's difficult to visualize that unless you see it for yourself. Diana's eyes in the photo are defiant. She almost looks as if she's been stripped of her humanity, as if her soul has retreated so far down it could never be pulled back up. She's lacking something. If, as the friend quoted in the epigraph to this chapter said, the SDS and its offshoots wanted to break a person, erase any sensitivity so they acted like robots, this picture supports that claim. The photo actually scares me a little. Whereas with every picture of Camilla I think, "She could be my friend," I look at this picture of Diana and I think I would want to run away.

———

Diana had a lover within the movement, but after her death no one suggested she was involved in the Weatherman just for love, as a way to stay close to Bill. People seemed to accept that she truly became radicalized and believed in revolution—through her experiences at Bryn Mawr, through her work in Guatemala, and through her involvement in the protest movement. Her experiences were similar to Camilla's, so it's not a stretch to think that Camilla also legitimately became more radicalized and wasn't drawn into the SLA only through her love of Mizmoon.

Diana and Camilla followed similar trajectories and exhibited similar behavior. They moved often and changed careers. Camilla went from social worker to artist to landscape laborer. Diana went from volunteer work to teaching to full-time activism. And in each move, they cut off friends they had known and started over again. Each stage in their lives was separate, each stage not clearly related to the others, but like a building block that led to something larger. After Bryn Mawr, Diana had little contact with college friends, and when she did, the meetings were tense as it became clear her life had diverged from the accepted social paths of her peers. Diana had little contact with Guatemalan friends after she left VISA. She had little contact with CCS friends and parents after the school closed.

Likewise, Camilla's friends at different ages lost contact with her. High school and college friends didn't know she had moved to California. In

California, she found a new set of friends, friends who didn't know much about her pre-California life. As in college, where few knew about her siblings' deaths, in California her friends didn't know much about her family, either. And both the Oughtons and the Halls knew little of what their daughters were doing.

Reading about Diana helps me see that Camilla's life, too, was more complex than an initial glance can show. But still, something is missing. I want to talk to someone who was alive during Camilla's time and who still is alive. I'm chasing down dead people all the time. So I turn to the woman who started me on this journey in the first place. Without the initial news reports about Sara Jane Olson, the SLA fugitive on the run finally discovered in St. Paul in 1999, I might have never learned about Camilla. My proxy for Camilla will be Sara Jane, another Minnesota girl who was also the daughter of a teacher, who also made her way to Berkeley in the 1970s. When I visited Sara Jane in 2008, she was in California, though her home at that point was a women's prison in California's dusty Central Valley.

CHAPTER 24

A Visit to Chowchilla

IN 1976, Kathleen Soliah was indicted on charges of planting pipe bombs on Los Angeles Police Department (LAPD) squad cars. The bombs were supposedly in retaliation for the deaths of the six SLA members killed in the 1974 shoot-out. Among the dead was Angela Atwood, Kathleen's good friend. Kathleen allegedly became involved in the SLA shortly after the shoot-out to aid the three surviving SLA members, Bill Harris, Emily Harris, and Patty Hearst. Kathleen and others were determined to continue the SLA's mission. As a member of the SLA, Kathleen was also allegedly involved in the Crocker National Bank robbery of April 21, 1975, in which a mother of four, Myrna Opsahl, was killed.

Instead of facing trial, Kathleen went into hiding and changed her name to Sara Jane Olson. She lived in Zimbabwe for a time with her husband, Dr. Fred Peterson, and gave birth to three girls. The family then settled in St. Paul, Minnesota. She volunteered in her community and acted in community theater. Her past caught up to her during an airing of the television program *America's Most Wanted*. She was arrested outside her home on June 16, 1999.

Sara Jane's arrest was a major story in Minnesota. The volatility of the 1960s and 1970s didn't seem so far away. Emotions about Sara Jane's case ran high, as evidenced by callers to radio talk shows and newspaper letters to the editor in the aftermath of the arrest. Who was Sara Jane Olson? A freedom fighter? A cold-blooded murderer? A domestic terrorist?

———

Perhaps Sara can give me some insight on that time and place. I'd met her briefly a couple of times shortly after her arrest, when she was holding fundraisers to help pay for her defense. At that time, she told me she had never met Camilla. But now I'd like a longer conversation with her about Angela and Berkeley in the 1970s. It might help me better understand Camilla. So through Sara Jane's husband, Fred, I make arrangements to visit her in prison.

"It's very cool and kind of courageous to schlepp to Chowchilla," Fred told me in an email. I wonder what he means by "courageous." Is he just paranoid? Or am I really going to be watched, surveilled, followed somehow by someone? Fred also tells me that when I fill out the visitor's form, on the line where it asks for relation to prisoner, put down "friend" instead of "writer" or "journalist." The less people know about what I'm doing there, the better.

He cautions me about nosing around for information regarding the Los Angeles shoot-out that left Angela, Camilla, and the four others dead. Four hundred Los Angeles and FBI officers against six people. The LAPD wouldn't want a writer coming around and reminding people of the obvious mismatch in firepower. Yet here I am.

You'd think thirty-plus years would seal the past. But you'd be wrong.

———

I leave the apartment I'm renting in Oakland just past 6 a.m. The July morning is already warm. Those incarcerated at the Central California Women's Facility in Chowchilla are allowed visitors only on weekends, and only from 9 a.m. to 3 p.m. Fred has told me to get there as soon as the visiting area opens. Don't wait too long, he says, or else Sara will have to stay until the next hourly yard count. If I arrive after 10 a.m., by the time I'm processed, Sara will be held for another hour, then she'll need to be processed, and it might be noon by the time I see her.

Interstate 580 cuts east through the Livermore ridge, a series of rounded hills the color of sunburned grass. I'm climbing up and out of the flat, sea-level bay area. Only a guardrail stands between zooming cars and the steep drop-offs that line the interstate. At the top of the hills are extended shoulders, where semi drivers pull off and check their brakes before careening down.

When I hit Highway 132, which will take me to Modesto, I'm greeted by the rich greens of agriculture. Irrigation brings life to this otherwise hot, barren desert. I pass stands of walnut, pecan, and almond trees. I see corn and cows, and if I ignore the stark hills that surround me, I picture myself home among southern Minnesota's farm fields. But the sky here is tinted an odd white, hazy from wildfires to the north and from California's notorious air pollution.

Fred gives me excellent directions to the prison. I exit at Chowchilla and drive five miles to the east. Fred tells me exactly what to bring and what to wear. For the past six years, he's been visiting his wife about every other month. He tries to go on holidays, when visitors are allowed an extra day on top of the usual Saturday–Sunday visit.

I pull into the prison's parking lot a little after 9 a.m. When I open the door, the hot, dry air rushes into my lungs and takes my breath away. I walk quickly to the check-in building, where air-conditioning awaits.

I do what Fred had instructed in an email:

Pick up a sign-in sheet at the corner of the guard's counter, write top line Sara Olson W94197, next line "friend," don't say writer. Then put the sheet in the little box. They will call you up in turn. The process is essentially airport TSA security, belts, shoes off, the addition is inverting pockets and pull down socks. They will give you a token [for a locker] for the car keys, and whatever stuff you can't bring in.

Here is what I can bring: A clear, small plastic bag with thirty to fifty one-dollar bills and my driver's license. The money is for food and drinks at the snack bar, the license is so I can get in and out to use the bathroom while I'm there. No pencil, no notebook, no nothing.

When the woman at Saint Sabrina's Parlor in Purgatory in uptown Minneapolis jabbed a needle through my navel in 1996, I didn't watch. It was my first piercing aside from my ears, my first stab at rebellion. I looked down at the silver hoop, the two ends curved and joined by a silver ball. I had no idea how she put the hoop in, no idea how it came apart.

I forget I even have it. It's become a part of me, like the birthmark on my leg or the mole on my face. So I don't take it out in Oakland before I drive to Chowchilla. All my other metal—earrings, the nose stud, the labret below my lip—lies on the bathroom counter in the apartment.

So when I lift my shirt to show the guard that I don't have a pistol or rifle tucked into my waistband, that's when I remember the piercing.

"That's got to go," the guard says, pointing to my navel with her pencil.

It's all over, I think. I've never taken out the piercing. The long drive is all for naught. They'll send me home because I didn't follow the rules. I look at the guard nervously.

"Just take it out and put it in another locker," she says. I had already put my keys in a locker, so she hands me another token. I head for the lockers that line this visitors' room. I get to stay, at least for now. But first, I have to get this piercing out.

I look at it. Ball. Hoop. It can't be that hard. I turn the ball. It spins round and round but stays in place. Nothing gets tighter or looser. I tug on the ring, on the ends where it meets the ball. I sigh and look toward the guards. A small group of visitors has formed at the counter. They flash their waistbands, as I have. They take off shoes and place them in bins. They get their wrists stamped with ink visible only under ultraviolet light, a stamp that allows them entry into an exclusive club. They're all going in, while I struggle with my jewelry. Will I have to drive back to Oakland without even entering the prison gates? A month of planning gone because I cannot remove my damn navel ring? I wonder if the guards have pliers. I envision a guard tugging at the jewelry with the sharp tool, scraping and stabbing the pale skin of my stomach. But I'll do anything to get inside that razor wire.

I attack my navel ring with renewed determination. I spin the ball some more. The skin turns bright pink in response to my twisting and pulling. I tug at the ring at each side of the ball, like I did before, but harder this time.

Ping! The ball sails through the air and lands on the floor. Bounce, bounce, bounce. I follow it with my eyes; it's so small. It comes to rest against a wall. I grab it and remove the rest of the ring from its twelve-year resting spot. I probably will not get it back in. That's all right. A small sacrifice for my first prison visit.

———

After locking up everything, I sit in a hard, molded plastic chair and wait. I study the guy in front of me. I had followed him into this building when I arrived. Russell, I hear the guards call him. Russell looks to be in his forties, tall, with thin hair, parted on the side, that flops over his head. He looks like a stereotypical insurance agent, maybe, or a computer programmer. He slouches in his chair and wears the look of a tired man. Emotionally tired from a hard life. He looks "tough," as my mom likes to say—not "beat-you-up tough" but "in tough shape," someone who drank too much, smoked too much, lived a life full of conflict and drama. I'll see this look repeated on faces throughout the day. I wonder whom he's here to see, if this is a trip he takes every weekend. He appears comfortable and seems to know the process well.

I wait only a few minutes before my name is called. I get my shoes back and walk through a metal detector. A guard stamps my wrist with invisible ink. He'll pass the wand over my wrist when I come back through at the end of the day. It's a pass that allows me to float between the free world and this contained one.

The guard presses a button, and a metal gate opens. I'm outside but boxed in by a high chain-link fence. I look up and see sky. I wait a few moments for another gate to buzz open. From here, I walk to the building where I'll meet Sara. If I could put on blinders and gaze only straight ahead, I could convince myself that I'm on a college campus or at a business complex. The visitation building, a nondescript one-story, is straight ahead. Green bushes line my path, and two bunnies scamper ahead of me.

But that high chain-link fence with razor wire atop is everywhere. Beyond that is an electric fence. If a prisoner trying to escape somehow gets past those two fences, she would need to scale yet another high fence capped by razor wire. But before reaching that last fence, she'd have to hurdle the spools of razor wire that lie on the ground. No one is getting out of here before her time.

At the visitation building's main desk, a cheery guard greets me. His is the first smile I've seen all day. The guards in the main building were all business, quick and to the point. I'm grateful to see a smile and I return it. I take my driver's license out of the Ziploc bag and give it to him.

"Minnesota!" he says. "Wow, you've come a long way." Smile.

He walks me to the door. Through its window I glance into the visitors' room, a large, square, cafeteria-like space. He pulls a key from a gigantic key ring attached to his belt. "What's the weather like there?"

I say it's hot and humid and tell him how much I like California weather because at night it cools off and I can sleep with the windows open.

"Humid, yes," he says, pondering the dampness as if it's an idea he can't quite grasp. He smiles as he opens the door and ushers me inside. "Have a good time," he says.

About a quarter of the round cafeteria tables are occupied by visitors, some of whom are already chatting with those they came to visit. At yet another guard's desk, I sign in and am assigned Table 29. A sign above the desk reads, "Inmates and visitors are allowed just one brief hug at the beginning and end of the visit."

My stomach rumbles. I look forward to coffee and a treat. The "concession stand" turns out to be two guys standing behind a collapsible table piled high with food in plastic containers. I was hoping for a doughnut, but the offerings mostly consist of greasy, fried lunch items such as egg rolls, pizza, or chicken fingers. The food is cold and entirely unappetizing. The only sweets are gargantuan slabs of cake—chocolate and cheesecake. I grab a plastic container of precut veggies—Fred said that's what Sara likes—and two coffees. The coffee comes out of a large metal coffeepot, like those found in church basements. The coffees and vegetables cost me ten dollars. With no competition, the prices are high. I had wondered why I needed so much money going in, but I realize I might be out fifty bucks by the time this is over.

Back at the table, I watch what I assume are routines. Parents, friends, children who visit each week. They know the drill. They confidently approach the guard desk, get their table number, casually walk to the concession stand, get their food, and wait. At the tables they keep their eyes on a gray metal door, the door that separates the visitors from the incarcerated. Two young men grab a Bible and sit down. Some pick up battered board games. A woman next to me lines up the pieces for Sorry!

I see Russell again. He's come in just before me and sits at the next table. He still slouches, does nothing except stare at the door. Three women who were with me in the processing building sit near me, too, elegant in their flowing flower-print skirts and muted blouses. At another table, an older couple wait. Parents, I assume.

It's mostly young women who emerge from the doorway, and they are prettier than I expected incarcerated women to be. Girls with long hair, eyes rimmed with liner, lips bearing bright colors. In another life, in their former lives, their breasts would strain at their shirts and their long toned legs would be revealed by short skirts, wreaking havoc on men who cross their paths. They'd be the girls lined up outside dance clubs, cell phones to ears, hair piled high. Here, they're allowed only baggy denim pants with loose blue shirts or thin white jersey shirts with navy blue sleeves, like they're on a recreation-league softball team.

Near me, one dark-haired girl greets her parents, tears filling her eyes. Mom and Dad grip her tightly in an embrace and plant kisses on her cheeks and head. Tears spring to my eyes. My emotion surprises me. What had I expected? That all visitors would be like me, distant journalists? I didn't think about the families, the people who come here once a month, maybe even every weekend, desperate for the only contact they can have with a person they love. Did I think love would be absent in this place?

After several minutes, still I wait. I wish I could have a newspaper or book; I have no idea how much longer Sara will be. Russell, at Table 28, stands up as he spots the woman he has come to see. She's small, with short blond hair. They hug only briefly, awkwardly. Siblings, maybe? Good friends? Husband who's lost his trust? Russell doesn't smile.

Then there's Sara.

She's immediately recognizable from the most recent pictures splashed across newspapers during her brief but mistaken release in March. But even without the pictures I would know her; there can't be many white-haired grandmotherly types in Chowchilla.

She's surprisingly bubbly and energetic; she pumps my hand enthusiastically and smiles widely. Fred had said in an email, "Sara would really appreciate the visit, more than you know."

Her energy will not wane during the entire day. She's grateful for the coffee and veggies that are waiting, but she wants to see what else is at the concession stand. Like a kid in a candy store, she surveys the available food, so much different from the standard prison fare. The grease and fat are pure treats. She picks out a container with thick, pink cuts of watermelon, and then spies the cakes. "Oh, that looks so good," she says. Her fingers hover over the boxed pieces, first over one, then another, like the tense crowning ceremony of Miss America. Which one will it be? She finally taps a container that holds a piece of rich chocolate cake with chocolate frosting.

We go back to the table. Sara launches into nonstop talk right away. Fred said she'd be "full of chatter." Without a notebook it's hard for me to take it all in. Mostly she talks about politics, and I hear a lot of "Bush" and "oil" and "Iraq," but I have trouble following. I'm aware of current events. I read a newspaper every day, but then I move on to other things. I don't drill deep into what's really going on.

Sara's face is malleable, like rubber. Her training as an actress is evident. Her eyes widen, then narrow, her mouth moving into different shapes. Her hands dance around and do not sit still. It was through acting that she met Angela. Both performed in Berkeley community theater, then later worked together at the Great Electric Underground restaurant in San Francisco. Later, Sara acted in numerous plays in the Twin Cities. She was on the run but still craved the spotlight.

By the time Olson's case came through the court system, three years had passed since her arrest. It was 2002. In any other year she might have been slapped with minimal jail time and parole, her case making headlines for a brief time but then fading quickly. But the September 11 attacks play a critical role in this narrative. Prosecutors around the nation vowed to bring to justice the perpetrators of any real or perceived act of terrorism on U.S. soil, whether foreigners or homegrown Americans, whether yesterday or twenty-five years in the past. The Los Angeles district attorney would make an example of Sara, would use her to prove the government indeed can be tough on terrorism, present *and* past. Sara was given twenty years to life for two counts of *attempting* to bomb police cars and received a sentence of five years to life for the murder of Opsahl.

The district attorney's office considered the sentence a major victory. In a 2001–2 annual "Report to the People" issued by the office, the successful prosecution of Sara's case is listed alongside the cases against Winona Ryder (shoplifting), Robert Blake (murder), and Paula Poundstone (child molestation). In a 2004 press release noting major awards for the Los Angeles County District Attorney's Office, Deputy District Attorney Eleanor Hunter was named prosecutor of the year in California, and the only case of hers mentioned by name is Sara's.

———

Earlier in 2008, I had written a letter to Sara, explaining who I was and that I was writing a biography of Camilla Hall. She wrote back, saying that she would be happy to visit but that she would not talk about her involvement in the SLA. At Chowchilla, she surprises me.

I ask her about Angela. Sara and Angela met at a play audition in 1972. Sara was looking for work, and Angela helped her get a job at the Great Electric Underground, a restaurant in the bowels of the Bank of America building in San Francisco. The two became inseparable. They worked together nearly every day, and in the evening they attended play rehearsals.

Sara recalls that Angela's husband, Gary Atwood, had a temper and went after Angela with his fists. They broke up, much to Sara's relief. Gary returned to Indiana for graduate school, and Angela continued to send him money.

"I would tell her, 'Stop doing that,'" Sara says, shaking her head.

Angela's involvement in the SLA came about quickly, Sara says, and pinpoints her entry to September 1973. Sara didn't notice any remarkable shifts in Angela's personality or behavior. She was political and was known to use violent rhetoric, but Sara says that was common in the early 1970s in the Bay Area. Looking back, Sara thinks Angela was trying to gauge Sara's convictions.

"She asked me what I thought of the Foster murder," Sara says. "I said I thought it was a dumb move."

That answer might have saved Sara from immediate involvement in the SLA. Sara thinks Angela didn't ask her to join because she knew Sara would try to convince her to leave the SLA.

Even though the SLA desperately wanted recruits, especially because the Foster murder sank their reputation, they were careful about the people they invited in. They needed people they could trust. And there must have been something about Sara suggesting that she was not serious or that she might squeal. Of course, after the shoot-out that killed six of their own, Bill, Emily, and Patty took anyone they could get, desperate to salvage their group and stay on the run. Sara was photographed at a rally at Berkeley's Ho Chi Minh Park after the shoot-out, sunglasses covering half her face, fist raised in defiance. She joined the SLA, and it became a family affair as her brother and sister joined, too.

———

Typically, people involved in an organization such as the SLA cut off their friends and family. But Angela did not reject Sara, as she may have with other friends. That was another reason Sara suspected, and hoped, that Angela was not involved. She figured that if Angela were in the SLA, that would be the end of their friendship.

Camilla, too, held on to her friends, even while becoming more and more wrapped up in the SLA. She had many friends over the years, but they didn't know each other. She kept her friends compartmentalized. Each friend knew a small portion of Camilla's life well, whether it was her passion for art, her dedication to music, or her love of gardening. But few knew where she was from, that her dad was a Lutheran pastor, or that her three siblings had preceded her in death. They didn't know Camilla's true politics, and few had met Mizmoon.

Keeping secrets was a way to protect her friends. The less Camilla's friends knew about her or her true politics or her family, the less they could reveal to police or to the FBI agents who eventually came knocking.

I hope Sara can help me theorize why Camilla became wrapped up in the SLA.

"The whole story confuses me," I say. "She wasn't involved in the Foster murder, and I don't know why she'd support the SLA after that happened."

Sara picks at the vegetables. It's nearing noon. The watermelon and chocolate cake remain untouched.

"Cin definitely had a mesmerizing hold over the women," Sara says of DeFreeze.

Perhaps Camilla subscribed to the theory of white guilt. The SLA exalted Cin, put him on a pedestal, anointed him as their leader even though he didn't have a track record of organizing activists. But he was black. And according to the SLA, any revolution against the power structure would have to be led by a black man.

———

The incarcerated women are allowed to use the bathroom once an hour. They line up for the restroom at the bottom of every hour, a sea of women in their standard-issue blues. After one break, just before 1 p.m., Sara suggests we walk outside. A small, square dirt yard with patchy grass adjoins the visitors' center. We walk the perimeter, next to the tall chain-link fence. We walk around and around and around. It takes us only about one minute to complete a lap. The high sun is hot; I'm wearing a black shirt. My skin sizzles. Sara's tan suggests that she gets outside whenever possible, that she's acclimated to this heat.

Here, away from other ears, Sara feels comfortable talking more about the SLA. Few people are out here. A couple of women also walk with their guests, and a couple more claim the only two picnic tables. It's not a welcoming environment.

Sara talks about writing a book when she's released. It wouldn't be a book about her SLA involvement; she sees no need to discuss that with the wider world. If anything, she'd write a book about the prison system. While in Chowchilla she's been actively writing essays about that topic, getting published in progressive newspapers and websites. These women don't have a chance, she says. Prisons are not for rehabilitation, and she decries the high recidivism rate.

She doesn't think anyone would be interested in a book about the SLA, whether written by her or by me.

"Even if they were," she says, "I wouldn't get published. Even a book I write about prisons probably won't get published." The powers that be are simply too strong, in her estimation. The world will keep silencing her.

A laugh escapes from me. I don't mean to laugh at her and when I do, I regret it.

"I know it can sound paranoid, but it's not far from the truth," she says, and I hear a little hurt in her voice.

I backtrack. "I realize that," I say. "I understand."

We go inside. Sara finally eats the watermelon and cake. We take turns stabbing the food with our forks and bringing the morsels to our mouths. Sara says she sometimes thinks about what the SLA would have become if not for the shoot-out. What would have been their ultimate fate? A few years in jail, like Weatherman members Bill Ayers and Bernardine Dohrn? Would the SLA have committed more violent crimes, more kidnappings and mur-ders? Or would they have quietly disintegrated as reality sunk in? Without the SLA, Kathy remains Kathy, Angela remains Angela, and Camilla remains Camilla, writing poetry, drawing, playing guitar. I see older women, women in their seventies with blunt bobs and glasses, stocky, mannish, smiling, and I think, *You could be Camilla.*

Soon it's three o'clock. I've been talking with Sara for more than five hours, and it seems no longer than five minutes. I had originally planned to stay a couple of hours. After all, I figured, how much can two strangers say to each other?

I wonder if she had put off eating the food for as long as possible. For when the food was gone, then I'd be gone, too.

CHAPTER 25

Nan

AT TIMES, months passed without me ever touching the computer files that became this book. In the spring of 2020, more than twenty years after I first came across Camilla's story, I'm still working on it. Lately the only time I can devote to it has been a weekend here or a weekend there. The third weekend in May finds me in Duluth, on my annual retreat with women from my writing group.

I'm sitting at the rental home's dining room table on Sunday morning, books and papers spiraling around my laptop, my own solar system of notes and writing errata. I'm editing an early chapter, addressing questions and comments left by readers the summer before.

My phone lights up with a text: "Just wondering how things are going."

It's Nan. I don't hear from Nan often, but when I do, it's always when all my energies are devoted to Camilla. She somehow senses when I'm working on the book. I like to think that through Nan, Camilla is urging me on.

———

George Hall's family was an island unto itself. Their frequent moves isolated them from their relatives. George had three siblings, as did Lorena. But they never lived near any of them, and communication was often sporadic—or nonexistent. Lorena's younger sister, Helen, moved to Boston and they fell out of touch. Lorena didn't even know Helen was dying of cancer until the very end.

As a result, Camilla didn't know her aunts, uncles, or cousins well. And because her siblings died before she did, there is no family left to remember Camilla. That concept is hard for me to grasp, growing up as I did with frequent family weddings, a smattering of funerals, and "cousin camp," where I would spend a week at my cousin Bernadette's house and she at mine. Another cousin, Karen, lived one mile away as the crow flies, and I spent more time with her than with my own sister, who was nine years older than me.

But it seemed important to find a relative of Camilla's who would be willing to talk to me. I wanted to give the family a voice. Maybe I was also looking for a blessing. One reason why this book was taking so long to write was that I struggled with the ethics of writing about someone I didn't know. Did Camilla even want her story told?

———

I visited Don Myers at the Hillstrom Museum of Art on the Gustavus Adolphus campus one summer day in 2014. The Hillstrom collection held a couple of paintings by Lorena, and I wanted to see them. Don and I discussed the possibility that, with enough material, perhaps one day there could be a show of both Camilla's and Lorena's art. For that reason, Don was looking to acquire more works by Lorena and shared with me contact information for some family members, including an elderly niece of George's and a grandniece. The grandniece, Nan, lived in Sioux Falls, South Dakota, and had an email address. I thought I'd start with her.

I sent this email to Nan on July 10, 2014:

Hi Nan,
I received your contact information from Don Myers at the Hillstrom Museum at Gustavus Adolphus. I'm looking to get in touch with relatives of George and Lorena and Camilla Hall, as I'm writing a biography on Camilla.

I first came across Camilla's story in 1999 and learned of the great resources George Hall had left to the Gustavus archives. I did my master's thesis on Camilla and the SLA, but now would like to write a more narrative account of her story.

Don had the names of some Hall relatives who may have art done by Lorena and/or Camilla. I am interested in seeing these pieces, but I also am interested in talking to family members who may have memories of George, Lorena, and Camilla. As you can imagine, now that forty years have passed since Camilla's death, and now that her immediate family has passed, it is difficult to find first-hand information about her.

Please let me know if you'd be interested in talking, or if you know of any other relatives who might be willing to talk.

Thank you for your time today.

Sincerely,

Rachael Hanel

Minutes after I emailed Nan, my phone rang. I had a feeling it might be her. I picked up the phone and looked at the number: Sioux Falls. It was Nan. I was planning to leave soon for an event in Rochester, Minnesota, but I had a few minutes to chat.

"That was fast," I told Nan after she introduced herself.

"I wouldn't be able to type as fast as my thoughts are coming," she said, explaining the phone call.

Her words came out in a rush, like they'd been bottled up for years. Since I had to leave, we spoke for only a few minutes. She wanted to know where we could go from here. I said that I would like to have a longer phone conversation with her but that ultimately I would like to meet in person. She mentioned that the family felt sensitive about Camilla, that some were still unwilling to talk about her or to make their connection to her widely known. To the family, Camilla's involvement in the SLA and subsequent death was shameful, embarrassing. Nan grew up wondering why people were so reticent. Why didn't her family speak freely of Camilla? Nan wanted to know more.

We ended the conversation with plans to meet. I finished getting ready for my Rochester trip and left the house. I got into the car, and no sooner had I turned on the ignition than my phone rang. Sioux Falls, again. Any worries I'd had about Nan's reluctance to talk dissipated. She was a reporter's dream. This time, Nan wondered if a story about Camilla would be enough to generate interest. Is there a larger story that Camilla illustrates? I said I was working precisely on that question.

We talked about her family's sensitivity. I assured her that I wasn't interested in criticizing Camilla or her family.

"Like what, that George and Lorena were bad parents?" she asked.

"No, not at all," I responded. "To make a long story short, I have had nothing but sympathy for Camilla and her family from the beginning." I hoped this would be enough to convince her to talk further to me.

———

Nan and I met for the first time two months later in Sioux Falls. We ate dinner at a nice restaurant downtown that offered views of the Big Sioux River. Nan was tall and slim, with chestnut hair and brown eyes, and bore no discernable resemblance to the photos I've seen of George and Camilla. We talked for hours and discovered that we had been born just months apart in 1974, the year Camilla died. Long after the sun had set, with the meal cleared away and coffee in front of us, Nan received a text from her husband, which she ignored. He called a few minutes later.

"He was just wondering if I was OK," she said when she hung up.

It turned out that Nan was exactly the family member I was looking for. She hadn't known Camilla, nor had her mom (who was Camilla's first cousin). But Nan had had a special relationship with George, one that began when she was very small, visiting his cabin on Lake Superior with her family. There, she found remnants of past lives, ghosts lingering of children no longer there. She found children's books with names printed inside—not only Camilla, but also her sister Nan.

"I could see how she used to write her name. It was striking to me that there was a little girl named Nan who died," Nan says, her voice soft and wistful. "It was sort of eerie, yet kind of unique since it's not a common name. It gave me a feeling of place."

She's right, it wasn't a common name in 1974. The closest variation is Nanette, ranked at number 804 in the Social Security's list of baby names. You're more likely to find a female born in 1974 named Venus, Flora, or even Matthew than you are to find a plain old Nan. It wasn't a popular name in 1947, either, the year Nan Hall was born, but it was on the list at number 520.

Nan says the story is that she was named after her great-grandmother on her father's side. "But her name was Nanny, not just Nan," she says. "I believe in my mother's heart, she named me after Uncle George's daughter who died."

Even though George didn't live near his siblings, he was close to his sisters, says Nan. His sister Dorothy was Nan's grandmother. Nan's mother was an only child.

As Nan grew older, she gravitated toward the Halls. At her grandmother Dorothy's house, things were much different than at the homes on her dad's side of the family.

"Even with the mannerisms, there was just such a different feel. Grandma had the table set just right. Eggs were in egg holders."

It was clear that George and his siblings valued education, culture, and travel. That filtered down to Nan's mother and to Nan.

"When I was little he'd send us artifacts from his travels. I remember seeing rosewood from Tanzania, and how different that looked from anything else. The things we'd get from Uncle George were defining for me. I knew that I wanted to see and explore the world."

And she did. She studied in Mexico, China, and England. The already-close relationship she and George had grew stronger as they bonded over her travels and education.

"I didn't have anyone who understood where I was coming from, but Uncle George did," Nan says.

Their relationship grew so close that when Lorena was getting sicker, George asked Nan and her mother to be there with him. Only Nan was there when Lorena died. Nan helped George write the obituary and organize the funeral. Repeatedly, in letters to Nan over the next few years, George thanks her for her help in those days. "You were with me when Lorena died and you may remember how we went to my computer and together composed the story of her life for the service bulletin. Then we went off to the universities to see what they had to offer [you]. Thank you again for spending those days with me. I was very proud to present you as my grand-niece. Thank you again."

That summer, Nan had just finished her second year of college. She contemplated transferring to a bigger, more rigorous school. George was living near Northwestern University, and they visited that campus as well as the University of Chicago. Plans began to take shape: George had access to a second apartment, where Nan could live for free. Throughout the summer of 1995, in letters to Nan, he expressed excitement at the possibility that she might move near him. But ultimately, she decided to stay where she was in Iowa. She was almost assured a role as student body president there and decided to stick with that path. But to this day, she wonders how differently her life might have turned out had she lived with George in Chicago.

I see Nan as a proxy daughter to George or as the granddaughter he never had. Here was a young woman he could have intellectual conversations with, a young woman to engage with as he followed her educational and early career path. It sounds a lot like the relationship he had with Camilla, where they exchanged ideas and carried on philosophical debates through their letters.

I ask Nan if she thought she played a daughter or granddaughter role in George's life.

Without hesitation she answers, "Totally. Completely. Yes."

———

As Nan got older, she worked up the courage to ask George about Camilla.

"At first I was hesitant. I grew up with not talking about it and it was brushed under the rug." But she was curious and could sense that George was willing to have an open conversation.

"I can just see him, the way he sat. How he crossed his legs, and he had a curve in his back. The way he clasped his hands in his lap, held his coffee cup. There was a reserved calm. He didn't have that shame or embarrassment." Perhaps he felt unburdened and grateful that someone, anyone, in his family dared to say Camilla's name.

He wondered if there had been warning signs that he and Lorena had missed. There was a letter or a phone call from Camilla—Nan didn't know exactly where or when—that gave George and Lorena the sense that their daughter was in something deep and wanted to get out.

"But they didn't know how to help her. It was too late to find her," Nan says.

George wondered out loud, too, if his and Lorena's busy lifestyle gave Camilla the wrong impression.

"He as a parent could see how busy their life was. Camilla took their busyness as 'they don't care about me.' But George's thought was that he and Lorena were role models—'Here's what you've been given. Do something with it, use us as an example.'"

George made it clear to Nan, and also in newspaper articles in which he's quoted after Camilla's death, that the police had had no right to shoot up the Los Angeles house. A few days after the shoot-out, he told Tom Fitzpatrick, a *Chicago Sun-Times* columnist, "If they hadn't killed them all they might have been brought to trial and we might have learned something from all this. We might have found out what they were against."

———

A few months after I first met Nan, we meet again, this time at a coffee shop in Jackson, Minnesota, a small town halfway between Mankato and Sioux Falls. Nan walks into the shop with a big smile, her brown eyes bright. She has a canvas tote bag filled with items to pass along to me. Copies of letters George had written to her over the years, along with some recent publicity she received in Sioux Falls as a result of her work for a citywide arts non-profit. I feel like it's Harvey all over again: documents related to the Halls sitting around, too valuable to thrown away, biding their time until they find the right home. Me.

I have developed an affinity with Nan. I see a lot of myself in her—a go-getter, hard-pressed to say no to requests, active in the arts community, and possessing a fervent belief that the world can be a better place and that we have a duty to make it so.

This time, in Jackson, we spend little time talking about George or Camilla. Nan has already explained the extent of her relationship with

George; there isn't much more to add. Now the conversation turns toward an idea Nan mentioned when she first called me a few months back. She and I will continue to have a variation of the same conversation over the years.

It's an echo of what George had asked her: What could we learn from Camilla? What was she fighting against? What's the bigger meaning of Camilla's story? What is the lesson learned?

Here Nan's tone becomes passionate and energized. Her eyes blaze; she straightens up. I wonder if this is how Camilla looked when filled with passion. I look at Nan's face and try to imagine Camilla.

Nan sees parallels between the issues Camilla confronted head-on in the 1960s and 1970s and the issues we face today: social injustice, racial injustice, lack of equal opportunities for women and minorities, dramatic political divisions. Camilla worked toward something better her whole life until she lost patience. But she never lost passion. That passion didn't have to die with her. Is this the time to finally learn from history and not repeat it?

"What story did [the SLA] have to say that we weren't ready to listen to? That's what Uncle George would have said, too. What do we need to hear?"

Nan's mother and aunts implore her to stay quiet, to keep stories like Camilla's under that rug. *If you bring that up, Nan, you will ruin your life. Just avoid this; otherwise you will ruin yourself,* she's told. She still wonders if it's a risk to talk about Camilla publicly, to claim her as family, as she heads into middle age and continues to build a career in community activism. Is there someone out there who will hear Camilla's story and wonder if there's a thread of insanity that runs through her entire extended family?

I tell Nan that it's hard for me to believe that any rational person would learn of a deed done in 1974 and, decades later, attribute the behavior that led to it to a first cousin, once-removed, who wasn't even born when the deeds took place. I try to be convincing, but I can hear a bit of doubt in Nan's voice. But I know that doubt is not enough to silence her.

"Share the story," she says, as if speaking to herself. "You never know who it might impact."

She's the family member willing to embrace the connection, to draw a line between George, Camilla, and herself. It's why she retained those letters. It's why she shared with me articles about herself and her form of community activism. George and Camilla desired a better world. So does Nan. Echoes remain.

———

On the afternoon of the day in May 2020 when I receive the check-in text from Nan, I go for a run along the shore of Lake Superior. Every time I'm in Duluth I think of Camilla. I wonder what it must have been like to live here for a few months in the late 1960s; I think about how different it must have looked, how many people needed her help, and the energy she spent here. It's a blustery day but the sun is bright. I start out with many layers—May along the big lake can be as bone-chilling as any winter day—but halfway through my run I shed my windbreaker. Heading back to the house, my feet in a steady rhythm, my mind goes into a meditative state, as it often does when I run. We are two months into the pandemic, and I am having trouble remembering what day or date it is. What is today? I think. It's Sunday, I remind myself. But what's the date? May 17.

May 17.

Camilla was killed forty-six years ago today.

When I get back to the house, I text Nan. *Did you know this is the anniversary of Camilla's death? Is that why you messaged me?*

She replies, *I wish I was that cool. But no, I had forgotten. I have goosebumps all over.*

So do I.

I take that as a sign that Camilla wants her story to be told.

CHAPTER 26

Good Girls Gone Bad

OCCAM'S RAZOR is a centuries-old principle that says the simplest explanation is the most likely explanation. In the absence of certainty, the fewer
assumptions we have to make, the better. I grew up reading stories about
crime and violence. When I was young, I thought the answer to why people
chose lives of crime was simple. Now I know better.

———

When I was eleven years old, I came upon a used copy of *Helter Skelter*,
the account of the Charles Manson "Family" murders written by the lead
prosecutor, Vincent Bugliosi (another native Minnesotan). Mom bought
the book for me. We lived in the country and my summer days were long
and isolated. I had hours of time at my disposal, a situation I would never
see again. I graduated rapidly from young-reader chapter books to thick
paperbacks hundreds of pages long.

I hardly put down *Helter Skelter* once I started reading it. Almost twenty
years had passed since the Manson murders, and I'm sure I was the only
student at Waseca Middle School who not only knew the names of Leslie
Van Houten, Patricia Krenwinkel, Susan Atkins, and Mary Brunner but
could also identify their photographs.

The Manson girls fascinated me. They were runaways, and I tried to grasp the concept of leaving home at such a young age. I didn't know any runaways myself, or any girls who had tried to run away. I couldn't fathom *why* someone would run away.

I judged those girls for their decisions. Couldn't they see how crazy Manson was? They must have known the risks that came with running off and living with strangers. Wouldn't they rather be in their own beds at home, near their siblings, their mothers, their fathers? *I would live my life differently*, I thought with smug satisfaction. I would not run off to live on a dirty, dusty abandoned movie set in the California desert, where I'd have to have sex with a wild, hairy little man.

As I grew older I reread *Helter Skelter* every now and again. I started to see the girls as more complicated beings. I looked for clues that might answer the unanswerable: Why did those girls go live with Manson, and what prompted them to fall under his influence? Why did they think they couldn't get out? I wanted to understand them and their motivations. I wanted to get into their minds.

And I wanted to save them. I reread the book hoping I'd find a different ending. I wanted to travel back in time, slip formless through the pages of the book and back to those girls' early lives. *Don't do it*, I would tell them. *Stay where you are. Don't run away.* I so much wanted it to be different for them. I longed for them to have the happiness and contentment I knew.

In many ways, before they met Manson they were much like me, girls who did ordinary things like go to school, ride the bus, play with friends, sleep at night, and wake in the morning. And if they were like me, did that mean I could be like them? What was saving me from getting wrapped up in a cult, from falling under the influence of a crazy personality? The Manson Family probably didn't seem too dangerous at first glance. Weird, yes, but dangerous? They weren't murderers from the beginning; that developed over time. They were hippies living in their communal way. When their lives became more outlandish and bizarre, did the girls even see the progression? Maybe they were too close to it, the proverbial frogs in the pot of slowly warming water. By the time the family crossed over into crime, perhaps the girls were in too far to escape. Rereading the book years later, I understood that my initial judgments had been too quick. How easily I had said to myself, *That would never be me.*

I didn't know how far I would be willing to go for someone I loved. Maybe I'm just lucky my lovers weren't revolutionaries. We have the benefit of hindsight regarding Manson as well as the SLA. We know what the Manson Family did. We know what the SLA did. It's easy to assess ourselves and say we would never have been them. But go back in time before any crimes were committed. Imagine we're looking for love, for a place to belong. Is there a possibility we might have been there, too?

———

I'm not the only one to develop a fascination with these girls. In *Role Models*, film director John Waters writes of his relationship with Leslie Van Houten, one of the Manson girls. The relationship developed through letters and during his visits to prison, where Leslie has served time for murder since 1971.

Waters became intrigued with the Manson murders as soon as the news broke. As details emerged about the gang, Waters wanted to know more. "How had these kids, from backgrounds so similar to mine, committed in real life the awful crimes against peace and love that we were acting out for comedy in our films?"

While Waters was in Los Angeles in 1971 for a film premiere, he attended the courtroom proceedings of some Manson Family members. (He was not the only celebrity drawn into the Manson trials: Dennis Hopper and Jack Nicholson were also courtroom visitors.) About fifteen members of the Manson Family were reunited in court, chained but joyous upon seeing each other after months of separation. Waters writes of the "group madness and insanity" he witnessed. "Heavily influenced, and actually jealous of their notoriety, I went back to Baltimore and made *Pink Flamingoes*, which I wrote, directed, and dedicated to the Manson girls, 'Sadie, Katie and Les'" (that is, Atkins, Krenwinkel, and Van Houten).

Rolling Stone magazine asked Waters to write an article about Charles Manson in 1985. Waters was less interested in Manson and more interested in the women who had followed him. He wanted to write about Leslie, whom he saw as "pretty, out of her mind, rebellious, with fashion daring, a good haircut, and a taste for LSD—just like the girls in my movies."

Waters expresses the same desire I do, the same desire Camilla's parents and friends had expressed: a wish, a longing to have been the one to reach out first. "Instead of being a 'good soldier' for Charlie . . . I wish [Leslie] had been with us in Baltimore on location for *Pink Flamingoes*," he writes, and, "If Leslie had met me instead of Charlie, could she have gone to the Cannes Film Festival instead of the California Institute for Women?"

Van Houten was not the only "bad girl" Waters became obsessed with. By 1990, he had handpicked a new actress for his film *Cry-Baby*: Patty Hearst.

———

How quickly do we dismiss entire groups of people? Individuals make up those groups, individuals who are human beings with emotions like love and anger and sadness, individuals who had a mother or father or grandparent who loved them. But if we see them as human, with emotions and family, then they become like us. And if they are like us, we can develop empathy. And empathy makes it hard for us to judge them. If we look at them collectively, as the SLA or as the Manson Family, the human element goes away and we can ignore them as the individuals they were.

Camilla represents choices any woman could make. Anyone can make a decision to become radicalized, to harm themselves or others. We don't have genes for terrorism; it's bred out of environment and develops slowly over time. Who hasn't felt angry or frustrated because of politics, corruption, or social issues? But most of us are willing to overlook the problems; we feel too small to make a difference. We ignore the bigger picture and instead focus on our little lives.

But who is becoming tired of feeling small? Who will be the next one to decide she will make a difference? Who will be the next one to turn? Your neighbor? Your sister? Your friend? Could you see it coming? Camilla was not the first woman in the United States to take up arms in the hope of violent revolution, and she won't be the last.

Stories like Camilla's still emerge. In August 2015, a young Mississippi girl name Jaelyn Young was arrested, along with her boyfriend, for allegedly making plans to go to Syria and fight for ISIS. Just nineteen, Jaelyn had been an honor student, a cheerleader, and a member of the homecoming court in high school. She was attending Mississippi State University, where she worked in a chemistry lab and had hoped to become a doctor. Her father was a police officer, and her friends were puzzled by the charges against her.

"Something must have happened to her," said one of Jaelyn's friends. "She's too levelheaded, too smart to do this."

What happened to her, indeed?

———

Where one person sees a terrorist, another sees a martyr. They are two sides of the same coin. Some people view Camilla as a terrorist. She was a kidnapper and an armed bank robber. She knew about the Marcus Foster murder and could have helped bring the killers to justice. To others she was a martyr, someone who gave up her life in a fight for the people, someone who took action while so many others sat on the sidelines. John Waters doesn't see a murderer when he visits Leslie. He sees a woman who fell under a spell through no fault of her own.

I don't agree with what Camilla did, just as Waters doesn't agree with Leslie's actions on August 10, 1969, when she took part in the murders of Rosemary and Leno LaBianca. Just as I wanted to save the Manson girls, I wish I could go back in time and save Camilla. If I had read the SLA story instead of *Helter Skelter* when I was young, I would have judged the women of the SLA in the same way I judged the Manson girls. How easily I would have dismissed them as crazy. How easily I would have said I wouldn't have made the same choices. That I would have known better.

But what I've learned by spending twenty years with Camilla's ghost is that she was complicated and complex. Many factors led her into the SLA. Take any one factor away, and she might have led a very different life. I don't think there's any way I could have spent this much time with her and not have developed empathy. Even more so than the Manson girls, Camilla was like me: white, middle-class, midwestern. She was outgoing and gregarious, someone with many friends. People could describe me that way, too. She had a loving family, but one clouded with grief, like mine.

I've learned that Occam's razor doesn't always apply. Occam's razor would say that because we are not certain why Camilla joined the SLA, we should look for the simplest explanation—for example, that she joined for love. She joined because it was her only option to stay close to Mizmoon; otherwise, she would have lost her forever. But that explanation completely dismisses Camilla's complexity and reduces her to a sad caricature. Something was brewing beneath Camilla's facade, no matter how determined she was to portray warmth and joy to those she met. There's something beyond all our surfaces, something beyond what we want to project to the world.

"It Has Been a Wonderful Life"

AT RESURRECTION CEMETERY, I walk up and down the rows of grave-stones. I cannot remember where the Halls are buried; it has been many years since I've been here. The six inches of snow that fell last night is not helping my search. I know their gravestones are low, and the white blanket of fluff is all but hiding the smaller markers. When I spot a mound of snow, I bend down to brush it away. I uncover names, not Hall but Anderson, Carlson, Lindstrom. There's no mistaking that St. Peter was once a Swedish town.

After several minutes, I become chilled. It's late March, but the cold and snow is not atypical for this time of year. I think this is the worst kind of snow, the kind that comes in early spring. By this point, Minnesotans have already endured about four months of winter. The rebirth of spring, which teased us with temperatures in the forties and fifties just a couple of weeks ago, now seems far away.

I make my way toward the north, working myself deeper and deeper into the cemetery. I thought the Halls were somewhere in the middle of this section, but I may have misremembered. By the time I get to the larger decades-old gravestones, I know I've gone too far. I turn around and decide to stick closer to the road on my sweep back.

I look back at my zigzagging footprints in the snow. I've made a mess of the pristine, sparkling white cover. If someone drove by and saw this, they might wonder why the owner of the footprints wandered so and what she was looking for.

———

Camilla's ashes were interred at Resurrection in July 1974. The Halls wanted a quiet ceremony and chose to wait a few weeks after the shoot-out until the media hype faded. Still, newspaper reporters and television cameras showed up from around the country. The thought was that there was a small chance Patty Hearst might make an undercover appearance to honor her dead comrade.

On arrival at the cemetery, George and Lorena discovered that their daughter's name was spelled wrong on her marker: Camilia. "Newspapers called this to the attention of everyone, how misfortune followed her to her gravestone," George wrote.

At the committal service, the Halls spoke: "God in His grace has given us His presence. Through it our love for Camilla and her love for us is sustained. We can forgive and pray for forgiveness. We sense a peace that passes understanding. Thanks to God for His gift. Thanks to everyone for intercessory prayer which undergirds our humanity."

The next day, George and Lorena retreated to their North Shore cabin, staying one night at a Duluth hotel on the way. "On our arrival at the hotel desk the front page of several newspapers carried the story of Camilla's interment," George wrote.

———

I'm almost back to where I started, near where I parked my car, when I bend down to brush snow from yet another gravestone. My fingers are getting cold despite my gloves, and the damp chill penetrates my coat and settles into my bones. But at last, I have found what I am looking for. Here's a Hall gravestone. I quickly uncover the other five, laid out as I had remembered: Two rows of three gravestones each. Terry, Peter, and Nan in one row, Camilla—the original gravestone's spelling error long since corrected—sharing a row with her parents.

I walk back to my car to get the flowers and card I brought. Today is March 24, 2015, Camilla's seventieth birthday. It's a Tuesday, and I have driven from Mankato on a break between classes.

I've been planning this for weeks. It seemed a shame that no one would know it's Camilla's birthday, and a milestone one at that. I grew up in cemeteries, and when I saw graves adorned with trinkets, balloons, and flowers, it showed me that someone still cared about those souls. Those graves stood in contrast to the plain graves of people who had long since died or whose families had moved away.

I grew up in a large extended family, and the thought of being buried in a place so far away from any relatives saddened me. My Grandma Zimny was buried at a cemetery just a couple of miles from us. My dad's dad was buried on the other side of the county, at a cemetery we drove past every time we visited Grandma Hager. In that tiny cemetery, Corpus Christi, rested not only Grandpa but also my uncle, Dad's infant sisters, and a baby cousin.

At the flower shop, I had picked out daisies for Camilla. They are white and yellow, wrapped in colorful cellophane imprinted with icons of flowers and butterflies. I know that my addressee is not going to read the card or see the flowers, but I believe in sending messages out to the universe. Inside the birthday card I include thoughts from the women in my writing group, who over the past decade have lived with Camilla just as I have. I pen my own message to Camilla: "People remember you and love you. Help me to write the story of your life that you want written."

———

On another late March day in St. Peter, in 1998, a storm rolled through town. Not a snowstorm this time, but a freakish early spring tornado. The powerful twister devastated the town.

I was working in the *Free Press* newsroom that day. It was a Sunday, usually a quiet day at work with just four or five of us on staff. I headed to the office at around 4 p.m. Rain had fallen off and on that day; temperatures were in the midsixties and the air was a little stuffy. On my drive to work, I heard reports of severe storms to the west. By 5 p.m. Mankato, St. Peter, and the surrounding areas were under a tornado warning. I went outside the newspaper office's back door with coworkers and watched angry clouds roil in the western sky while the sun shone above us. Back inside, the police scanner started to squawk. A quiet Sunday night shift soon turned into an all-hands-on-deck situation, with every reporter and editor there to chronicle the damage. Trees were ripped from the ground, hundreds of homes were torn apart, and a little boy in St. Peter died.

The beloved Gustavus Adolphus campus took the brunt of the storm. Almost every tree there was knocked down. The iconic spire of Christ Chapel broke off, its sharp point buried downward in the lawn.

I waited about a week to go to St. Peter, giving space to residents and cleanup crews. What struck me most as I drove down the hill into the river valley was how much I could see. I had taken the trees for granted. But without them, I could spot Gustavus's Old Main building from more than a mile away. It looked so sad, naked, and vulnerable.

Resurrection Cemetery also stood in the tornado's path. The storm had come roaring up from the southwest. The cemetery sits on the southwest side of St. Peter, not far from the Gustavus campus. All the trees disappeared from the cemetery, too, giving the place the look it must have had when it was first established on the prairie.

Today you can hardly tell what happened in 1998. In many ways, St. Peter looks the same as it did when the Halls lived there. Main Street retains its old-world charm. Buildings and houses have been lovingly restored. Minnesota Square Park remains a central gathering space for the community.

How quickly scars can heal. A town can cover up a tornado's aftermath. A hole for a casket is dug, then filled in, the grass eventually stitching itself back together. It takes time, but at the surface, it's as if nothing happened. But people who were there witnessed these things and can tell the truth, stories of grief, pain, and loss that have long been rendered invisible.

———

Lorena died in 1995 at the age of eighty-four, outliving her last surviving child by more than twenty years. In "I Remember Lorena," George writes of sitting at Lorena's side at the hospital.

"She said we had never thought of divorce but that she had only loved me always. I assured her of my love." I imagine two elderly people, holding hands across a hospital bed, one dying, knowing their shared grief and love of nearly sixty years is coming to an end. George's tender words, which finally reveal his simple understated passion, catch me by surprise, as do my tears.

George was a man who thought he had to keep his feelings under control. At Lorena's memorial service at the Swedish Retirement Home in Evanston, Illinois, where he and Lorena had been living, he decided to say a few words.

"I feared that I might break down and embarrass everyone. But given strength, I did not do so."

And He led them out as far as Bethany, and He lifted up His hands and blessed them. Now it came to pass, while He blessed them, that He was parted from them and carried up into heaven. And they worshiped Him, and returned to Jerusalem with great joy, and were continually in the temple praising and blessing God.

Luke 24:50–53

May 22, 1974, was Ascension Day eve. Ascension Day, an important feast in the Christian church calendar, marks Jesus's bodily rise into heaven forty days after Easter. It is considered one of the five milestones of Jesus's life, along with baptism, transfiguration, crucifixion, and resurrection. Camilla was born during the Holy Week preceding Easter; now she was being memorialized on the eve of another major Christian date. This may have given George, a man of deep faith, a reason to cling even more firmly to his God during this time of darkness rather than push Him away.

At St. John's in Lincolnwood, parishioners gathered to honor Camilla's life and support George and Lorena. At the service, George and Lorena spoke these words: "In the Sacrament this evening, we experience love and fellowship for each other while we sense just as deeply our fellowship with the Saints.

"Last Christmas Eve, at midnight our family with many others communed. Camilla was home with us and you. As we remember Christ this night in his Ascension, we thank you one and all for the power coming from our communing together. We sense just as strongly the abiding love and relationship with Camilla, her brothers Terry and Peter, and her sister, Nan."

———

George ends his memoir with this:

> In the presence of the loss of Lorena and my lonely existence, I strangely sense a great peace. It is a veritable gift from God. Those last days, Lorena and I often mentioned how blessed we had been. While we had lost our children, had reverses in fortune, yet both of us experienced good health until the last few weeks. We were not suddenly torn from each other but had time to talk and share our deepest thoughts and memories. There were no known unforgiven blemishes on our relationship. I remember especially Lorena's comment, "<u>It has been a wonderful life</u>." (Emphasis George's)

George lived another five years after Lorena's death. He stayed active until the end, ministering to fellow residents at the Swedish Retirement Home.

He died in 2000. Fifty-two years after he bought the plots, he was the last of his family laid to rest at Resurrection Cemetery.

ACKNOWLEDGMENTS

I first came across Camilla's story in 1999 and started research immediately. My gratitude and thanks go to the many people who have helped me along the way. I apologize in advance if I've forgotten anyone; twenty-plus years is a long time to be working on a book.

Harvey Honig was most generous in sharing many materials he used for his dissertation on Camilla. I've lost track of how many times I have read that dissertation over the years. Harvey and I are in a little club of two who have spent the most time with Camilla's spirit.

Finding a family member like Nan has been a blessing. She was just as curious as I was to learn about Camilla. She knew George Hall well and didn't hesitate to share her stories and insights with me. I've gained a friend.

Don Myers at the Hillstrom Museum of Art at Gustavus Adolphus College first put me in contact with Nan. I've appreciated Don's interest in Camilla, George, and Lorena.

I am indebted to the archives at Gustavus Adolphus College and the wonderful archivists. Mike Haeuser was the first I worked with, and Adrianna Darden has been an enormous help, especially in locating many of the photographs that are reprinted in this book.

Thanks to Jessica Becker and Ruth Einstein at the Nicollet County Historical Society for their help in locating photographs. I had heard a rumor that there was a photograph of the Halls with all four children, taken just months before their oldest died. Eileen Holz was the first to share the photograph with me; it was in St. Peter, Minnesota, all this time. Pat Christman at the *Mankato Free Press* did this girl a tremendous favor by finding the picture of Camilla's interment in the newspaper archives.

Cheryl Brooks, what a find! I'm so grateful she reached out to me after reading my blog posts. She generously shared her memories of Camilla as well as several pieces of Camilla's art and snapshots of Camilla. Cheryl is truly a researcher's dream, and I'm so glad we had a chance to meet in 2021. Sara Jane Olson was also a valuable contact, and I appreciate the time she gave to me.

The faculty at Bath Spa University gave me valuable feedback as I submitted a version of this book as my PhD dissertation: my thanks to Kate Pullinger, Gerard Woodward, and Tracy Brain. Many thanks also to my cohort of Dr. Heather Sharfeddin and Dr. Jennifer Militello. We did it!

My colleague Chuck Lewis at Minnesota State University, Mankato, offered valuable weapons information and served as a general sounding board. Not everyone is interested in the military-like actions of a domestic terrorist organization, and I'm happy that he is!

My friend and former colleague John Gaterud served on my committee when Camilla was the subject of my master's thesis. I appreciate his encouragement of my writing, going back to when we first met in 1994. Thanks also to the other people on my thesis committee, Chuck Piehl and Matt Loayza.

What would I do without my dear Siblings in Ink? I don't publish anything that they haven't read first. I wholeheartedly trust the collective wisdom of Kirstin, Becky, Nick, Shelley, Michelle, Melanie, Kandi, and Angie. A special thanks to Kirstin, who always shared my excitement whenever I saw a blue Volkswagen bug and knew it was more than coincidence. Nick and Bruce generously provided their expert eyes during the proofing process. Any remaining errors are mine alone. I thank Lisa for her overall support and her research skills.

I received support from the Jerome Foundation in the form of a travel grant to the Bay Area in 2008. Seeing where Camilla lived and conducting research in archives there remain highlights of the entire research and writing process. I have also been supported by the Prairie Lakes Regional Arts Council for this project.

Thank you to Allison K. Williams and Ashleigh Renard for Writers Bridge. I spent my sabbatical year attending their biweekly sessions about all things writerly and promotional. Time will tell if I'm making the most of what I learned!

Kim Loomis, I am grateful for your early read of the manuscript. It was so valuable to have a smart reader who knew little about Camilla or the SLA go through it. Your comments were so helpful. I expect to see your book soon.

I appreciate the writings by others about the SLA. Brad Schreiber's book *Revolution's End: The Patty Hearst Kidnapping, Mind Control, and the Secret History of Donald DeFreeze and the SLA* took on a different meaning each time I read it, and I appreciate our phone conversations about the SLA. *American Heiress: The Wild Saga of the Kidnapping, Crimes, and Trial of Patty Hearst*, by Jeffrey Toobin, was a welcome update to the SLA story. Vin McLellan and Paul Avery's *The Voices of Guns* remains my bible for all things SLA.

Thank you to Erik Anderson and the entire team at the University of Minnesota Press. I'm thrilled that you decided to take me on again.

My family, as always, has been so supportive and encouraging. Thanks especially to David for putting up with all he has had to put up with. "Wendy, let me explain something to you: Whenever you come in here and interrupt me you're breaking my concentration." I apologize for all the times I've channeled my inner Jack Torrance.

NOTES

Prologue

Page 2, On behalf of the families, noted attorney Leonard Weinglass: Lake Headley, Elizabeth Schmidt, and Jeanne Davis, *Investigation Report: An Inquiry into the Events of May 17, 1974* (n.p.: August 1, 1974).

Pages 2–3, "Looking at the site, it also became clear to a visitor": editorial, *New York Post*, May 24, 1974, George Hall Archives, Folke Bernadotte Memorial Library, Gustavus Adolphus College, St. Peter, Minnesota.

Page 3, The witnesses said Camilla had acted like a den mother: Vin McLellan and Paul Avery, *The Voices of Guns* (New York: G. P. Putnam's Sons, 1977), 351.

Page 4, "I want you to remember that I'm with really good people": Camilla Hall to George and Lorena Hall, no date, George Hall Archives.

Introduction

Page 11, Next to my article was a smaller story: Joe Tougas, "The FBI Wanted SLA Members; St. James Chief Kept the Posters," *Mankato Free Press*, July 3, 1999.

Page 11, "A small clique of young, self-absorbed, guilt-ridden, emotionally scarred white men and women": Gregory Cumming and Stephen Sayles, *The Symbionese Liberation Army and Patricia Hearst, Queen of the Revolution* (Pechanga, Calif.: Great Oak Press, 2019), 5.

"We Begin When We First Met"

Pages 20–22, Information about the Halls' courtship and marriage taken from Hall, "I Remember Lorena—A Love Story" (typescript, 1995), chap. 2, p. 21, George Hall Archives.

Pages 23–24, "[We] were always welcomed": Hall, "I Remember Lorena," chap. 1, p. 9.

Page 24, "As I went on in the lecture": Hall, "I Remember Lorena," chap. 4, p. 9.

Page 25, "Less publicly, at home": Hall, "I Remember Lorena," chap. 4, p. 9.

"Their First Concern"

Page 27, "We thought about it for a few days": Hall, "I Remember Lorena," chap. 5, p. 3.

Page 28, Rather, "their first concern": George F. Hall, *The Missionary Spirit in the Augustana Church* (Rock Island, Ill.: Augustana Historical Society, Augustana College, 1984), 149.

Page 29, "It was a wonderful family time": Hall, "I Remember Lorena," chap. 5, p. 3.

Page 30, George wrote that Africa would change the family: Hall, "I Remember Lorena," chap. 6, p. 12.

Page 30, "The girls were ridiculed": Hall, "I Remember Lorena," chap. 7, p. 2.

Page 32, "It was difficult for Lorena": Hall, "I Remember Lorena," chap. 7, p. 7.

Page 32, "It was an irrational decision": Hall, "I Remember Lorena," chap. 8, p. 1.

"It Was a Troubled Spring, Heavy with Grief"

Page 35, "I sat by her bedside": Hall, "I Remember Lorena," chap. 8, p. 10.

Page 35, "The lights were on": Hall, "I Remember Lorena," chap. 8, p. 11.

Page 36, "A new future in Chicago was inviting": Hall, "I Remember Lorena," chap. 8, p. 12.

Page 37, "I'm your only child left": Hall, "I Remember Lorena," chap. 9, p. 2.

Page 37, "Everyone but not us was taking pictures": Hall, "I Remember Lorena," chap. 9, p. 2.

Camilla Goes to College

Page 41, "The powers that be determined": Frani (Peterson) Anderson, interview, April 11, 2014, St. Peter, Minnesota.

Page 41, "We were shocked": Hall, "I Remember Lorena," chap. 9, p. 4.

Page 45, "Was getting as good an academic education": Harvey H. Honig, "A

Psychobiographical Study of Camilla Hall" (PhD diss., Loyola University Chicago, 1979), Dissertation 1788, 112, https://ecommons.luc.edu/luc_diss/1788.

Page 45, But in other courses, such as art: University of Minnesota transcript.

Page 45, "My theater arts teacher is a very enjoyable lecturer": Camilla Hall to George and Lorena Hall, October 5, 1964, Harvey Honig personal collection, now in author's possession.

Page 45, "This was my first real experience with budgeting money": Honig, "A Psychobiographical Study," 112.

Camilla Gets a Job

Page 46, "I'm pleased with your work": Camilla Hall to George and Lorena Hall, December 4, 1967, Harvey Honig collection.

Page 46, "Let's hear it for me": Camilla Hall to George and Lorena Hall, December 4, 1967, Harvey Honig collection.

Page 46, "As I said, these would be the last resorts": Camilla Hall to George and Lorena Hall, November 7, 1967, George Hall Archives.

Page 47, "Tremendously challenging and scarey": Camilla Hall to George and Lorena Hall, August 17, 1967, George Hall Archives.

Page 47, "While at school together": Honig, "A Psychobiographical Study," 105.

Page 47, "We prepare the cases": Camilla Hall to George and Lorena Hall, January 10, 1968, Harvey Honig collection.

Page 47, "I've been reading up on adolescent psychology": Camilla Hall to George and Lorena Hall, December 16, 1967, Harvey Honig collection.

Page 47, Looking forward to a symposium on unwed mothers: Camilla Hall to George and Lorena Hall, March 7, 1968, George Hall Archives.

Page 48, "Do you have room in your home / For homeless children—": Camilla Hall to George and Lorena Hall, February 23, 1968, George Hall Archives.

Page 48, "Last I heard, they were also scheduling me": Camilla Hall to George and Lorena Hall, February 23, 1968, George Hall Archives.

Page 49, "The hill ghettoes reminded me of the favellas": Camilla Hall to George and Lorena Hall, August 17, 1967, George Hall Archives.

Page 49, She told her parents that she could have moved: Camilla Hall to George and Lorena Hall, August 17, 1967, George Hall Archives.

Page 49, She told her parents she did not want to be thought of as a spy: Camilla Hall to George and Lorena Hall, August 17, 1967, George Hall Archives.

Page 49, "This makes me very angry": Camilla Hall to George and Lorena Hall, March 7, 1968, George Hall Archives.

Page 50, "Somewhere along the line casework services failed for them": Camilla Hall to George and Lorena Hall, November 7, 1967, George Hall Archives.

Page 50, "Work steadily fluctuates": Camilla Hall to George and Lorena Hall, October 9, 1967, Harvey Honig collection.

Page 50, "I'm having a hard time keeping a professional distance": Camilla Hall to George and Lorena Hall, November 7, 1967, George Hall Archives.

Page 50, "DFL caucuses were this week": Camilla Hall to George and Lorena Hall, March 7, 1968, George Hall Archives.

Page 51, "[Camilla] was very witty": Honig, "A Psychobiographical Study," 172.

Page 51, "I never once saw her depressed": Honig, "A Psychobiographical Study," 168.

A Turning Point

Page 52, "People have forgotten already": Camilla Hall to George and Lorena Hall, October 25, 1968, George Hall Archives.

Page 52, "Gee, he's handsome!": Letter, October 25, 1968, George Hall Archives.

Page 53, "They gripe a little": Letter, October 25, 1968, George Hall Archives.

Page 53, "Mis-use of democracy": Letter, October 25, 1968. George Hall Archives.

Page 53, "When I first knew her": Honig, "A Psychobiographical Study," 179.

Page 53, The Hatch Act still forbade political activity: Camilla Hall to George and Lorena Hall, August 9, 1968, George Hall Archives.

Page 53, "Camilla was always into revolution": Honig, "A Psychobiographical Study," 196.

Page 54, "Very disappointed to watch Nixon win": Camilla Hall to George and Lorena Hall, August 9, 1968, George Hall Archives.

Page 54, "Unfortunately, more often than not P&F people": Camilla Hall to George and Lorena Hall, August 9, 1968, George Hall Archives.

Page 54, She recommended that her parents read: Letter, August 9, 1968, George Hall Archives.

Page 54, "The southern states react to poverty": Camilla Hall to George and Lorena Hall, September 1968, George Hall Archives.

Page 55, "If she questioned": Honig, "A Psychobiographical Study," 171.

Page 55, "I think that relates to Candy's maverickness": Honig, "A Psychobiographical Study," 170.

Page 55, "And I think the reason she gave up her work": Honig, "A Psychobiographical Study," 159–60.

Page 55, "She never came off as an angry person": Honig, "A Psychobiographical Study," 173.

Page 56, "These days I'm getting my annual California fever": Camilla Hall to George and Lorena Hall, March 1, 1969, Harvey Honig collection.

Page 56, "It seems like San Andreas fault is mentioned": Camilla Hall to George and Lorena Hall, March 26, 1969, Harvey Honig collection.

Page 56, "I think she had done a lot of thinking": Honig, "A Psychobiographical Study," 185.

Page 56, "She didn't present this trip to California": Honig, "A Psychobiographical Study," 174.

Part II

Page 57, "We want so much to make a movie of ourselves": Fred Soltysik, *In Search of a Sister* (New York: Bantam Books, 1976), 45–46.

Camilla Moves to California

Page 60, "That's the best I've ever done": Camilla Hall to George and Lorena Hall, February 5, 1971, Harvey Honig collection.

Page 60, "So it looks like I'm on my way!": Camilla Hall to George and Lorena Hall, February 5, 1971, Harvey Honig collection.

Pages 60–61, "Friends who had moved to California": Hall, "I Remember Lorena," chap. 9, pp. 10–11.

Page 61, "Camilla told her mother the pain had stopped": Honig, "A Psychobiographical Study," 159.

Page 61, "I still can't get over the weather here": Camilla Hall to George and Lorena Hall, April 8, 1970, Harvey Honig collection.

Page 62, "Her art was unique": Hall, "I Remember Lorena," chap. 10, p. 9.

Page 62, By November her sales had slowed: Camilla Hall to George and Lorena Hall, November 3, 1970, Harvey Honig collection.

Page 62, "I've been out here for a year": Camilla Hall to George and Lorena Hall, February 21, 1971, Harvey Honig collection.

Page 62, "I've decided to try the market in San Francisco": Camilla Hall to George and Lorena Hall, March 10, 1971, Harvey Honig collection.

Page 63, "After I saw Berkeley": Honig, "A Psychobiographical Study," 127.

Page 63, She told friends she liked Berkeley's "respected socialism": McLellan and Avery, *The Voices of Guns,* 121.

Page 63, California friends remember her criticizing: McLellan and Avery, *The Voices of Guns,* 121.

Page 64, A burgeoning food co-op movement: McLellan and Avery, *The Voices of Guns*, 116.

Page 64, "It's really been an experience": Camilla Hall to George and Lorena Hall, June 7, 1971, Harvey Honig collection.

Page 64, She and Camilla soon became lovers: McLellan and Avery, *The Voices of Guns*, 117.

Camilla and Mizmoon

Page 65, "They didn't come in and announce it": McLellan and Avery, *The Voices of Guns*, 117.

Page 66, "Fourteen happy years" of marriage: Soltysik, *In Search of a Sister*, 20.

Page 66, "I guess, now that I practically died": Soltysik, *In Search of a Sister*, 18.

Page 66, "Hardly a meeting transpired": Soltysik, *In Search of a Sister*, 21.

Page 67, "After attending Women's Caucus meetings": Soltysik, *In Search of a Sister*, 27.

Page 67, "Today Tele [Telegraph Avenue] is the last big 'hippie' scene": John Bryan, *This Soldier Still at War* (New York: Harcourt Brace Jovanovich, 1975), 69.

Page 67, Berkeley became home to the largest group of "vintage" New Left radicals: McLellan and Avery, *The Voices of Guns*, 29.

Page 68, "This Bay Left is a unique environment": McLellan and Avery, *The Voices of Guns*, 32.

Page 68, "Pat and I went camping": Camilla Hall to George and Lorena Hall, October 8, 1971, Harvey Honig collection.

Page 68, "Sisters, none of us are free": Soltysik, *In Search of a Sister*, 32.

Page 68, "We were concerned about the large number of young people": Hall, "I Remember Lorena," chap. 10, p. 8.

Page 69, George described Mizmoon: Hall, "I Remember Lorena," chap. 10, p. 8.

Page 69, "The experiment is being lovers again": Soltysik, *In Search of a Sister*, 46.

Page 69, "Went to a Greek tavern": Camilla Hall to George and Lorena Hall, August 8, 1972, Harvey Honig collection.

Page 69, "She had expected to find a utopia": McLellan and Avery, *The Voices of Guns*, 121.

Page 70, "Maybe renting a villa on an island": Soltysik, *In Search of a Sister*, 43.

Page 70, "It really sounded as if she'd been writing this all down": Soltysik, *In Search of a Sister*, 44.

Page 70, "Howdy! Well, Mizmoon got to Denver safely and we're having a wonderful holiday. . . . I'm all well now": It is unclear what illness Camilla was suffering at the time.

Page 70, The postcard is signed "Mizmoon and Golden Mane": Camilla Hall to George and Lorena Hall, January 25, 1973, Harvey Honig collection.

Page 70, "We plan to go to Europe together in one year": Soltysik, *In Search of a Sister*, 49.

Page 70, "She noticed how natural Camilla was": Soltysik, *In Search of a Sister*, 50.

The SLA Forms

Page 72, "I remember planting a kiss": Soltysik, *In Search of a Sister*, 55.

Page 73, "The legal system accommodated him": Brad Schreiber, *Revolution's End: The Patty Hearst Kidnapping, Mind Control, and the Secret History of Donald DeFreeze and the SLA* (New York: Skyhorse, 2016), 21.

Page 73, "This person is a high-risk danger to society": Schreiber, *Revolution's End*, 30.

Page 73, Inmates who wanted to escape punishment: Schreiber, *Revolution's End*, 44.

Page 74, PA&E is thought to have been a CIA cover in Saigon: Schreiber, *Revolution's End*, 40.

Page 74, Used various means to infiltrate the Viet Cong: Schreiber, *Revolution's End*, 41.

Page 74, "In reality, it became a cover for an experimental project": Schreiber, *Revolution's End*, 42.

Page 74, Perhaps he was just the type of pliable and easily manipulated person: Schreiber, *Revolution's End*, 43.

Page 74, "DeFreeze was told he would be a new black leader": Alex Constantine, ed., *The Essential Mae Brussell* (Port Townsend, Wash.: Feral House, 2014), 8.

Page 75, In DeFreeze, Westbrook found a prison insider to mold: Schreiber, *Revolution's End*, 50.

Page 75, "Willie was no leader": Schreiber, *Revolution's End*, 49.

Page 76, "We're writing a serious document": Soltysik, *In Search of a Sister*, 63.

Page 76, That was the only time the sisters spent together: Soltysik, *In Search of a Sister*, 63–64.

Page 76, "Therefore, we of the Symbionese Federation": McLellan and Avery, *The Voices of Guns*, 505.

Page 77, "I couldn't seriously recruit for him": Cumming and Sayles, *The Symbionese Liberation Army and Patricia Hearst*, 32.

Page 78, "It [the SLA] didn't have nothing to do with reality": Cumming and Sayles, *The Symbionese Liberation Army and Patricia Hearst*, 34.

Page 78, She also received regular checks from a securities fund: Hall, "I Remember Lorena," chap. 10, p. 11.

Page 79, DeFreeze, who had been standing back: Cumming and Sayles, *The Symbionese Liberation Army and Patricia Hearst*, 41.

Page 79, Hearst testified at her trial: McLellan and Avery, *The Voices of Guns*, 132.

Camilla Moves to Francisco Street

Page 82, "I'm finally able to check out": Camilla Hall letter to George and Lorena Hall, April 26, 1972, George Hall Archives.

Page 83, "She really was an incredible woman": McLellan and Avery, *The Voices of Guns*, 123.

Page 84, And after a few minutes they all would be laughing: McLellan and Avery, *The Voices of Guns*, 123.

Page 84, "This kind of work has been mystified": Carol Shull, "At Last—A Feminist 'First Lady' Surfaces," *Argus* (Fremont–Newark, Calif.), November 20, 1973.

Page 84, Which employed 470 people: East Bay Regional Park District board meeting minutes, October 16, 1973.

Page 84, "I've been meeting regularly": Camilla Hall to George and Lorena Hall, August 26, 1973, Harvey Honig collection.

Page 85, "If you are asking for complete fairness": East Bay Regional Park District board meeting minutes, October 16, 1973.

Page 85, "Management claims the union does not . . . represent the temps": Camilla Hall to George and Lorena Hall, August 26, 1973, Harvey Honig collection.

Page 86, "Look, the point I'm trying to make": East Bay Regional Park District board meeting minutes, October 16, 1973.

Page 86, "The motion's failure seems to me": East Bay Regional Park District board meeting minutes, October 16, 1973.

Camilla Joins the SLA

Page 88, At this point, nearly half of all homes in the United States have guns: Statista Research Department, "Gun Ownership in the U.S., 1972–2021," Statista, December 1, 2021, https://www.statista.com/statistics/249740 /percentage-of-households-in-the-united-states-owning-a-firearm/.

Page 88, He'd estimate maybe 10 percent of all women own a gun: Violence Policy Center, "The Long-Term Decline of Gun Ownership in America: 1973–2018," June 2020, https://www.vpc.org/studies/ownership.pdf.

Page 89, "Some of the men challenged me": Shull, "At Last."

Page 89, Emily Harris helps us pin down the time frame: Bill Harris, Emily Harris, Russell Little, and Joseph Remiro, "The Story of the SLA," as told to Susan Lyne and Robert Scheer, *New Times* 6, no. 8 (April 16, 1976), 30.

Page 89, Atwood was the last to join the SLA: McLellan and Avery, *The Voices of Guns*, 151.

Page 91, "When I'm in town": Soltysik, *In Search of a Sister*, 78.

Page 91, "Tragedy? The guy was in it with the pigs": Soltysik, *In Search of a Sister*, 75.

Page 92, "There were a lot of people who would have joined the SLA": Emily Harris, Bill Harris, Russell Little, and Joseph Remiro, *The Last SLA Statement: An Interview with Russ, Joe, Bill and Emily* (Berkeley, Calif.: Bay Area Research Collective, 1976), 25.

Page 92, "Because Camilla was a lesbian": Harris, Harris, Little, and Remiro, *The Last SLA Statement*, 8.

Page 92, Joe Remiro bought his gun: "Guns Used by SLA Traced," *Oakland Tribune*, May 2, 1974.

Page 93, Camilla checked into the Chabot Gun Club's firing range: "Guns Used by SLA Traced."

Page 93, Nancy and Mizmoon; the Harrises, Nancy, and Mizmoon; Remiro and the Harrises: Don Martinez, "2nd Weapon Tied to Foster Killing," *San Francisco Examiner*, May 23, 1974.

Page 93, "I had known for some time": Soltysik, *In Search of a Sister*, 95.

Page 93, "I remember feeling": Harris, Harris, Little, and Remiro, *The Last SLA Statement*, 15.

The SLA Kidnaps Patty: February 4, 1974

Page 95, Specifically named Patty Hearst as a potential kidnapping victim: McLellan and Avery, *The Voices of Guns*, 72.

Page 96, The SLA had initially planned to kidnap Patty on January 7: McLellan and Avery, *The Voices of Guns,* 172.

Page 99, Camilla visited her good friends Paul and Joyce Halverson: Information about Camilla's visits with the Halversons is taken from McLellan and Avery, *The Voices of Guns,* 125.

Page 100, Camilla visited her former boss Eddie Collins: Information about Camilla's last visit with Eddie Collins is taken from McLellan and Avery, *The Voices of Guns,* 124–25.

Page 101, Years later he would talk about Camilla with fondness: Information gathered from personal interviews with East Bay Regional Park District workers Britt Thorsnes, Joan Suzio, and Jerry Kent, July 2008.

Camilla Slips Away

Page 103, Two men in suits showed up at Cheryl Brooks's office: Cheryl Brooks, phone interview, August 2016.

Pages 103–6, Information in this chapter taken from Larry Hatfield, "How a Chance to Trace Patty Was Missed," *San Francisco Examiner,* June 30, 1974.

Camilla inside the SLA

Page 107, "Poor Gabi": Patricia Campbell Hearst, *Patty Hearst: Her Own Story,* with Alvin Moscow (New York: Avon Books, 1988; originally published as *Every Secret Thing,* 1982), 146.

Page 109, "She had a soft, warm voice": *Hearst: Her Own Story,* 79.

Page 110, No one told employees to watch: McLellan and Avery, *The Voices of Guns,* 219.

Page 110, Agents don't make the connection: McLellan and Avery, *The Voices of Guns,* 219.

Page 110, "On the left side was Gabi": *Hearst: Her Own Story,* 111.

Page 111, Say "bang-bang" and "rat-a-tat-tat": *Hearst: Her Own Story,* 78.

Page 111, "The SLA would be ready to do battle with the pigs": *Hearst: Her Own Story,* 90.

Page 111, "Gabi sort of lumbered about": *Hearst: Her Own Story,* 123.

Page 113, They have taken $10,692.51: McLellan and Avery, *The Voices of Guns,* 322–28.

Page 114, "Warning to the FBI": McLellan and Avery, *The Voices of Guns,* 338.

Page 115, "Our team would be crippled from the start": *Hearst: Her Own Story,* 199.

Page 115, "Death filled the center room": *Hearst: Her Own Story,* 201.

Page 116, "Who the hell do you think you are": *Hearst: Her Own Story,* 215–16.

Pages 117–18, Day 102: The Last Day: Information on the shoot-out taken from McLellan and Avery, *The Voices of Guns,* 349–64.

Page 118, "Our support is from the people": Camilla Hall to George and Lorena Hall, no date, George Hall Archives.

Page 119, "Sunday morning our church was jubilant": Hall, "I Remember Lorena," chap. 10, p. 12.

Crumbs on the Trail

Page 123, Close has said, "I want people to see": Jessica Backus, "Beyond the Portrait: The Many Categories of Chuck Close," *Artsy,* September, 16, 2013, para. 13, https://www.artsy.net/articlejessica-beyond-the-portrait-the -many-categories-of.

Page 126, "There was a tremendous fascination": Honig, "A Psychobiographical Study," 4.

Page 126, "What we heard of these two": Honig, "A Psychobiographical Study," 4.

Page 126, George and Lorena were willing to talk to him: Honig, "A Psychobiographical Study," 6.

The Missing Letters

Page 127, "She wrote home much more": Honig, "A Psychobiographical Study," 151.

Page 128, "For a while the FBI was coming around": Honig, "A Psychobiographical Study," 163.

Page 129, "I am much more of the view": Jeffrey Toobin, personal communication, November 3, 2014.

Page 130, Thanks to Harvey, we know that Camilla was changing her rhetoric: Honig, "A Psychobiographical Study," 163–64.

Page 131, "I'm sure that Mr. Bates": McLellan and Avery, *The Voices of Guns,* 211.

"A Perfect, Loving Daughter"

Page 132, "These letters are too good to be true!": Honig, "A Psychobiographical Study," 70.

Page 132, "After that, we have a perfect, loving daughter": Honig, "A Psychobiographical Study," 70.

Page 133, "The personal images are all positive": Honig, "A Psychobiographical Study," 71.

Page 133, In a July 7 letter, Camilla signs off: Letters dated July 7 through December 30 from the Harvey Honig collection.

Page 135, "Severely withdrawn, preoccupied, and depressed": Albert Cain, Irene Fast, and Mary E. Erickson, "Children's Disturbed Reactions to the Death of a Sibling," *American Journal of Orthopsychiatry* 34, no. 4 (1964): 749, https://doi.org/10.1111/j.1939-0025.1964.tb02375.x.

Page 135, The children in one study were often immature and fearful: Cain, Fast, and Erickson, "Children's Disturbed Reactions."

Page 135, "Parents may simultaneously withdraw": R. Krell and L. Rabkin, "The Effects of Sibling Death on the Surviving Child: A Family Perspective," *Family Process* 18, no. 4 (1979): 475, https://doi.org/10.1111/j.1545-5300.1979.00471.x.

Page 135, "An over dependent relationship": Camilla Hall to George and Lorena Hall, July 14, 1969, Harvey Honig collection.

Page 136, "Add to these beautiful qualities your varied life experiences": Camilla Hall to Lorena Hall, March 26, 1969, Harvey Honig collection.

Page 136, "In a psychological sense she was never free": Honig, "A Psychobiographical Study," 73.

Page 138, "Part of her was really attached to her family": Harvey Honig, personal communication, July 2, 2015.

The Last Christmas

Page 139, "We just felt there was something different": Honig, "A Psychobiographical Study," 164.

Page 139, "Everything was normal": Hall, "I Remember Lorena," chap. 10, p. 11.

Page 140, "She assured us . . . that she was all right": Hall, "I Remember Lorena," chap. 10, p. 11.

Page 140, "We didn't quite understand that": Honig, "A Psychobiographical Study," 164–65.

Page 141, "There was tragedy": Honig, "A Psychobiographical Study," 86.

Page 141, "These are . . . problems to be borne individually": Honig, "A Psychobiographical Study," 86.

Page 143, "But maybe she didn't see it that way": Honig, "A Psychobiographical Study," 185.

Page 143, She loved her mother very much: Honig, "A Psychobiographical Study," 184.

Page 143, "And he was always so right": Honig, "A Psychobiographical Study," 194–95.

Page 144, Harvey saw another side of George: Honig, "A Psychobiographical Study," 195.

The Sole Survivor

Page 145, "'Sister,' / that's what your button said": Honig, "A Psychobiographical Study," 122.

Page 146, "No family, no matter how religious or how integrated": Honig, "A Psychobiographical Study," 87.

Page 147, And the more one feels pressure to live up to outside expectations: Honig, "A Psychobiographical Study," 88.

Page 147, "It is not that Reverend Hall is a man who hides behind his role": Honig, "A Psychobiographical Study," 89.

Page 147, "The child's confusion about God's portrayal as benevolent": Cain, Fast, and Erickson, "Children's Disturbed Reactions," 746.

Page 148, "Since she could not believe": Honig, "A Psychobiographical Study," 92.

Page 150, "For the survivor can never, inwardly, simply conclude": Honig, "A Psychobiographical Study," 89.

Page 150, "The children, of course, had a generally heightened awareness": Cain, Fast, and Erickson, "Children's Disturbed Reactions," 747.

Page 151, "The older child seems overwhelmed with guilt": R. Rogers, "Children's Reactions to Sibling Death," Proceedings of the First International Congress of Psychosomatic Medicine, Spain, *Excerpta Medica (Amsterdam)*, ser. 134 (1966): 215.

Page 151, "She did have this problem": Honig, "A Psychobiographical Study," 150.

Page 151, "They insisted they should enjoy nothing": Cain, Fast, and Erickson, "Children's Disturbed Reactions," 743, 746.

Page 151, The beginning of a child's "existential anxiety": Helen Rosen and Harriette L. Cohen, "Children's Reactions to Sibling Loss," *Clinical Social Work* 9, no. 3 (1981): 212.

Pages 151–53, Harvey interviewed an unidentified friend: All unattributed information from "Linda," the unidentified friend, comes from Honig, "A Psychobiographical Study," 197–222.

Page 153, "Camilla certainly had reason to fear death": Honig, "A Psychobiographical Study," 82.

Page 153, "I will cradle you / in my woman hips": poem written by Camilla Hall, in *Poem-Maker Soul-Healer: Poems Made by Members of the Radical Psychiatry Community* (Berkeley: n.p.).

"She Was a Pacifist"

Pages 154–60, Harvey interviewed Linda for his dissertation: All information from "Linda," the unidentified friend, taken from Honig, "A Psychobiographical Study," 197–222.

Pages 155–58, He interviewed . . . Jean Bigelow and Alan Carlson: All information from Jean Bigelow and Alan Carlson taken from Honig, "A Psychobiographical Study," 168–78.

"I'm Not Surprised"

Pages 161–64, Bette sat down for an interview with Harvey: Information from Bette Esbjornson taken from Honig, "A Psychobiographical Study," 179–96.

Page 163, Harvey said that the personality test Camilla took when she started at the University of Minnesota: At the time, incoming students at some universities across the country took the Minnesota Multiphasic Personality Inventory (MMPI) as part of the admission procedure. By the late 1960s, a manual for college counselors was developed using data from thousands of tests.

Camilla Reveals Herself

Pages 165–76, "Please don't say no / Until you know . . .": All poems are from the Harvey Honig collection.

Page 167, "When she first started doing her little drawings": Honig, "A Psychobiographical Study," 188–89.

Page 168, "[Calisch's] impression was of a person": Honig, "A Psychobiographical Study," 68.

Page 168, But Calisch "experienced her as someone": Honig, "A Psychobiographical Study," 69.

Page 170, "The other time I saw her in a kind of depression": Honig, "A Psychobiographical Study," 218.

Page 174, Who wrote that Mizmoon was devastated: Soltysik, *In Search of a Sister*, 50.

Page 175, "They erupt from the page": Honig, "A Psychobiographical Study," 72.

Page 175, "I would not be at all surprised": Honig, "A Psychobiographical Study," 72.

Page 175, "Is the clearest expression of her psychological state": Honig, "A Psychobiographical Study," 72.

Page 176, "The lines themselves reflect": Honig, "A Psychobiographical Study," 74.

A Parallel Story

Pages 177–84, Diana Oughton died in a townhouse explosion: All information in this chapter taken from Thomas Powers, *Diana: The Making of a Terrorist* (Boston: Houghton Mifflin, 1971).

Page 183, I look at this picture of Diana: The photographs can be seen in Lucinda Franks and Thomas Powers, "Diana—The Making of a Terrorist—Part I," UPI Archives, September 14, 1970, https://www.upi.com/Archives/1970/09/14 /Diana-The-Making-of-a-Terrorist-Part-I/6414752448101/.

Nan

Page 198, Lorena didn't even know Helen was dying of cancer: Susan O'Brien notes, p. 27, in George Hall Archives.

Page 201, "You were with me when Lorena died": George Hall to Nan, February 12, 1998; letter from Nan, in the possession of the author.

Page 203, "If they hadn't killed them all": Tom Fitzpatrick, "Father Asks, 'Why?'" *Chicago Sun-Times*, May 20, 1974.

Good Girls Gone Bad

Page 208, "How had these kids": John Waters, *Role Models* (New York: Farrar, Straus and Giroux, 2010), 48.

Page 208, "Heavily influenced, and actually jealous": Waters, *Role Models*, 49.

Page 209, "Pretty, out of her mind": Waters, *Role Models*, 52.

Page 209, "Instead of being a 'good soldier'": Waters, *Role Models*, 52.

Page 210, "Something must have happened": Richard Fausset, "Young Mississippi Couple Linked to ISIS, Perplexing All," *New York Times*, August 14, 2015, http://www.nytimes.com/2015/08/15/us/disbelief-in-mississippi -at-how-far-isis-message-can-travel.html?_r=0.

Epilogue

Page 213, "Newspapers called this to the attention": Hall, "I Remember Lorena," chap. 10, p. 13.

Page 213, "God in His grace": Transcript of memorial service for Lorena, as back matter in Hall, "I Remember Lorena."

Page 213, "On our arrival at the hotel desk": Hall, "I Remember Lorena," chap. 10, p. 14.

Page 216, "She said we had never thought of divorce": Hall, "I Remember Lorena," chap. 12, p. 5.

Page 216, "I feared that I might break down": Hall, "I Remember Lorena," chap. 13, p. 4.

Page 216, "In the Sacrament this evening": Transcript of memorial service for Lorena, as back matter in Hall, "I Remember Lorena."

Page 217, "In the presence of the loss of Lorena": Hall, "I Remember Lorena," chap. 13, p. 5.

Rachael Hanel is associate professor of creative nonfiction and journalism at Minnesota State University, Mankato. She is author of *We'll Be the Last Ones to Let You Down: Memoir of a Gravedigger's Daughter* (Minnesota, 2013).